A Handbook
   of CHURCH
     Public
     Relations

RALPH STOODY

A Handbook of CHURCH Public Relations

ABINGDON PRESS
NEW YORK
NASHVILLE

UNITY SCHOOL LIBRARY
Unity Village
Lee's Summit, Missouri 64063

A HANDBOOK OF CHURCH PUBLIC RELATIONS

Copyright © MCMLIX by Abingdon Press

All rights in this book are reserved.
No part of the book may be reproduced in any manner whatsoever without written permission of the publishers except brief quotations embodied in critical articles or reviews. For information address Abingdon Press, Nashville 2, Tennessee.

The Library of Congress has cataloged
this book as follows:

Stoody, Ralph. A handbook of church public relations. New York, Abingdon Press [1959] 256 p. 23 cm. 1. Public relations—Churches. i. Title: Church public relations. BV653.S84 254.4 59-8201 ‡

SET UP, PRINTED, AND BOUND BY THE
PARTHENON PRESS, AT NASHVILLE,
TENNESSEE, UNITED STATES OF AMERICA

DEDICATION

Dedicated to three esteemed associates in church public relations:
ARTHUR WEST,
ORVILLE B. FANNING, and
WILLIAM M. HEARN
and to an unexcelled administrative assistant,
CHARLOTTE HAINEY O'NEAL,
each of whom in the spirit of one ordained to the task has consecrated talent and time without stint or limit toward making the church more widely known and more fully understood.

PREFACE

"Sometimes it is more important to emphasize the obvious than to elucidate the obscure."

This observation by Oliver Wendell Holmes seems the perfect text for the preface of this book.

Since we must, in honesty, disclaim competence to elucidate anything very abstruse, it is no little comfort to be assured by so profound a scholar that the simpler task may be quite as useful as the more complex, and probably to a much larger number.

The mass media in all their aspects have of late been subjected to intensive examination. In laboratories, in homes, and at their desks erudite researchers are conducting investigations, analyses, syntheses, measurement and testing procedures. Attempts are being made to formulate both a philosophy and a theology of Christian communication. Magazines and books have been reporting their findings, not always in terms fully comprehended by the average reader. Sometimes, a little dazed, one catches himself as he seeks to interpret the reports, asking, "What's that again?"

But, understand it or not, this kind of psychoanalysis of the media must be made. In the same way that the development of pure mathematics preceded application of this knowledge to the new problems of physics, brought forward by the atomic age, theorizing on communication is a necessary preliminary to its improvement.

All those who are elucidating the obscurities in the realm of communication have this in common. Their conclusions implant in their readers one clear and inescapable idea: effective communication is such tremendously important business that upon it depends the happiness of mankind and the peace of the world.

This book is concerned with better public relations in church life. Good public relations obviously involves successful communication. It is as practitioners, not as metaphysicians, that we will be approaching the communications media.

Happily the nature of public relations is such that a practical treatment of its problems will be most likely achieved by "emphasizing the obvious."

The practice of public relations seems to have attained full professional status with dignified organizations fostering it. Universities not only are set up to teach it, but in some the subject has the status of a department. But with all this, the content of the curricula, the subject matter of what is taught, is completely out in the open, hidden from no one.

There are professions that do seem deliberately to surround their procedures with a touch of the mysterious. In dealing with their patients or clients their practitioners seldom employ simple words of Anglo-Saxon derivation if more impressive technical nomenclature of Latin or Greek descent is available. The kindly but often slightly condescending efforts of these men of the learned professions to answer questions usually leave their listeners both confused and impressed. Try to remember what you told your wife when she asked, "What did the doctor say?"

If this seems a bit unfair, decode the next cryptic prescription your specialist hands you. Ask yourself what possible reason he could have had for writing beside some odd-looking symbols *acidum acetylsalicylicum* when all he ordered was aspirin. Or struggle through some of the fine print on your insurance policy which in ponderous legal language guards not only your rights under the contract, but with special consideration the rights of the company.

Public relations, whatever comments may be made about it, kindly or caustic, is in no way like this, at least where persons of normal analytical powers and discernment are concerned. Everything is out on the table for all to see. The working tools and their operation are familiar. The so-called "hidden persuaders" are actually not so hard to find, and the unseen motivation is not as difficult to identify as some would make out.

Were public relations next to impossible to comprehend, it wouldn't be *public* relations.

Actually almost everyone thinks, were he to give the subject enough thoughtful attention, that he would do rather well at public relations. In holding this opinion almost everyone is right, provided he doesn't overlook the part about giving it thought. This is the crux. Bad public relations comes not from the absence of an awe-inspiring vocabulary or from lack of a bag of tricks or because one has not mastered certain esoterica. Bad public relations results from not having given a situation enough thought.

Usually this deficiency of thought comes not because of too brief cerebration but from concentrating on only one narrow sector of the problem, your side of it. One can never achieve good public relations, no matter how long and how hard he belabors his gray matter, if he does not circle the situation, see it from the standpoint of all parties involved, major and minor, and with understanding and sympathy.

A farmer was approached by a salesman. "This book on agriculture," he said, "will teach you how to be twice as good a farmer as you are now." "Shucks," replied the prospect, "I don't need no such book. I ain't farming now half as well as I know how."

The book that you hold in your hand has been written in the belief that every minister, church worker, public relations chairman, organizational press secretary, and the publicity director for every church institution has tremendous potential for effective public relations. Many are demonstrating this insight and these skills every day. But few of us could not improve. We are not practicing public relations half as well as we know how.

This is why this book seeks to "emphasize the obvious [rather] than to elucidate the obscure."

A Texas church leader, Bishop A. Frank Smith, once wrote: "Again and again I say to my men privately and I say it to them in conferences, 'Given character and a modicum of ability, nine-tenths of the success and failure of a minister can be charted in the field of his public relations.'"

What is true of a minister is also true of a church. Nine tenths of the success of a church on the human side is the result of good public relations.

This brings us to the question of definition. Exactly what is meant by "public relations"? First of all, it is not something you can have or not have at will. Whether or not you like it, you and your church have public relations. You cannot escape. You can, however, determine whether your public relations practices are good or bad.

Forget the pompous and complex approach to the subject. Among professionals in the general field may be those who aspire to be "propagandistic manipulators" or "engineers of consent," but this type of practitioner is extremely rare. In general, PR people seem sincerely committed to standards of truth and good taste and to objectives that are in accordance with public welfare. Their definitions, which may help churchmen in their understanding of "public relations," are simple and straightforward.

These definitions require little adaptation when applied to the public relations of churches and churchmen, if any. Singly or collectively they may help bring us all to a common understanding of "public relations." (Other definitions of public relations may be found on pp. 228-29.)

Good public relations means obtaining merited recognition and understanding for the causes you represent.
Good public relations is doing a job well and getting credit for it.
Good public relations is basically good internal relations made public.
Good public relations is the creation and carrying out of ideas which result in good will.
Good public relations are those procedures by which an individual or an institution becomes more widely and more favorably known.

In the framework of religion good public relations can be thought of as doing whatever contributes toward making a church deserve and receive the confidence and co-operation of increasing numbers of people—in still simpler form: making friends for Christ and his Church.

RALPH STOODY

CONTENTS

PART ONE
HEADLINING THE CHURCH

CHAPTER I. The Church—A Public Relations Natural 17
    Message Conveyed by Fine Arts—Church First to Broadcast—Invitation Set to Music—Relation to Life's Crises—The Church and the Printing Press—Growing Hospitality Toward Church News

CHAPTER II. What Makes News "News"? 26
    Most Church Happenings Not News—Importance Versus News Value—The People's Interest in News—Ingredients That Add News Value—Finding the News in Your Church

CHAPTER III. How to Write News 35
    News Writing Versus Homiletic Style—Writing the Lead—Why the "Inverted Pyramid" Formula?—Editorializing and Moralizing—Fact Sheet—Feature Stories

CHAPTER IV. Releases: How to Prepare and Present Them 44
    Mechanical Details—Identification of Source—Release Date—No Headlines—Date Lines—Typing the Release—Accuracy Essential—Handling Names—Deadlines

CHAPTER V. Dealing with Editors and Reporters 56
    Newsmen's Dim View of Clergy—Newspapermen—The Papers' Preferences—Promptness with Reporters—Condescension—Pitfalls of a Church Editor's Job—Respect for Newsmen's Professional Status—Building Up a Beginning Reporter—Boners—Changes—Trusting the

11

A HANDBOOK OF CHURCH PUBLIC RELATIONS

Reporter—Possibility of Being Quoted—Exclusives—Following Through—Ministers Let Down the Press—News Tips—When It's Bad News—Fighting the Evil, Not the Editor—Saying "Thank You."

CHAPTER VI. Camera in the Service of the Church 77
Ideas Conveyed Quickly from Good Pictures—Working with News Photographers—What It Takes to Make a Photo Click—Appointing an Official Church Photographer—Some Warnings and Some Hints—Watching Your Backgrounds—Captions and Cut Lines

CHAPTER VII. How to Make News When There Isn't Any 89
Anniversaries—Interest in Notable Numbers—Someone for Honors—Doing Something Differently—Tying in with Current News Events—News Interest Magnified by Dramatizing

CHAPTER VIII. Covering Conferences and Conventions 103
Conventions in the News—Preparing for Convention Coverage—Coverage at the Convention—Reaching Outlets Not Represented—After Conference Chores

PART TWO

RADIO AND TELEVISION SERVING THE CHURCH

CHAPTER IX. You, Your Church, and the Networks 127
Obligation of Churches to Broadcasters—Influence on Network Broadcasting

CHAPTER X. If You Want Air Time 131
Why Time Is Hard to Get—Hints That May Help—A Strong Promotion Plan—Relations with Stations

CONTENTS

CHAPTER XI. Program Formats Are Many 137
    Talks and Sermons—Interviews—Panels—Documentaries—Dramatic Programs

CHAPTER XII. Broadcasting the News of Religion 149
    Newscasters—You as Church Newscaster

PART THREE
YOUR CHURCH MEETS ITS PUBLIC

CHAPTER XIII. Buildings Can Invite or Repel 159
    Landscaping and Lighting—Adequate Parking Provisions—Signs of the Times—Immaculate Housekeeping—Equipped for Worship, Training, and Service—How Comfortable Are Thy Dwelling Places?

CHAPTER XIV. Public Relations and the Church School 172
    Keen Sense of Public Relations Values—Neglecting to Use Press—Plenty to Publicize—Creating News—Still and Motion Pictures—Handling News—Teachers

CHAPTER XV. The Parish Paper in the Public Relations Program . . 179
    Public Relations Values in Parish Papers—Financing the Paper—Editing the Parish Paper—Make-up, Layout, and Style

CHAPTER XVI. Ushers—Hosts for God 190
    Few or Many Ushers—Appearance "Given to Hospitality"—Front and Center—Courtesy Toward Guests—Some Do's for Ushers—And, of Course, Some Don't's—Names on the Dotted Line—Training Your Ushers

CHAPTER XVII. Telephone and Post Office Work for the Church . . 200
    Telephone Manners—"May I Tell Him Who's Call-

ing?"—*Reaching Your Families by Tele-Corps—Art of Letter Writing—Conversational Letters—Length of the Letter—To the Editor*

CHAPTER XVIII. Sermon Titles Have Public Relations 211
    Titles—Anticipation—Universal Problems—Truth in Advertising

CHAPTER XIX. Public Relations Pointers for Pastors 217
    Dependence on Good Public Relations—A Pastor's Inward Look—Personalized Pastoral Remembrances—Birthdays—Wedding Anniversaries—Anniversaries of Sorrow—Obtaining Birth Dates—Finding Time

CHAPTER XX. A Live Public Relations Committee 227
    Public Relations Committee: How Many and Who?—Meaning of Public Relations—General Objectives—General Policy Principles of Committee—Public Relations Subcommittees and Their Duties

CHAPTER XXI. Getting Personal About Public Relations 238
    Good Rumor Man—Believers and Communicators—Society of Aaron and Hur—Church of a Thousand Pastors—More Than Techniques

    Glossary 245
    Index 251

PART ONE

HEADLINING THE CHURCH

CHAPTER I

The Church—A Public Relations Natural

WHY SHOULD CHURCHES BE INTERESTED IN PUBLIC RELATIONS? Here is the answer to this frequent question: Why shouldn't they?

Churches were among the earliest practitioners of the arts and techniques that are now the arsenal of the modern PR professional. Many of the methods which the mid-twentieth-century publicity man mistakenly thinks he invented actually had their prototypes in early religious life.

Increasingly during the past hundred years governments, the military, manufacturers, merchandisers, hotels, colleges, and the entertainment industry have all set up offices of public information

17

in a deliberate and studied effort to "make friends and influence people." While departments so labeled have been a part of the organizations of our several church bodies for only a few decades, the church in general has been utilizing all known communications media to further its cause for many centuries.

Some interesting practices of the church have come down to us from the past. Because of our familiarity with them, we accept them simply as customs and traditions. A moment's reflection will reveal these usages as evidence of the keenest public relations understanding on the part of the church fathers.

Were these policies revealed to them, or are they the product of sheer promotional genius? Whichever is true, they worked. They continue to compel attention to the church, to develop loyalty to it, and to interpret its message.

Had more recent church leaders been as alert as the founding fathers in appropriating the newer communications media developed during the last century and in adapting them to reach the hearts and minds of the age, the church would be much further on its way.

Message Conveyed by Fine Arts

The earliest churches we can find anywhere in Europe look like nothing else but churches. Their wise builders constructed them according to designs that required no identifying signs. Their architecture spelled out unmistakably c-h-u-r-c-h to every passer-by. We are so accustomed to this today that it is easy to overlook its PR significance.

The first builders of village chapels and town churches and urban cathedrals were not compelled to give them a form that distinguished them from all other structures. When they did do this, knowingly or not, they erected in effect not only sanctuaries but huge, four-sided outdoor signboards which all day long and through the shadowy moonlight wordlessly reminded men of the worship of God.

They built these temples loftier than was needed for the accommodation of the congregation. Thus they could be seen farther. That this visual influence might reach even greater distances, they surmounted their churches with vaulted domes and upreaching spires.

These churches, architectural testimonies to their faith, they placed as conspicuously as they could, where radiating streets converged at the town square, or on an eminence. The church was the first structure to meet the farmer's eyes as he slowly journeyed to the market city.

If the spire on the skyline suggested prayer or praise to him as he slowly approached, isn't it likely that this possibility was in the minds of those who raised it there?

Public good will was created by making these churches beautiful within and without, whatever the other good motives. Inside were paintings, sculpture, tapestries, and colorful windows.

In a day when only a small minority could read, the illiterate were taught by picture language and by symbols. A father and mother on a Sunday afternoon might stand with their family before a tapestry or a painting of Jesus blessing the little children. As a generation ago they had been told the story by their own parents, they now communicated it to their own boys and girls with the help of what today we call "visual aids."

Similarly the Stations of the Cross almost explained themselves to untutored worshipers. The symbolism, the vestments, the drama of the liturgy, were all used as media of interpretation.

Church First to Broadcast

Not only did the public relations genius of our church fathers show itself in reaching men through their eyes; it capitalized on audio communications as well. Broadcasting—we think—started soon after World War I, or at the earliest with Marconi. Didn't it actually originate with medieval churchmen?

Someone in those days before noon whistles, when watches and clocks were possessed only by the wealthy, suggested that a bell would be helpful in notifying parishioners of the arrival of the hours for divine services. The first church bells were erected on platforms in front of or alongside the sanctuary.

Then someone else, with a still-higher public relations I.Q., suggested that the range of this broadcasting station could be considerably increased by elevating the bell. Towers were built for the purpose and the desired result obtained. Now with a favoring wind the sound could be heard for several miles.

Millet in his painting "The Angelus" shows on the distant horizon the bell tower from which such a broadcast came. In the foreground the peasant couple heeds the summons of the bells. They stop their work in the fields to offer their evening prayer.

Through the centuries music has been an almost-essential component of both Jewish and Christian worship. The psalms and the hymns are so much a part of our religious practice that it may seem to some almost improper to point out the genius of those patriarchs who realized that melody and poetry and harmony could be used as mechanisms of religious communication. Hymns are not used solely to pray, to praise, to confess, and to meditate. They are employed as well to declare beliefs, to teach doctrines, and to evangelize.

Invitation Set to Music

Centuries before Madison Avenue, U.S.A., even thought of implanting desires for merchandise by singing their virtues over the airways, the church harmonized its appeals, its advantages, and its invitations. The men in the gray flannel suits have obviously borrowed the idea for the singing commercial. They should at once double their subscriptions to their several churches as a method of paying this debt.

The church has for years been singing this invitation to men: "Come we that love the Lord, and let our joys be known." Here is a hymn that summons to repentence: "Come, ye sinners, poor and needy."

Certain melodious health broadcasts are today aimed at specific types of sufferers, and prescriptions proffered. Even so the church long, long ago directed some of its harmonized verses to particular audiences.

As an example of such selectivity here is a hymn "pitched" to the disheartened and discouraged. It recommends a remedy in confident terms and gives specific instructions to persons so afflicted:

> Come, ye disconsolate, where'er ye languish,
> Come to the mercy seat, fervently kneel;
> Here bring your wounded hearts, here tell your anguish:
> Earth has no sorrow that heaven cannot heal.

Churches understand basically how to get through to the human being. They reach him through his vision, through his hearing, through his emotions, and through his intellect.

In the pre-Christian background days of our faith, and later in large sections of the church continuing today there is communication even through the sense of smell by the use of incense. No approach has been overlooked.

The distinctive garb of the clergy and of others dedicated to the religious life serves not only its primary purposes. Worn at all times, it also advertises the church and is a constant reminder of the availability of the particular type of service each wearer is prepared to give. This, too, is good public relations.

Relation to Life's Crises

The church with admirable wisdom has tied itself to the several crucial experiences of human life. There is a sense of responsibility that comes to young parents. In the case of the first baby particularly and to some degree with the advent of every child, parents feel inadequate.

At this critical moment religion steps in, depending upon the century and the practices of the group, to provide ceremonies of dedication at the temple or church. Here the parents promise to rear their offspring "in the nurture and admonition of the Lord." At the same time the religious authority offers directly or by implication its interests, assistance, and blessing.

In whatever way the doctrinal significance of such a ceremony is construed, one result is that parents feel an increased sense of gratitude, dependence, and endearment toward the institution. To them the rite constitutes formal assurance that they have the total resources of the church as their ally in their parental joys and duties.

In much the same way the church anticipates the transition from childhood to youth and its responsibilities with various appropriate rites. These increase the sense of "belonging." The young person learns to speak with assurance of "my church."

When love comes with its promise of the founding of a new home, the church makes itself significant. Its ministry on such occasions is indispensable to those who regard marriage as a sacrament. Other churches regard their blessing upon the marriage contract as no less meaningful. Here again, however one regards the doctrinal or legal aspects of wedlock, the fact that it became "holy" matrimony indicates in addition to everything else an amazing sense of good public relations. What better step toward acquiring the loyalty of the home than to become essentially related to the home's authorization and foundation?

Similarly, in other life crises such as serious illness and death the church is on call with rites and ministries of strength and comfort. Its services at such seasons of dire need and human helplessness cannot help producing grateful loyalty.

It is interesting to observe, too, how holiday observances in the home have been tied in with happy religious anniversaries: Christmas, Easter, and Thanksgiving. Of course the degree to which these days have been secularized is deplorable. Even after discounting this, though, in these festivals there are immense educational and promotional values for the church. Public relations men would give anything to have millions of people the world around give comparable time and attention to occasions related to their clients' institutions and observances.

Consciously or unconsciously, by deliberate planning or as accidental by-products, those who patterned church life through the centuries provided the world with its best and first lessons in productive public relations.

The Church and the Printing Press

When Martin Luther hurled the inkpot at the devil, if we can credit this tradition, he initiated the use of a new missile in the age-long war against evil. Ink was to become as revolutionary, as powerful and of as long-range effectiveness in the centuries that followed, as the I.C.B.M. is today.

It is no accident that the rapid spread of the Protestant Reformation followed so closely in point of time the invention of printing from movable type, and that the Bible was the first book to be published.

Martin Luther's hammer, as he defiantly nailed his ninety-five theses to the church door in Wittenberg, was presently widely echoed by crude wooden presses. Their platens were noisily implanting printer's ink on paper, proclaiming the new, revolutionary doctrines.

The publication of propaganda and counterpropaganda soon developed into what church historians have called the "pamphlet war," made possible by this new, effective communications medium, the printing press. The several religious movements that were the offspring of the Reformation depended heavily upon the printer's ink for the dissemination of their distinctive tenets.

Throughout the succeeding centuries the art of printing has been the constant ally of religion. Particularly in colonial America where population was sparse, the circuit rider's saddlebags were loaded with small books and tracts. Left with their pioneer followers, this reading matter answered questions and kept faith and loyalty alive between pastoral visits.

One "apostle of the long trail," Francis Asbury, evaluated religious publications thus: "The propagation of religion by means of the press is next in importance to the preaching of the gospel."

Unfortunately, however, the influence of church publications tends to be confined to a constituency already committed to the Christian life. To reach the unreached is one aim of the church in seeking to make the largest possible use of the nation's 1,875 daily papers, of its 10,000 weeklies, its magazines, and its radio and TV.

Another reason why the churches frankly desire to utilize the secular press is for the information of their own members. Denominational periodicals reach but a minor fraction of total memberships. They are read by a still smaller proportion. This means that the only place that many professed Christians are reading news of their own communions or of the larger world of religion is in their newspapers.

Growing Hospitality Toward Church News

Newspapers and magazines have never devoted more space to religion than they are giving now. In 1930 Professor Talcott Williams of the Columbia University School of Journalism said:

Sixty years ago (1870) when a New York daily began to print news of religious organizations, report sermons and follow the affairs of churches, almost every religious body in the city protested against the desecration. Today American dailies print more religious news and give more space to affairs of the churches than any other newspapers in the world.

If Professor Williams was gratified in 1930, it would be interesting to know what he would say today. Publisher James A. Linen of *Time* gave some indication in his issue (September 6, 1954) of the reaction of the press twenty-four years later to a gathering of world churchmen held in Illinois:

The Evanston meeting was important news.... Some 3,000 reporters applied for accreditation.... Reluctantly, the council cut the list of accredited correspondents and photographers down to 600, representing 36 countries. Warned by the flood of applications for press passes, the council was prepared to give more than casual help to reporters.... There was also a full-time staff of 54 public-relations experts to see that the press got its share of 6½ tons of speeches, reports and papers. . . .

In a broad sense, the meeting might be said to signal the arrival of a time in which the U. S. press in general recognizes that religious news has become news in the accepted city-room sense of the word. Scores of reporters who had never before written a religion story were on the job for wire services and major dailies around the world.

Evidence of increasing hospitality on the part of newspapers toward religious news and the enlarging understanding between these two influential institutions, the press and the pulpit, can be found in addresses of many noted publishers.

Just before he died in 1951, Edwin L. James, speaking as managing editor of *The New York Times*, declared that America's largest newspapers "are giving more and more space to the major developments in the religious world." His reason for this changed policy was that the papers are beginning to realize that religious news interested readers. "I think the church is, even if belatedly, finding it has an important ally in the newspapers," he said, "and it seems to me that the press, on the other hand, is perhaps also belatedly coming to a more complete realization that there is important news in religion."

Magazines have also thrown out the red carpet to the churches. It was not long ago that a rather rigid taboo against religion prevailed. Editors who did not shrink from differences of opinion in other areas avoided the subject.

"Religious loyalties are too deeply seated to take a chance," they said. "People get emotional when the subject is discussed. We would lose subscribers by the thousands. Religion is just too controversial to touch."

This attitude is almost completely reversed today. The photojournalism magazines have carried lengthy and profusely illustrated articles on the several church bodies. They have published question and answer series on the doctrines and practices of the denominations. Hundreds of thousands of reprints of such articles have been circulated. The demand has been so great that series have been brought together in book form.

A study was made by a seminar group in Hartford Theological Foundation of articles in *Reader's Digest* throughout a year. From each of twelve successive issues the five articles were selected which were thought "to be most likely to release Christlike conduct." At the end of the year these sixty articles were checked with the *Digest's* own readership survey. It was found that these "religious" articles all had registered from one and a half to twice the reader appeal of the average article and that forty of the sixty fell in the highest category of reader interest.

These evidences of the changed attitude of the nation's dailies and weeklies toward news of the churches and the new hospitality of magazines toward religious subjects is cited to encourage you and your church to take the fullest possible advantage of the situation.

There is hospitalty for religious news, but it must be *news*.

To transfer the event from where it happened to the printed page requires some skills which, if you do not presently possess them, are easily developed.

How to recognize news, how to write it, how to prepare and present it, and how, when it is running low, to make it are subjects of subsequent chapters.

What a pity it would be if in this technological age the church were to make less imaginative, less effective use of the media available to it than did the churches of the middle ages with their primitive but perfectly utilized resources.

CHAPTER II

What Makes News "News"?

"A BETTER UNDERSTANDING ON THE PART OF CHURCH OFFICIALS as to what constitutes news would, I think, serve both the churches and the newspapers." This conviction, voiced by Jonathan Daniels, is widely held and often expressed by editors.

Whether or not the newsman's definition of his commodity coincides with the minister's judgment, it is the editor's decision that the churchman will have to accept if there is to be the fullest cooperation between his church and the news outlets. When one is making use of another's medium, he must realize that the owner and controller of that medium makes the rules and defines the terms.

While this principle prevails in general, it should be stated in tribute to the kindness of editors that there is no category of their many publics where they stretch their otherwise rigid definitions of "news" as leniently as they do with religion. A vast amount of linage is devoted to the churches each week by the newspapers of the nation. Much of this, though a valuable public service, cannot by any construction be regarded as "news."

"There are three kinds of news," the religion editor of *Time*, Douglas Auchincloss, once told a ministerial press seminar. "First is 'Gee Whiz' news." This type of news story is summarized by a banner head and is calculated to evoke expletives of amazement when the story is read. "Gee whiz!" the reader will say, or a reasonably accurate facsimile, depending upon his state of grace.

"Fun news" is the second category. Sports pages, amusements, the woman's section, and the back-of-the-book departments of magazines like *Time* and *Newsweek* are examples.

The third classification of news is "for edification"—news that is good for one's mind. Unfortunately most church news falls into this category.

Most Church Happenings Not News

Much that happens in the church obviously is not "news" in the sense of being "something new." Routine church procedures rarely come under the dictionary definition of "hitherto unknown facts, fresh tidings."

It is not news when a science teacher lectures on the laws of falling bodies, even if he has just returned from a convention of physicists. Nor is it news when the ancient history professor discusses the Peloponnesian Wars, even with new insights from last summer's cruise in the Mediterranean.

The city editor does not print stories of routine lectures in a school because they are merely part of the curriculum. It is the business of the teacher to be giving such instruction. By no definition can it be regarded as news.

By just the same reasoning, it is not news that the minister of First Church is about to preach a series of sermons on the Ten Commandments or on the Beatitudes. The city editor regards this as part of the preacher's curriculum. Everyone expects the church to be against sin and the church school to desire record-breaking attendance. "I was lured to regularity with gold and silver pins, picnics, and Christmas candy myself," the editor tells the pastor, "and they've been seeking larger numbers ever since."

When newspapers do publish items dealing with the routine and expected activities of a church, the pastor should gratefully recognize this evidence of newsmen's concern in the public welfare. The publishers are trying to help the church by giving it some free advertising. Never assume that they regard material of this kind as news.

To decide whether an item about your own church is news, ask yourself whether you would be interested in reading a similar story about a church of another denomination over on the other side of town. If the story in itself doesn't interest you, then it is not news.

Importance Versus News Value

It is understandably difficult for a minister to realize that to the editor the *importance* of an event and its news value may be completely unrelated. The pastor is inclined to equate the two. The more important anything is, he reasons, the greater its news value.

Because he is engaged in what he regards as the most important task in the world, the clergyman cannot understand how the newspapers can devote so much space to trivialities and so little (sometimes none at all) to the important matters that fill his thoughts.

Unfortunately, importance alone does not make news. It is but one of a long list of factors. Many news stories have value solely because of the importance of an event; other stories, quite as newsworthy, are based on completely unimportant happenings.

A cat climbs a tree in the park in front of the courthouse. She goes so high that now she can't get down. A kind soul sees her predicament and calls the S.P.C.A. The society's light truck arrives but isn't equipped for this situation. The man in charge knows what to do next. He calls the fire department. By the time the long red fire truck arrives, a crowd has gathered. Extension ladders begin reaching up. Newsmen, alerted by the fire station alarm, are there almost as soon as the hook and ladder. Police cruiser cars roll in. More and more people strain to catch sight of the frightened cat. A fireman makes sure progress up the steps of the ladder. The crowd is breathless. He scoops up the cat and brings her to the ground. Speed graphic shutters click madly. Cleverly written feature stories and the pictures are on page one of the evening papers.

WHAT MAKES NEWS "NEWS"?

This saga of a stray alley cat certainly was not important yet it was definitely regarded as being newsworthy. Why? First, the crowd it attracted proved that people were interested in the event. Next, an animal was involved. Every news photographer knows that animals rank with pretty girls and children as subjects of universal interest. Everyone who had ever had a pet would be interested in this event.

The story was also newsworthy because it was not something that happens every day: the dilemma of the cat, the use made of the fire ladders, and the nature of the service rendered by the fireman added elements of the unusual. And at least in the eyes of some of the spectators, the fireman seemed to be risking his life on a hazardously insecure ladder to save a cat.

When Senator Glen H. Taylor first came to Washington, photo editors of the wire services remembered how as the "Singing Cowboy" he had played his guitar at political rallies during his campaign. They persuaded him to put on the broad-brimmed Stetson which he had worn back in the state of Idaho and to be photographed on the Capitol steps accompanying himself as he sang a western ballad.

The Senator reported that "the atomic age had wrought no revolution in American press standards of news judgment." When he obliged the reporters by singing on the Capitol steps, "they put the picture in every newspaper, including the *New York Times.*" But when he did something of real importance and introduced a resolution calling for a world republic to save mankind from mass extinction, he got "practically no space at all." "I don't know what kind of moral to draw from this," he told the Senate.

The People's Interest in News

Newsmen do not accept responsibility for the well-established criteria of news value; many of them would like to see the criteria changed. News is what interests people. The public, they say, determines what is news, not the editors.

A western newspaper deliberately tested its policy of making full use of the news from Asia. For thirty days nothing with an Asiatic date line was published. There was not a single protest, not even an inquiry. During this period it skipped "Little Orphan Annie" just once. There were five thousand letters and innumerable phone calls.

The late Bishop Lewis O. Hartman challenged newspapers because they gave major space to three daily-double ticket holders at a New

Hampshire track who had won $8,614 apiece. They ignored the fact that on the same day in the vicinity of Worcester, Massachusetts, twelve hundred persons had embraced the Christian faith.

Among the many papers which commented was the *Daily Courier* of Waterloo, Iowa. Their editorial said:

> Every newspaperman recognizes the sincerity of such criticisms and accepts the responsibility of presenting news of real community significance, as well as that of merely superficial interest. But it is a difficult problem. If fifteen thousand Waterloo husbands behave themselves and don't beat their wives, that fact isn't news. But if one Waterloo husband does beat his wife, that is news. In other words, it is much more significant for the welfare of the community that fifteen thousand husbands don't beat their wives than that one does; yet the public is interested in the one who does.

The editor adds:

> If Bishop Hartman can devise some way to make the conversion of twelve hundred people to Christianity as interesting as it is important, he will win the sincere gratitude of every newsman.

The classic illustration of journalism lecturers is not repeated here to labor the point. However, it does show clearly that factors other than basic significance weigh heavily in determining the space and position of news coverage.

Rudolph Valentino's death coincided with that of ex-president Eliot of Harvard University. There were yards of space for the movie idol, and inches for the great educator. Did this mean that Eliot was less important? No newsman would have said so. Yet they were quite content to use the wire service announcement of Eliot's death, the obituary in their files, and perhaps a one-column halftone. Meanwhile, they were making over page one to give room to the Valentino story, a review of his life and loves, pictures from his roles, and photos of the block-circling queues which moved slowly through the funeral chapel day and night.

The contrasts between President Eliot and Valentino highlight elements that make for news interest: Eliot died a very old man; Valentino, in his thirties. There was no shock in the death of a tottering and feeble man; no one, on the other hand, anticipated the death of Valentino, robust, virile, the very symbol of vitality. For every

WHAT MAKES NEWS "NEWS"?

hundred who knew of Eliot there were tens of thousands not only who had heard of Valentino but who felt almost that they knew him personally. The name Valentino had the matinee idol appeal of romance. And in this last illness, there had been the element of conflict—would he or the disease conquer? This combination of elements made the man who had entertained millions one of the most written about and read about personalities of all time.

We would not wish to outrage the feelings of the many admirers who swooned at Valentino's bier, but regardless of the elements which so obviously made him newsworthy, he could scarcely be called important.

Churchmen are coming more and more to realize that importance is only one of several factors that affect the news judgment of city editors. To understand this is to avoid disappointment in your relations with the press. It will help keep you from expecting the impossible.

On the positive side, to know news when you see it will aid you in co-operating understandingly and profitably with newsmen.

Ingredients That Add News Value

Here are some of the ingredients that give news value to a happening.

PROXIMITY—There is more interest on the part of villagers in the process of regilding the weather vane on the town hall than in a revolution in Indonesia. Should your mayor drive his car into a tree and fracture his collarbone, it would produce a bigger story in your local paper than an earthquake in New Zealand that makes ten thousand homeless.

TIMELINESS—There is nothing as perishable as news. Don't discount the phrase "News while it is news." The same newspaper that you selected from the newsstand last night with eager expectation, you will use this morning, if it is cool, to start a blaze in the fireplace.

NAMES MAKE NEWS—An old city room instruction is that if a dog bites a man, it isn't news, while if a man bites a dog it is news. But observe that a sufficiently well-known name can upset otherwise fixed standards. Should the vicious dog happen to be a Rin Tin Tin or a Lassie or a Fala or a Checkers, even if the victim is an unknown wayfarer, it will probably make the papers in spite of the rule. Moreover, if a famous dog nips a famous man, Gromyko, for example, the news value is double. Names are newsworthy.

VARIATION FROM NORMAL—Ordinary temperatures are recorded in small type in a tiny box in the paper. Extremes of heat and cold make front page stories. Columbia University once had a chaplain whose learned discourses were rarely, and then but briefly, reported. In his undergraduate days, however, he had been a member of the rowing crew. Each year on his birthday to prove his continuing prowess he stripped down to T-shirt and trunks and rowed a shell up the Hudson to Poughkeepsie. This renewal of his youthful athletic specialty by reason of the contrast with the way the chaplain spent the other 364 days of the year was always good for photos and interviews in the metropolitan papers. The space he commanded for this birthday exploit probably surpassed his newspaper attention for the rest of the year.

LARGE NUMBERS OF PEOPLE—Occasions that interest huge crowds are newsworthy for that reason even if for no other. Examples are the "Festival of Faith" that brought 125,000 to Chicago Soldier Field, huge Reformation services that overflow municipal auditoriums, and Billy Graham's speaking in Times Square and in Yankee Stadium.

WIDESPREAD INTEREST—For the same reason, anything of interest to large numbers of people, such as a change in postal rates or the discovery of a possible help for the common cold, may be news. The item in itself does not have to be important if it interests almost everybody at least a little bit. Conversely, matters important to but a few people have little news value, even though the facts may be highly significant to the few who are interested.

MAGNITUDE—Vast figures, immense dimensions, celestial distances, extreme age—all influence an editor's news judgment. Several cathedrals claim to be the world's largest. The standard of comparison in one case is over-all length, in another the number of square feet covered, in another the cubic content, in still another the height of the dome. There seems to be a universal interest in record-breaking "new highs." A new "longest tunnel" or "fastest ship" or "highest-flying jet plane" or "tallest building" always rates a story.

DISASTER—The same factors that produce a crowd from nowhere when a street accident occurs lead to a desire to read about catastrophes

WHAT MAKES NEWS "NEWS"?

—accidents, conflicts, cruelty, crimes, floods, fires, tornadoes. Dr. H. A. Overstreet wrote in *The Mature Mind:*

> Newspapers have a vested interest in catastrophe. Planes that fly safely, the trains that reach their destination, the individuals who live together without murdering each other, the rivers that flow between their banks, and the men and nations that transact their affairs and resolve their differences without fighting are not news.

CONFLICT—STRUGGLE—A happier expression of the same interest that puts war news on page one is responsible for the great attention given by newspapers to sports. The struggles of man against man in the ring, on the mat or track, or on the clay courts; the hotly contested games of team play; the racing of horses; the struggle of man against bull in the arena: all make big news. Opposing forces, such as man versus the machine, add news value.

MYSTERY AND DISCOVERY—Man may struggle against the unknown. Expressed in popular language accounts of scientists making new discoveries, of explorers probing new areas, of archaeologists unearthing secrets of the past, and of crime sleuths ferreting hidden clues are all of interest to many people and hence are news.

BASIC INTERESTS—These general categories of news interest are not the only ones. In addition, a number of basic needs and concerns of human beings compel almost universal attention and often get into the news. Among these interests are children, romance, marriage, pets, homes, food, sex, money, travel, health, and self-improvement. There are many more.

Finding the News in Your Church

The foregoing paragraphs describe primary elements that enhance the news value of a happening or a set of facts.

At first thought it may seem that by these standards there isn't much in your church that would qualify as news. If you mean "Gee Whiz!" news, you are probably right. It is true that most of what goes on, including some of the most significant activities, do not classify as news.

A large number of common church happenings still remain, however, that in all but metropolitan dailies will stand a good chance of publication if properly presented.

The following suggestions for news stories, grouped under obvious topics, are not a complete list. Let them serve only as a self-starter. You will immediately think of more.

For less obvious news possibilities see the chapter on "How to Make News When There Isn't Any."

THE MINISTER—His call, appointment, installation, reception, resignation, retirement, speaking engagements, denominational duties, hobbies, vacations, travels, attendance at conventions, pastors' schools and retreats, civic recognitions, community service, interchurch participation, counseling programs, articles, pamphlets, or books written.

ORGANIZATIONS—Staff changes, annual meetings, meetings of governing boards, elections of officers, adoption of budget, reports of financial progress or membership growth, choirs, ushers' clubs, church school teacher elections, teacher installations, graduation ceremonies, leadership training, vacation church schools, curriculum changes, mission, Bible and stewardship study groups, outings, men's clubs, women's organizations, youth fellowships, Boy Scouts, Girl Scouts, conferences and conventions.

UNUSUAL PUBLIC SERVICES—New Year's Eve, February patriotic days, Ash Wednesday, Lenten missions, Holy Week, Maundy Thursday, Good Friday, Easter, Whitsunday (Pentecost), Commemorative days, Children's Day, Mother's and Father's days, Independence Day, Labor Sunday, World Communion, Veterans Day, Thanksgiving, Harvest Festivals, Advent Sundays, Christmas Eve, Christmas Day, Student Recognition Day, Evangelistic Services, Founders' Day, Laymen's Sunday, Temperance Sunday, Rallies, Pageants, Oratorios, and dramatic programs.

PROPERTY—Bequests, new church plans, landscaping, new education wings, new parsonages, renovations, redecoration, new furnishings, organs, carillons, memorial windows, new recreational facilities indoor or outdoor, new kitchens or kitchen modernization, and nursery.

SERVICE ACTIVITIES—Children's and teen-age programs, recreation, assistance to displaced families, young marrieds, baby sitters, get-acquainted and fellowship projects, child study groups, audio-visual utilization, panel programs, forums, drama and choral groups, work programs, paint-up and cleanup crews, and every-member canvasses.

CHAPTER III

How to Write News

MANY MINISTERS BECOME EXCELLENT NEWS WRITERS THROUGH training and observation. It is not at all surprising that many others don't. Good reporting and good sermon writing involve totally different principles. To excel in one, it is necessary to forget almost all that has been learned about the other.

The homiletic approach to a theme is likely to be gradual. The minister will ease into the subject a little at a time, like a bather inching into the water because he shrinks from a sudden icy immersion. He may move into the topic historically, or he may open by stating a problem which he will later seek to solve.

A minister may discuss a doctrine, telling first what other men in other ages have believed, pointing out why he cannot accept their reasoning, and ultimately stating and supporting his own conclusions. Again, he may dissect a text word by word or phrase by phrase, seeking to discover its full meaning.

Only toward the end of the sermon does the preacher tie his facts and his arguments together, pleading for a decision or for the acceptance of his point of view, or challenging the listener to take some action or to adopt some policy.

This procedure is well suited to a church. The congregation is there for a stated period. There is adequate time to proceed little by little to the peroration. Nothing prevents the preacher from arranging his material in whatever order may seem most logical and convincing. His captive congregation will hear him through. While the minister speaks, there are no rival voices to divert attention.

News Writing Versus Homiletic Style

News writing is an entirely different problem. A story is only one of a dozen on the page. Each clamors to be read.

Analyze for a moment the way you read your paper. Your eye catches a headline. You read the first paragraph, then the next until the final word. Some stories you turn away from after a few paragraphs; others you read no further than the headline and the first paragraph. Some you give only a glance.

Every news story is in competition with every other. Probably no one reads everything in the paper. Newspaper reading is an extremely selective process.

The reporter knows that the reader will go only as far as his interest takes him. Just as quickly as he can, he gives prospective readers as much insight into the nature of his story as he can. He tries to arouse curiosity. He uses every lure to get the reader as far into the story as possible.

The good reporter has another reason for packing the opening sentences with the essential facts that will be developed later in the story more fully. He knows that many newspaper readers only "skim" the paper because their time is so limited. If reporters scattered basic facts throughout their stories, readers who spend only seconds on each one might miss the point or come away with distorted or incomplete ideas of the day's happenings.

HOW TO WRITE NEWS

The news writer is like a diver going off a diving board—he plunges head first into his story. He tells what has happened as simply, as directly, and as briefly as he can. He presents most conspicuously whatever facet of the story seems to him to have the widest interest.

Writing the Lead

The important first sentence or two in journalese is called the "lead" (pronounced to rhyme with "seed"). The news writer answers directly or by implication in this lead the questions in the reader's mind.

Who is involved in this story? *What* occurred? *When* and *where* did it happen? *Why* did it take place? In many stories the question "How?" must also be answered.

In a meeting when one action greatly outweighs in importance everything else that happened, that decision should, of course, constitute the lead.

Example: Provision for a new community youth center has been made by First Presbyterian Church. The trustees, meeting at the Parish House last night, voted to purchase the mansion at 810 Main Street, adjacent to the church. They appropriated $35,000 to renovate the building and equip it.

Should you be reporting a meeting where no item of business greatly exceeded another in interest a budget lead might be indicated. Here, in the briefest possible terms, you would list several of the subjects upon which action was taken.

Example: Trinity Church officials last night in their annual meeting re-elected officers, authorized minor improvements in the church plant, and reviewed reports from eight church organizations.

Leads may begin with a quotation provided it is striking and is pertinent to the general theme of the address or the occasion.

Example: "Not apostolic succession but apostolic success is the true criterion of the validity of ministerial orders." This was the point made by Dr. Ralph W. Sockman of New York in an address before the Faith and Order Conference in Westminster Theological Seminary here this morning.

"Shoot the works in the first paragraph," the city editor tells reporters. At the same time he blue-pencils leads crowded with too many details. Work these in later.

There are many types of leads. Study your newspapers.

When the story has been condensed into capsule form in the lead, the writer seemingly makes a second start. This gives news writing a certain repetitious quality.

The reporter selects the most significant of the elements set forth in the lead and develops its important details. Then he treats another element, already set forth, in greater detail. All the important facts are supplied in this way, in order of diminishing importance.

You can see why news stories *must* be written with each paragraph somewhat less important than the preceding one. They must be flexible.

No one knows in advance how many column inches of type will be produced in a day by the local staff. Nor can anyone foretell how much space in tomorrow's paper will be demanded by important world and national happenings. Since newspapers depend upon advertisers, the total news space in a given edition is often enlarged or diminished by the business office.

Until the last minute before press time demands for space must not be too rigid. Type cannot be compressed, and the chases that frame the pages cannot be stretched. The only "give" in the whole operation is in the length of the news stories.

Why the "Inverted Pyramid" Formula?

If there is more material than space, some of the stories must be eliminated, or else enough of them must be shortened so that they will fit into the space. This is easily done when news is written in the "inverted pyramid" formula.

The final paragraphs contain only the least important details. They can be quickly discarded if less space is available. Since the essential information has all been supplied in the early paragraphs, the reader will not be aware of the missing paragraphs.

Lengthy stories already in type are often cut to two or three inches under pressure of banner head news that comes in just before press time. This would be impossible if news stories were written like sermons.

If the climax came at the end of a news story, laborious editing, cutting, rewriting, and resetting would be required to reduce the story's length. There would not be time to do all this, and the story might be discarded.

Many churchmen waste hours puzzling self-consciously over the proper word choice and sentence structure. Writing for the press does not demand getting into a tension.

The "inverted pyramid" formula, for example, is not complicated. It is actually the simple, natural way any normal person would announce news to members of his own family. First he would tell in as few words as possible what happened. Then he would add details.

Relax when you write a news story. State the important facts as clearly and conciscly as possible. Concentrate on helping the newspaper or newscaster get the news of your church to the public.

It may help relieve nervousness to remember while writing that your story may not be used at all. Then keep in mind that even if it is eventually published, it will first pass through the hands of at least one newspaper editor. These, as their reporters know, are never quite as happy as when they are cutting out words. It's neither a sin nor a disgrace if you still have a few things to learn about a profession that isn't your own.

Editorializing and Moralizing

Reporting differs from preaching in content as well as in the order in which facts are presented. A pastor is expected to voice his personal opinion on a great number of matters for the guidance of his congregation.

In the pulpit the minister's function is like that of the editorial writer. He is to counsel and advise, to pronounce judgment and express opinion. He is engaged to give his people the benefit of his professional training and specialized knowledge.

When ministers turn news writer, they bring their well-practiced critical faculties to the task. They find it almost impossible to avoid making judgments, assessing praise or blame, and moralizing as they write.

Occasionally, of course, pastors are asked to contribute guest editorials or to supply signed columns or weekly sermonettes. Here opinion is in place.

When writing *news*, however, the writer must not play up his own personality, convictions, or judgments. Probably nine out of ten editors would begin advice on news writing to ministers by saying, "Don't editorialize!"

Adhere strictly to the provable, observable facts. If you call a preacher "eloquent and soul-stirring," you may find that others differ from your opinion. When you say that he is a former moderator of his denomination or that he has delivered the Lyman Beecher lectures on preaching, you are giving information rather than opinion.

News writers are free, of course, to introduce personal judgment into a story. This may be in the form of quotations from authorities or even from bystanders. It must, however, always be attributed to someone.

Sometimes a writer isn't aware that he is editorializing. Adjectives and adverbs often express value judgments. In consequence editors are chary of these modifiers. Don't say, "The lecturer is well qualified." Cite briefly his experience and let your reader determine.

You may even unwittingly color a story by your choice of nouns. Calling a group of men in front of a house a "mob" prejudices the situation. It would be more objective not to use that particular word, but to provide the facts and let the reader make his own judgment. Reporting that the men were carrying shotguns and rifles, that one of them brandished a torch, that they were shouting and shaking their fists, would doubtless persuade the reader that they were there for no benevolent purpose. The facts would speak without the help of opinion.

Churchmen have to make particular efforts to leave a subject without tying it up neatly with a summarizing moral. They have developed their pedagogical instincts professionally to a point where it actually pains them not to point out the lesson inherent in each particular situation.

The reporter, it has been said, stops when he runs out of facts. He does so without embarrassment or apology or discomfort. As desirable as it is for a minister to moralize in the pulpit or lecture room, he should store up his minuscule homilies until an editor asks him to do a guest editorial. They have no place in news writing.

Fact Sheet

No matter how professionally you write a news story, the average editor or copyreader will find it hard to keep his hands off. Don't let this worry you. It's his business. You probably wouldn't be quite satisfied with his idea of a sermon.

What the newspaper does to your story will probably add to its

HOW TO WRITE NEWS

readability and clarity. Study the changes that are made and profit by them.

Most church and city editors are rushed and shorthanded. They will be grateful if you can supply them with usable copy that requires little editing. Do not hesitate to ask for their suggestions. In the first place, you will probably learn something of value; in the second, it will do them good to see a teachable churchman.

Some newspapers have the policy of rewriting everything that comes in. Sometimes they do this to prevent exactly the same story from appearing in a rival paper. Talk this over with the church editor. If he does not plan to use your story anyway, you may provide him with a "fact sheet" and avoid laboring over the news story formula. He will get what he wants more easily from such a fact sheet than from a story written out by you.

Begin the fact sheet as you would any release, with your name, position, address, phone number, and name of the institution you represent in the upper left-hand corner, unless you have a letterhead or special release head which contains this data. Put a release date in the right-hand corner, telling when you would like the story used: "For release Friday A.M. papers." "For immediate release." "Release at will."

A quarter of the way down the sheet on the left or across the page summarize the story in a short sentence, as:

> CALIFORNIAN LEAVES $100,000 TO
> ST. MARK'S, HIS BOYHOOD CHURCH

The simplest way to supply the necessary facts might be to use the five "W's" as an outline:

WHAT? —a bequest of $100,000 to St. Mark's Church, King City, Mass., for a community service building.

WHO? —by John Tinker of Alameda, Calif., retired rancher. Died January 22, aged 79, in California no family.

WHEN? —notification received this morning (Tuesday, March 15) from probate court by the Rev. Mr. Jason Snider, minister of St. Mark's.

WHY? —the will indicated Mr. Tinker desired to commemorate parents who were lifelong members of St. Mark's. He revisited King City two years ago after a fifty-year absence.

> *Showed interest at time in work being done with inadequate facilities for youth in neighborhood he lived in when a boy. Bequest, however, was unexpected.*

HOW? —*monthly meeting of trustees March 27 will appoint a building committee in order to have plans in readiness when funds from bequest become available.*

Another way to prepare a fact sheet is to anticipate in simple short statements all the questions you think a reader may ask. Leave plenty of space between sentences. The reporter may want to reshape your sheet into a kind of working outline. Don't crowd the page.

Some reporters and church editors do not like to take stories over the telephone, except, of course, in cases where they are of high importance and it is near the deadline. Other newsmen seem quite willing to get their news by phone.

If you use the telephone, it pays to prepare a rough fact sheet before calling the city room. Be sure you have all the data, including full names and addresses of persons involved. Stories that are phoned in carry an extra error hazard, so be patient with the editor when he spells back to you, "N as in 'Nicholas.'" Don't say Yes about spelling or initials unless you are sure.

Feature Stories

Newspaper editors like to brighten their pages and to break the monotony of a run of straight news stories. Feature or human interest stories provide this variety. Most of them have a touch of emotion, bringing a smile or a chuckle, arousing pity or producing nostalgia. Now and then you may have the makings of one.

Sometimes a feature story relates definitely to news happenings, but its value usually lies more in its human interest content. It may have no bearing on news at all but will appeal through humor or sentiment.

Feature stories demand a specialized technique. Often it is best to pass ideas on to a reporter or feature writer. If it clicks, he will appreciate your tip. From his long experience and through trial and error, he knows just how the editor would like to have the story handled. Your feature will probably get better play if a professional handles it than if you write it yourself.

Sources for feature stories are endless. If you can spot the dramatic, if you can tell a story effectively, if you have a vivid command of language, you will find feature writing not too difficult. Unexpected opinions and incidents, amusing happenings, strange coincidences, little dramas, embarrassing accidents, repartee—with imagination you can use any of these in a human interest story.

Style is particularly important if you decide to attempt such writing yourself. You need follow no fixed formula. Indeed, you may temporarily forget what you have learned about ordinary news writing. You have complete freedom as long as you handle your material with taste and artistry.

Feature-story style may have much in common with fiction. Mood and atmosphere may be created by the use of details that would be quite irrelevant in a straight news story. Historical order, taboo in news writing, may be acceptable. So may suspense. The reader's curiosity may be sustained as long as possible, with a snappy last line yanking the veil from the mystery.

The human interest story, it will be seen, is not so subject to the editor's privilege of cutting it at any point he wishes. It is more likely either to be carried in the paper as an artistic entity or else to be scrapped completely.

Your feature story is a literary creation in which you capture your reader's imagination. You may use the news writer's lead or the short-story writer's surprise ending. You may not, however, forget that you are writing for a *newspaper*. You will need to give the same attention to short sentences and short paragraphs and to use the same concrete words and crisp style that you would use in any news story.

CHAPTER IV

Releases: How to Prepare and Present Them

YOU CAN HANDLE CHURCH NEWS MORE ACCURATELY AND EXpeditiously by following a few well-known, practical mechanical principles. Probably you are already familiar with most of them. They are included here both for completeness and to enable the chapter to serve as a kind of check list. "Old stuff" as they are, it will pay to look them over.

A church publicist may be doing nearly everything just right, but by overlooking some single detail give the impression of being less adept and understanding in his press relations than he really is.

RELEASES: HOW TO PREPARE AND PRESENT THEM

Mechanical Details

ONE SIDE OF PAPER—For example, it would not seem necessary to mention that for any "copy" intended for the press, only one side of the paper should be used. This rule has greatly been stressed in schools and workshops, but still every church editor receives news notes each week written not only on both sides but around the margins!

Those who see no point in observing this taboo against both sides of the paper would perhaps understand its importance if they were to watch an editor at work.

One of the editor's tools is a pair of shears with rather long blades. Another is a paste pot and brush. He types two or three lines at the top of a sheet, cuts a usable section from a release, and then pastes it under what he has written. He proceeds in this fashion to prepare the copy for the Linotype operators.

If the editor wants to use part of a release written on both sides of a page, he will destroy what is on the back. His alternative is to stop everything and copy the release. Usually he has neither the time nor the disposition for this.

LETTER-SIZED PAPER—The kind and size of paper isn't as important as the "one side only" rule. Copy paper used by reporters in most city rooms is "newsprint," salvaged from the ends of the rolls that feed the presses.

This newsprint is usually cut 8½ by 11 inches. Because of this most agencies releasing news to the press use this size. It stacks up properly with what the editors are handling.

Occasionally, however, releases from news services, government agencies, and other headquarters are 15 inches long.

RELEASE HEADS?—There is no need for costly stationery. Any good opaque white paper will do. It is well worth checking on erasability, however—unless you never make mistakes! Papers vary greatly in their ability to stand up under corrections.

Should you have a release head designed and printed? There are two schools of thought on this. Most organizations that regularly release to the press do have a special form. The advantage is that the releases can be quickly identified.

This quick identification, in turn, can work two ways. If for a time the stories lack interest or are otherwise not usable for publication, the editor will soon lose interest and find the distinctive heading a help in discarding them without reading. On the other hand, if the editor finds the releases well written and newsy, he becomes favorably predisposed to meeting the attractive release head in his mail like an old friend.

Don't think that an investment in special release headings is necessary. Some organizations, which could well afford anything that might make releases more acceptable, go to great pains to give their releases a minimum of institutional billing. They want their stories to look as much as possible like copy written by a reporter in the newsroom to which it is sent. Of course they aren't trying to fool anyone, since their releases are all properly identified. They simply don't add anything to the release that will make the editor say to himself, "This piece I'm handling is a publicity story."

A great university and one of the South's greatest industries both use plain newsprint for their releases. The nation's oldest and richest college runs the first pages of its releases through a multigraph for the simplest kind of identification.

DOUBLE SPACE—Business correspondence is properly written on every line, but newspaper copy must never be single spaced. Double spacing is the minimum requirement. Triple spacing is preferable.

The reporter or editor who handles your story needs room between the lines to make additions or to alter the sentence structure. This preference for plenty of white space on a release is quite general among editors. One put it this way: "Frequently we discard a release that might have been usable in part, but was single spaced and therefore not easily edited."

You can give an editor even more room for adding to or revamping your story by leaving wide margins on both sides. It is desirable to keep ordinary releases to one page, but not at the expense of crowding and skimping on margins.

The editor's decision will be made on the news value of your story, but the general appearance of the release can't fail to influence his opinion of you and your church. Too often what he receives from you is his only basis of judgment.

MAKING IT LEGIBLE—Don't skimp on typewriter ribbons. They become dim so gradually that you may not be aware when one is worn and faded. Make it a point to change yours as often as it is necessary to turn out sharp copy.

RELEASES: HOW TO PREPARE AND PRESENT THEM

If you find your ribbon is faint and a new one is unavailable, the first copy from a fresh sheet of carbon will be crisper that the original from the dried-up ribbon. Of course the editor will know it's a copy, but he will be able to read it without eyestrain.

WRITING BY HAND—It is a rare happening these days, but there are occasions when a typewriter or a typist is not available and news has to be sent in handwritten. The rules for written releases are the same as for typed copy, but some editorial safeguards must be taken in the interest of accuracy.

Often a secretary or publicity chairman of a women's organization mails news from her home. In such a case, since the writing is done with a pen, it may be too easy to switch into the moods and habits of correspondence. By all means save your fancy-shaped, gay-colored Christmas stationery for your friends. It will not impress the editor.

If you must use social stationery, do not use it as the pages of a book, or worse, in any of the several possible trial and error deviations from normal in which some ladies delight. Open the paper up to its fullest surface, write on one side only and number the pages.

Of course only others write poorly. But remember that to the editor who must handle your copy, you are one of those "others." Always print out names. Carefully distinguish u's and n's. Unless you are positive that there is not the slightest possibility of error, help the editor by drawing a short line over n's and under u's. Carefully close the tops of o's so that they will not be mistaken for u's.

Study your writing for any departures from copybook standards that may have developed. Your friends will appreciate originality in this matter more than the editor will.

Identification of Source

After putting the paper in your typewriter, your first step in preparing a release is to identify its source. The facts should be typed compactly in the upper left-hand corner of the page. Include the name of the writer, the church or department he represents, his position or the capacity in which he is sending the release (secretary, publicity chairman, PR director, and others), mailing address, and telephone number. Of course if you use a church letterhead or a special release head, you do not need to repeat what is already printed there.

Newspapers do not publish hearsay as news. They want someone who will take responsibility for everything they print. Your name on the release is regarded by the editor as your personal guarantee of the facts as they are stated. You may be sure that if he hears from his readers to the contrary, they will be referred to you for explanations.

A second reason why a release source must be identified is that someone with an ailing sense of humor occasionally tries to embarrass friends by sending untrue or premature news about them to the paper. Editors ignore anonymous communications, and they check unknown news sources against the possibility of hoaxes, practical jokes, and the activities of busybodies.

It is to your own advantage to be as easy to find as possible. You may inadvertently leave out of a release some factor so important that it can't be used without this information. The editor may need more details. Sometimes he wants pictures. That's why your telephone number must appear on the release. In dealing with a morning paper, be sure to give your home number as well as the office number.

Make it as easy as possible for the editor to help you.

Release Date

The second step in writing your release is to give it a release date. When do you want the news printed? If there is no pressing time value, you can write "Release at Will." If you want it used as soon as possible, mark it "For Immediate Release."

If the story deals with something happening on a particular date, write "Release Thursday (July 17) A.M. Papers." If your story is an "advance" on a speech, the release date can be stated as the hour of delivery. If there is special reason to guard against premature usage, mark it "Future Release—Note Date."

One important reason for using a release date is that it enables you to treat all papers and all media fairly. This is not always easy. Many church events happening in the evening seem to break more advantageously for the A.M. than for the P.M. Consequently, those announcements which you can easily control might be kept for first release in the afternoon. If you have both morning and evening papers in your community, try to keep a balance between them as much as you can.

Do not forget to keep radio and TV newscasters in mind as well when you are setting a release date. The more nearly balanced you can keep your stories, as far as advantageous release dates, the better for you.

Weekly editors constantly are faced with news that has already been in the dailies. If your town has both a small daily and a weekly, you can give the weekly editor a boost by releasing stories so that they will appear in both simultaneously. If your town has only weeklies, the same principle is particularly true. Whenever you can, synchronize what you send directly or through a correspondent to the daily in the nearby city with the day it will come out in your weekly paper.

Data pertaining to release dates should be written in the upper right-hand corner of your release. Put it in caps, if you wish, or underscore it so that it will be noticed.

Newspapers will respect your release dates.

No Headlines

Don't waste time thinking up a good headline for your release. Some editors resent them. Professional reporters rarely write the heads for their stories.

Procedures vary on newspapers. This duty, though, usually falls to the copyreader, who writes the head after the city desk has indicated by letter or number what style head is to be used. This code will also indicate whether the story is to run in one or two or more columns.

No one can anticipate what size and style of headline type an editor will order for a particular story. Suggestions, therefore, are useless.

Headline writing is a highly skilled art in which its experts take a proper pride. There are special usages of tense, right and wrong places for two-line sentences to break, and the most exacting requirements of letter counting to make a head of given type size fit the space allotted to it.

Most editors would regard a suggested head on a news release simply as the mark of an amateur. However, a panel appearing in *Editor and Publisher* revealed that there are those editors who consider such suggestions presumptuous.

There are differences of opinion among editors, but most of them appreciate an informational guideline at the top of the page at one side or the other indicating the subject covered in the fewest possible words. "We get so many releases in the mail that the guideline is about all we read in the course of discarding them," one editor said. "Once in a great while, one of these guidelines halts the throw-away process."

Date Lines

"Chicago, March 5—" "London, November 19—" Data such as this precede the opening sentence of all but local news stories in most dailies. Place and date together are referred to as the "date line."

Each paper has a style sheet listing fifty cities, more or less, so well known that neither the state nor the country needs to be included. All other places require the added information in the date line.

Typing the Release

WHERE TO START—Start your story from one third to halfway down the page. This gives the city desk or copyreader in the newsroom a place to write instructions or a headline. Often the editor will use this space to write a new lead. He may think he can improve yours, or he may want to make certain that the lead in his paper differs from the one in the competing daily.

KEEPING PARAGRAPHS SHORT—Remember that each typed line will make two lines in the printed column. To avoid long, dull-looking paragraphs in the newspapers, you must keep each paragraph in the release to three or four lines at most whenever possible.

BREAKS—Try to avoid hyphenating words at the end of a line. Don't worry about the irregular right-hand margin that this produces.

A more important rule is not to carry a paragraph over a page. Again, do not be disturbed if this leaves some blank space at the bottom of the sheet. One reason for not breaking paragraphs is that copy is often divided among Linotype operators even in the middle of stories. With full paragraphs, it can be put together properly again, but this is impossible with continued paragraphs.

"MORE" AND "END"—At the end of the page if the story is not completed, write the word—more—. This indicates that there is more to come. Repeat it at the bottom of each succeeding page until the end. Here write —end—, two or three hatch marks ###, a long rule ——————, or the newsman's traditional -30-.

There are numerous explanations of the origin of this widely used symbol -30-. One is that when newspaper stories were handwritten, x meant the end of a sentence, xx the end of a paragraph, and xxx the end of the story. The Roman numeral xxx easily took on the Arabic form "30."

Another version is that Associated Press member papers in the early days were entitled to thirty telegrams daily. The last of each day's news budget was marked "30."

SLUG PAGES—When a release requires a second page or more to complete the story, it is important to write at the top of each page an identifying phrase along with the page number. This is in case the sheets should become mislaid or mixed. For example, "Westminster Church Anniversary, p. 2," or "New Pastor First Baptist, p. 3."

Accuracy Essential

The highest rated virtue in newsrooms is accuracy. Newspapers occasionally correct mistakes, particularly when a libel suit threatens, but they hate the necessity of having to inform the public that they were wrong. Every effort is constantly being made to avoid errors.

"Get the facts" is a phrase often posted where reporters will see it. Joseph Pulitzer's famous newsroom motto was:

> "GET IT RIGHT!
> GET IT NOW!
> BUT GET IT RIGHT!"

You might expect Dr. Rudolf Flesch to put readability in first place, but even he warned Associated Press reporters in the opening paragraph of a manual he wrote for them, "Never sacrifice accuracy for readability."

Mistakes will happen. When you think how a newspaper is put together in less than twenty-four hours, however, it actually seems amazing that there are as few errors as there are. The high record for accuracy is the result of consistent vigilance on the part of the entire staff.

Each writer on *Time* Magazine has at least one well-trained researcher whose duty is to read critically her principal's copy. Every name, place, date, and statement of fact must be verified from responsible sources. Even with all these ringed and underscored, checked and double checked, there are errors, as you are regularly made aware if you read the popular *Letters* department.

Every publisher wants to build a reputation for dependability. Other criteria of success depend on this basic factor.

Your own press relations will be helped if you remember that newspapers do demand accuracy. It's easier to be patient with a reporter who seems to be repeating his questions in a slightly different form if you realize that he is checking to be sure he's right. Help him get it straight—it's to your interest too.

Sometimes a vivid imagination is required in checking a story to see that it answers all the questions that readers might ask. The late

A HANDBOOK OF CHURCH PUBLIC RELATIONS

James Supple of the Chicago *Sun-Times* turned down a story which seemed complete but wasn't.

The announcement came in on a Sunday afternoon in plenty of time for Monday morning's edition. A church had purchased a large apartment house, which it would demolish to erect a new parochial school. The site was at the intersection of two prominent residential avenues.

Supple checked a directory and found that on each corner of the intersection was a large apartment house. Which building had been bought? Frantically he tried to get in touch with someone who could give him this information. No luck.

The paper went to press without the story. Supple had the imagination to foresee the deluge of calls from tenants of all four apartments buildings who might be dispossessed if the story went out lacking just that one important fact.

Almost right is not enough. Do you remember the man who said he had just come from Penn State and was staying at the Park Central? The facts were not very different. He had just come from the state pen and was sleeping in Central Park.

Handling Names

Be particularly on your guard in handling names. People love to see their names in print, but how it nettles them to be given a wrong initial! Many read their names in type only once or twice in a lifetime. It spoils the thrill if it isn't correct.

An acquaintance has in his desk drawer a collection of mispellings of his own name which he has cut from letters addressed to him. Why does he keep them! He would probably tell you that he thinks they are funny. A psychoanalyst might have another explanation.

So important is it to people that their names be spelled right that the Kansas City *Star*'s style book devotes ten pages to an alphabetical list of prominent persons and places, mostly in its area, whose names have spellings tricky enough to throw the most painstaking reporter.

One example is William Ljungdahl, a livestock man. This is correct. Kindly disposed helpers all along the route from reporter to pressman think they have caught an error and miscorrect it to read William L. Jungdahl.

Where you fear an odd-looking but accurate spelling may suffer a similar miscorrection, write the word "folo" (short for "follow copy") over it or the word "correct" in parentheses immediately following the questionable word. Some reporters draw a short line under the doubtful letters to indicate that appearance to the contrary it is correct.

Before including names in a story, be sure you know whether it is the custom of the paper involved to publish local names with or without street addresses. Most dailies want a street number for every name.

Don't expect someone in the city room to look up names in the telephone book for your story. First of all, there isn't enough time. Second, there are frequent duplications of names. Be as accurate with the street address as you are with the name itself.

Women's names should always be preceeded by "Miss" or "Mrs." Use the husband's name for a married woman or a widow. Divorcées ordinarily use their given names with their married surnames when there are children.

Editors object particularly to being handed a list of names of officers of a women's organization on which some appear with the husbands' names and others have given names.

Newspapers differ in use of the title "Mr." Many never use it except in combination with "Mrs." Others use the title with the surname on second mention. Follow the usage of the paper for which you are preparing news.

Most newspapers will not allow a name to appear with a single initial ("H. Berg"). They require either the full given name or at least two initials; however, the preference and customary usage of the owner should control the form in which his name appears.

Editors consider the use of nicknames in copy as an annoyance. Only a few country weeklies tolerate them at all. Most editors must check on each nickname and substitute the proper name. This is not always as simple as it seems.

Nicknames can be real trouble makers. "Bill" may be short for any one of five first names beginning with the syllable "Wil." Many nicknames are completely deceptive. A famous authority on country church life was always called "Pat" by his friends. His official name was Charles M.

A reporter or editor cannot afford to guess at names. Every incomplete or doubtful name in an amateur news story causes delay. Each one has to be substantiated by an authority. And the newsman cannot be blamed for considering the publicity person who sent in the story with nicknames inaccurate and unreliable.

Grammarians are almost ready to concede defeat in their long battle against the use of the adjective "Reverend" as a term of address. This error is so common, particularly in rural regions, that it threatens to become accepted usage in spite of professorial and editorial protests. Occasionally this abomination appears even in church printing.

If this term troubles you, test it with this rule: Never use the adjective "Reverend" in a grammatical construction where you could not use another suitable adjective. For example, you might say, "The Honorable Mr. Sparkman" or "The Honorable John M. Sparkman," but you would never say, "Honorable Sparkman will now address us." The reason: "Honorable" is an adjective, not a title.

You might say "the versatile Ralph Bellamy" or "the versatile Mr. Bellamy," but you would never say, "Versatile Bellamy has a new play." Versatile is an adjective, not a term of address.

Write or say, "The Rev. Jaspar Jones," "the Rev. Mr. Jones," or "the Rev. Dr. Jones," but never "Rev. Jones." In speaking to him say "Mr. Jones" or "Dr. Jones" if he rates it. "Mr." and "Dr." are titles of address. They are nouns.

Deadlines

"Deadlines are our biggest problem," a church editor from Florida told a group of ministers. Then he turned the tables on his clerical audience: "If Sunday after Sunday, year in and year out, I marched into church a half hour after the sermon began, I think sooner or later the pastor would become quite irritated. Yet we have ministers who treat us just that way, only they aren't late by half an hour, but by as much sometimes as a day and a half."

Don't tell an editor about an event in your church that happened yesterday. Tell him the day it happens. If it's important enough or if it has photo possibilities, tell him a couple of days before it happens.

The worst offenders are those who disregard deadlines. But those who make a habit of getting their copy in just under the line do not deserve congratulations. Nor are they playing the system that is most likely to win.

Remember what a deadline really is: the latest possible minute that a story could be presented, edited, set into type, and published.

Put yourself in a church editor's place. Suppose you receive a dozen

RELEASES: HOW TO PREPARE AND PRESENT THEM

important stories just as the clock hands are pushing toward press time. In other departments last-minute news is also taking form. Teleprinters are tapping out the very latest world happenings.

Everyone is working frantically during these last minutes. When the bell rings, there must invariably be a residue of stories which in the rush were too late for today and which will be stale and outdated by tomorrow.

You must know the deadlines for the rare emergency. If you don't abuse the privilege, a city or church desk will help take advantage of last-minute copy *once in a while*, if there is good reason for it.

To be really appreciated in the newsroom, though, you should get your copy in early. Anticipate what is to be said and done, as far is is possible, so that the story can be ready to go in the editor's desk tray. Then all you need do is confirm by telephone that everything took place as forecast "with these slight exceptions and additions."

Many churchmen always have stories in the editor's hands well before the last minute. Church news is fairly slow paced. There is little justification for stimulating an editor's incipient ulcers.

Some thoughtless publicists may be unaware of or insensitive to what in the aggregate they are doing to the editor's health and peace of mind. They should reform for a less noble reason: Over the months the church that chalks up the space is the one that files its copy as far ahead of the deadline as possible, not the one that habitually crowds the critical hour.

CHAPTER V

Dealing with Editors and Reporters

LET'S FACE IT FRANKLY. WHILE THERE ARE FREQUENT EXCEPtions, in general, ministers and newspaper people do not understand each other too well. This is a most unfortunate situation since both preachers and editors are valuable members of a community. Sympathetic comprehension of each other's professions would increase their usefulness to each other and their influence among their several constituencies.

To those churchmen whose relationships with editors and reporters are congenial and co-operative, it will seem incredible that there could exist gradations of hostility between these two important kinds of publicists, ranging from mild misconceptions to open feuding. Ministers who vibrate on the same wave length as newspapermen enjoy their relationships. They find journalists alert, well informed, analytical, and stimulating.

Occasionally, of course, by reason of the pressures under which newsmen work, there are moments when they are on edge. Being themselves direct in discourse, they often do not conceal their impatience with circumlocutory callers. Neither do they find it ever easy to be tolerant of pretense and pomposity. They are the world's best deflators. But these are qualities which ministers as a class will both understand and admire, having their own occupational seasons of tension and being committed, if not always by nature at least by professional principles, to the virtues of humility, sincerity, and forthright speech.

Newsmen's Dim View of Clergy

Pastors whose relations with the press are ideal will probably not believe without proof that their own happy experience is not typical. There is, unfortunately, plenty of evidence.

Stanley Walker, who once headed the newsroom of the *New York Herald Tribune*, in his book *City Editor* warns cub newsmen:

> In reporting the sayings of the clergy, great care should be used to quote them exactly. They are the most touchy set of quibblers who ever plagued a well-intentioned editor. Some will even find fault with a stenographic report attested by a dozen albino notaries swearing on a Gutenberg Bible.

While it is to be hoped that this is an exaggeration, it would be difficult to explain why Mr. Walker expressed himself as sharply about it, had his indignation not sprung from a background of unpleasant experiences with unreasonable parsons.

City editor Walker is not the only plaintiff. Another newsman, Maynard Kniskern, writing in *The Christian Century* (September 19, 1951), also distrusts clergymen. "Newspapermen stand in a curious, gingerly relationship to Protestant ministers. City-room people are accustomed to a shadowy Greek chorus of preachers fretting in parsonage studies, ready upon the slightest stimulus to launch, via telephone, anything from a rebuke to a holy war."

Charles Francis Benson's description of the difficulties of his job as religion editor of the *Tampa* (Fla.) *Tribune* was quoted by a University of Florida professor of journalism at a workshop on religious news reporting:

A church editor's job includes reconciliation of an anti-newspaper ministry and an anti-clerical newsroom.

Most clergymen, bless them, are newspaper readers and many newspapermen are devout churchmen. But when acting in a professional capacity, I find very few who have a true understanding of both fields of endeavor.

The professions can be likened to two stately mansions facing in opposite directions with adjoining back yards: the occupants judge each other by the kitchen smells and refuse containers.

In brass tack terms, few clergymen appreciate a newspaper's deadlines, techniques, or its duty to be all things to all people and to hew to the single line of publishing the truth; few newspapermen give ministers their due for being all in all the most sincere, self-sacrificing and withal efficient of professions.

One editor, Lloyd M. Felmly of the *Newark (N.J.) News*, in commenting on the attitudes that separate his profession from the clergy, referred to ministers as "a group of men who, though they may possess commendable motives, are nonetheless rather naïve Simon pures who really don't know what the score is." On the part of the church, he says, "there has been too much lack of understanding of the function of a newspaper, how it operates and what actually is news, and too much insistence on the use of unwieldy technical terms, confusing the general public and understood by only a few."

These misconceptions, Felmly believes, "can be resolved, or at least reduced to a minimum, through mutual contact and understanding."

Newspapermen

Make friends with the men and women who handle religious news on your papers and in your broadcasting studios.

If you are a minister, upon arriving at a new parish, even before paying your respects to the president of the board of trustees or your lay leader, make yourself known at the newspaper office.

In doing this there are a number of things to remember. If it's an afternoon paper, inquire when it goes to press, then time your call after, never just before, press time. If you must make a morning call,

DEALING WITH EDITORS AND REPORTERS

go early, as the tension builds up with the approach of press time. Each minute becomes more valuable than the one before.

In no case stay more than a few minutes. Even though an editor or reporter may seem to be at leisure, despite his courtesy there are always many matters pressing for his attention. Every day in many newspaper offices, as many words as in a novel are written, edited, put into type, and printed. It's an amazing accomplishment.

Little time is wasted in a city room. One feels the pressure as a paper is being put together, and a sensitive person will do his errand quickly and move on.

But don't let this high-pressure situation delude you into thinking that personal contacts are not valuable. They will be worth much to you. And so long as you do not make a nuisance of yourself, they will be appreciated by the news staff.

Morning paper people work different shifts. Some are on duty days, others come on in early afternoon; and still others not till late afternoon. It is best in calling on them to make an appointment at their convenience by telephone. Tell them that you are new in town and that you want just long enough to get acquainted. Then don't stay any longer than is necessary to accomplish this. Leave the editor or reporter wishing you had stayed another minute or two instead of feeling jittery that your visit was crowding his hour.

The same principles hold good in the case of the weekly paper. Often the whole staff works at printing and mailing out the paper. You will find the editor and reporters much more relaxed and receptive to visitors when the paper is in the post office.

One warning: The occasional minister who has never mastered the art of making a graceful and timely exit may find when he has overstayed his welcome that his dignified titles and his "cloth" are no protection from a curt dismissal from a high-strung city editor.

In spite of all this, know your newsmen. They are human. They have names. They have families.

The Papers' Preferences

As soon as possible, ask how you can be most helpful in reporting the news of your church. Learn their deadlines. Know the answers to the following questions.

"Are there kinds of news not used?

"What is handled on the woman's pages, what by the city desk, and what by the church editor?"

"What kinds of news could be used that are not now being provided?"

"Is it preferable to phone in the news, or should it be written?"

"Should written items be in news style or by fact sheet?"

Promptness with Reporters

Never refuse to see a reporter. When he asks for an appointment, the hour should be set at *his* convenience if possible. When he comes, don't keep him waiting.

Don't make him wait for information either. Have all the data likely to be needed in hand.

This may sound as if the reporter is a royal visitor. Perhaps you think he does not rate quite this much deference. A moment's reflection, however, will make it clear that this procedure does not make you subservient. It is quite as much in your own interest as in the reporter's.

Remember that when the reporter checked into the newsroom that morning, he found half a dozen assignments.

He looks at the clock—it's eight. He figures that he must allow about two hours to write his stories. With a one o'clock deadline he must be back at his typewriter by eleven. That leaves him three hours to make his contacts.

If all goes well and the schedule works out, he will have just time enough to knock out acceptable stories and, as fast as they are finished, hand them on to a satisfied city editor.

But human beings are not clocks, and even clocks get erratic. If some of the reporter's interviewees are off schedule or prove hard to find, the reporter may be out of breath when he pushes Dr. Blank's bell.

Suppose the minister has an important caller in his office and keeps our newsman waiting. After a time the reporter looks at his watch and begins to fidget. Will he make his other assignments? Will he get back to his desk in time to avoid the city editor's stinging wisecracks? No wonder he feels driven!

Finally Dr. Blank is ready to see the reporter. He begins hurriedly: "Who made the bequest for the new organ?"

"Her name was Temple. She was brought up here, but moved away long before I came."

"What was her first name?"

"Cissie. That's what I think they called her at the meeting."

"I doubt if that was her real name."

"I don't believe so either. I'll call up one of the older members."

Dr. Blank fumbles through the directory. He tries a number. Busy. He tries another. No answer. Finally he has an informant. She proves to be a talkative lady who wants to make the most of her pastor's call.

The reporter finds the extended pleasantries maddening. Finally Dr. Blank hangs up with the air of a mission well accomplished.

"It's Mrs. Ed Temple."

"But, Dr. Blank, 'Ed' could be Edwin, Edward, Edgar, Edson, or Edsel. We can't print it just 'Ed.'"

"That's right. I'll call her back."

The obliging pastor begins to dial. This time the reporter, certain that the minister hadn't given a thought to anticipate the need for basic data, reminds Dr. Blank to ask where Mrs. Temple was living when she died.

Throughout this imaginary interview, the minister doubtless felt that he was being quite helpful. But his lack of understanding that reporters ought not be kept waiting sent the newsman into a fever of resentment.

"Why did he have to keep me waiting? Why didn't he have the facts when he knew I was coming? Why did he take up my time with all that irrelevant talk about the trouble they had installing a new organ in his last church?" the reporter is asking himself angrily.

The minister who is ready for a visiting reporter at the appointed time, who has his data in hand, who has put the important facts in writing, and who shows that he understands the time element involved in printing a paper has done more than a favor for the newsman.

He has served his own interest as well. He has contributed to the accuracy of the story. He has expedited the reporter's arrival and departure and facilitated the writing of the story. Best of all, he has built up good will for himself and his church in the mind of the newsman.

Condescension

Treat reporters as equals. Don't try to impress them. There may be occasions where you ought to be on your professional dignity—

when for one reason or another you may ride a high horse. By all means dismount when you meet the press!

These newspapermen are hard to impress. They meet important people daily. Titles, honors, degrees, travel, and high position mean little to them. As a class they are the world's best balloon prickers. And it's easier than you think to be labeled a "stuffed shirt."

The one time it is wisest to be your own open, frank, natural friendly self is when you come in contact with the press.

Because a reporter may not be familiar with your own denominational religious vocabulary and procedures, it is easy to talk down to him. He will be quick to discern and resent this.

Actually the reporters hired today are likely to be high-grade young people. The old taboos against academic journalistic training as something to be lived down are gone. Almost all modern reporters are college graduates who have majored in journalism. Many have their master's degrees.

They are professionally qualified for their jobs. You will be wise to keep this in mind and in your attitude when dealing with reporters. They have chosen their profession, have prepared themselves for it, and are proud of it.

Approach them with the same respect and on the same level as you would certified practitioners in any other field.

Pitfalls of a Church Editor's Job

It is easy to become impatient with a reporter. How could a person possibly be so ignorant of ecclesiastical procedures and nomenclature? If a sports reporter were as unprepared for covering a ball game as some press representatives are for their religious assignments, he would be dropped from the payroll before the next edition banged against the front door!

Stop and think for a moment, however, of the complications of a church editor's job. Many of his trouble spots are not at all the fault of the poor editor, but are consequences of our religious divisiveness.

Is the minister's residence a parsonage, a rectory, a manse, or a vicarage? Indeed, how shall the occupant be designated? The different denominations have their preferences.

The governing bodies of the churches may be quarterly, district or annual conferences, conventions, synods, presbyteries, vestries, general assemblies, convocations, triennials, or congresses. Women's organizations may be anything from Ladies' Sodalities to Woman's Societies. "And please remember that the first word is spelled with an *A* not an *E*."

Titles of church officials are hard to keep straight. At the upper levels of some denominations there are bishops. That should make it easy, but no! There are bishops, suffragan bishops, bishops coadjutor, and even a presiding bishop, all in one communion. These particular bishops are addressed in letters as "the Right Rev." To add to the confusion, the moderator of the United Church of Canada is also a "Right Rev." even though he is not a bishop!

A Methodist bishop rates no embellishment of his title. He is simply called "Bishop."

The Episcopal bishop and the Roman Catholic each administers a diocese. A Methodist bishop has no diocese; he administers an "episcopal area."

Think of the other inconsistencies that face a church editor, even within churches of the same family name. Wesleyan and Primitive Methodists have no bishops at all. Neither do British or Australasian Methodists. Most Lutheran bodies don't have bishops, but there are some that do.

If you were a beginning religious reporter, wouldn't you be confused if an occasional Protestant Episcopal clergyman, despite his denomination's name, resented being called a "Protestant"? And just to prove that he really is "Catholic," he will insist on being referred to as "Father."

How can you expect a reporter to know the many baffling words whose meanings differ from communion to communion? For example, in the Roman Church, The Methodist Church, the Episcopal Church, and some others, "deacon" is a lesser order of clergy, the last step preceding full ordination. In Baptist and Congregational churches, deacons are lay officers with no expectation of ever taking up a clerical vocation.

In The Methodist Church a candidate is ordained "elder" as the final ordination that qualifies him for the ministry. An elder in the Presbyterian Church is a layman, who (with others) governs the local church.

Lay officers in various denominations are called stewards, trustees, vestrymen, wardens, lay leaders, and so on, ad infinitum.

These inconsistencies of nomenclature and organization are detailed here for but one purpose: to point out the tangle of terminology a young newspaperman or woman gets into when assigned to the "church beat."

We all find our own terms and systems so simple, so "just right," that it's difficult to understand the vague, confused, uncomprehending look that appears so often on the face of a reporter who has come to cover an annual conference for the first time. Move mentally into his totally confusing world for a minute, and you'll suddenly find it very easy to be patient with his questions.

Respect for Newsmen's Professional Status

Don't tell a newspaperman how to do his job. No wise person would drop into a physician's office, diagnose his own ailment, and prescribe for it without expecting the doctor to get ruffled. And it would require a rare state of sanctification for a preacher to accept graciously an unqualified layman's unsolicited suggestions on improving Sunday's sermon.

Lean over backward in this respect, even if you possess a considerable knowledge of newspaper technique and style. Give the reporter the facts. Have them written in an orderly way to make sure of names, dates, titles, committees, and needed phrases or quotations.

It will pay to be modest in presenting a story you have prepared as you would like to have it appear. Say, "I've written it out for you here, if this will be of any help. You will know how to fix it up and make something of it. I'm pretty much of an amateur at this."

You can use this approach in suggesting a possible subject for news or feature treatment too. Don't overflow with enthusiasm: "I've a wonderful idea for a story—you'll love it!"

You'll see the reporter or editor freeze up. Before he has even heard the suggestion, it has two strikes against it, because *you have unwittingly invaded his domain.* The newsman is the one who decides questions of news value. This is a matter that from his point of view lies outside your province.

Begin again, "Joe, I was calling on old Mrs. Pender on Cedar Street the other day and found she's going to be eighty next week. She still comes to Sunday school and claims she hasn't missed a Sunday since she was five years old. I don't know whether it has any news interest, but we thought we'd like to plan some kind of public observance. You don't have any ideas, do you?"

Joe is far ahead of you. "Why don't you have a pretty little girl just five years old, the age Mrs. Pender was when she started Sunday school, present her with flowers? We'd send a photographer and caption the picture "Between Them Seventy-five Years of Church School Attendance."

By this time it is Joe's story. He may even come up with a better idea before Sunday. By respecting his professional status you have won the co-operation of one of the most useful allies you can have in the community.

Building Up a Beginning Reporter

The reporter looked forward to relations with community leaders like you during his college days. Now he is meeting you. Anything you can do to show your appreciation of his professional services is all to the good. Build him up as much as you can.

Christian leaders ought to build up others as a matter of principle, and it is always a duty of older people to exercise every influence that will help younger ones to become their best possible selves. In the case of the press, however, there is a less noble reason, but one that is important to you, to your church, and to churches in general.

What kind of image is the editor or reporter forming of you through his contacts with you? Will he think of you as distrustful and irritating, eager to diminish his efforts? Or will he always remember you as one who gave his morale a boost on every occasion, who recognized his status and abilities as a newsman, and who showed confidence in him?

Remember that today's eager young reporter may turn out to a "natural." A few years of rapid progress and he may be sitting at a city editor's desk deciding what and how much about your church goes into the paper.

Boners

Sooner or later a reporter's story about your church will contain a "boner." It's inevitable. When it happens, don't go over his head, either in complaining or in seeking a correction.

You will find it so easy at the Rotary Club, sitting alongside the managing editor, to say, "That young fellow Joe on your church desk certainly got me into a mess. All morning long my phone has been busy with women complaining because their bazaar date is listed for Friday instead of Thursday." It's easy, but don't do it!

Call Joe directly. Share some of the blame. (As a matter of fact, the mistake may actually have originated in your office, or you may have misspoken.) Laugh with him about the Ladies' Aiders who are hounding you. Ask, "Is there anything we can do about it, Joe?"

A sympathetic, understanding approach will accomplish much more than going over the reporter's head. Your ill-spirited demand for a correction would undoubtedly get a four-line notice at the bottom of an obscure column. If Joe is on your side, he will try to find a better way.

Perhaps he will dig up a fresh angle on the bazaar and write a new story that the ladies wouldn't have had otherwise. Of course he will stress the correct date in this one. Or he may do a pleasant little feature about the women worrying the pastor because they feared no one would be around Thursday to buy their embroidery and eat their chicken pies. Letting Joe handle it himself will produce good immediate results, probably better than complaining to the editor.

Incidentally, many editors have a policy of standing by their reporters, right or wrong. Insistence may produce a "correction," but these are always made somewhat grudgingly.

You have a more persuasive reason for going directly to Joe. Of course, doing things the kinder way always gives a real satisfaction, but in this case you have retained Joe's good will, for he knows from bitter experience that less thoughtful persons would have gone over his head.

Changes

If he thought through the implications, no churchman would ever say to an editor or reporter, "Print this just as I've written it. Don't change a word." This demand may look well grounded, but it ignores the fact that the use of another person's medium is involved.

The rules, style, and policy are controlled by the proprietor. He alone is responsible for what ideas are printed and for the language in which they appear. Writing for and editing a newspaper is a highly specialized task.

While the parallel is not exact, it is quite as presumptuous for a minister to tell an editor not to change copy as it is for an editor to hand the minister a few paragraphs for his next Sunday's sermon with the instructions, "Say it just as I've written it. Don't change a word."

You may appreciate a helpful contribution to your discussion of an announced theme, but you alone are responsible for what is said from your pulpit. You might conceivably use such a contribution just as it was written, but you would be far less likely to do so if you were so instructed. You would alter it if for no other reason than to preserve your prerogatives.

There are times, to be sure, when the phraseology of matters relating to theology, ecclesiastical procedures, and legal acts needs to be exact. In such a case, your explanation of the reason would prevent the editor's taking offense.

Trusting the Reporter

Another request that it is better never to make of an editor is to see his report or interview before its publication.

You may not mean it that way, but to the reporter who takes pride in his work this request is equivalent to saying, "I think you are an incompetent reporter, and I do not trust you, all by yourself, to write a reliable, accurate, satisfactory story."

Of course minor errors might be caught by submitting a story to its source. But this occasional possibility of preventing what otherwise would be a mistake is not worth the risk of jeopardizing future relations with the reporter. It is far better to trust the newsman than to insult him unintentionally.

Conscientious reporters, when in doubt, will check back. Often they themselves will suggest submitting the script if they have doubts. But unless it is a matter of extreme importance or unless you have real reason to distrust the reporter's judgment or comprehension, you will have a better story by relying on him rather than by driving him into an unpleasant mood.

Incidentally, a request to see his story before it is published involves more than the personal dignity of the reporter. There is the time problem as well.

Many times the story would miss one or two editions if it were delayed by being sent out for approval. Perhaps the maximum news interest would be lost by too long a delay.

Possibility of Being Quoted

Of course no clergyman would be in danger of either unfeeling sentiments or violent language. Next time you're tempted to some outburst against a reporter, though, it will help you to remember that Commodore Vanderbilt one time made one, not only to his own lifelong regret but to that of big business as well.

A reporter called at Vanderbilt's home to obtain a statement regarding a pending strike on the New York Central Railway, of which he was president. Vanderbilt, angry at the invasion of his privacy and wanting to avoid the press, refused to answer the reporter's questions.

"But, Mr. Vanderbilt," the reporter insisted, "the public has a right to know."

"The public be damned!" shouted Vanderbilt as he pushed the newsman out and slammed to door.

The reporter did not get the statement he was after, but he did make page one with an eight column banner head. Great corporations have been trying for years to live down the impression Vanderbilt confirmed so dramatically, that in their passion for profits the welfare of the public is their last concern. Even though this impression is almost entirely untrue today, the rabble-rouser still has a weapon created for him long ago by a man who was foolish enough to lose his temper with a reporter.

Exclusives

Should a reporter come to you for help on what he expects to be an exclusive story, never pass his idea on to other papers. A story idea is the personal property of whoever originated it. Don't betray his confidence by letting others hear of the idea.

On the other hand, your own releases ought to treat all papers alike.

Following Through

Some ministers seem to editors like men with split personalities. The Rev. Dr. Blank, who wants a record-breaking crowd next Wednesday night for the annual parish meeting, petitions the editor for an advance notice with smiling assurance of grateful appreciation.

But when the occasion is over and a late-working reporter calls him for news of what happened, he finds a different person. Dr. Blank's personal worries are over—the room was filled, the reports were praised, the pulpit committee unanimously asked for the pastor's return for another year, and the relaxed parson is listening to the late news. He wants to forget the annual meeting that has been bothering him the past ten days.

Irritated by the interruption, Dr. Blank is further annoyed when he is asked about the meeting and what was said and done. He stalls. "I'll ask the secretary of the board to send you a copy of the minutes when he gets them written up."

The reporter explains patiently that that will hardly do. "We announced the meeting for tonight at your request, Dr. Blank. We have created an expectation on the part of our readers that important decisions were to be made, and they will be looking for the news in tomorrow morning's paper. You don't want us to let them down, do you?"

"Well, I suppose you are right," Dr. Blank replies resignedly. "Actually, nothing very important happened. It was just like every other annual meeting." He reluctantly stretches his mind to recall the few matters that by generous definition might be called newsworthy.

It never occurs to the Rev. Dr. Blank that the city editor had every right to expect his co-operation in furnishing the news of a meeting for which the minister was so eager for advance publicity. Again and again newsmen are puzzled over the chameleon changes of attitude between the minister who wants something from the newspaper and the same man when the editor seeks his co-operation.

If the pastor is so blind as to fail to recognize that cheerful co-operation with a newsman on all possible occasions is like putting money in the savings bank, he should at least respect the obligation that the Golden Rule puts upon him. The wise pastor will regard every occasion to be of service to the newspapers of his community, whether of immediate advantage to his church or not, as a welcome opportunity to strengthen his press relations.

Ministers Let Down the Press

The president of one denomination's woman's society in a southern state probably wondered why her organization fared so poorly in the press. The reason was simple. "This reporter came in just after our meeting had adjourned," she sputtered. "I certainly fixed him! He asked me if anything important had taken place. 'Well!' I said to him, looking him right in the eye, 'if it wasn't important enough for you to get here for the meeting, it wasn't important enough for me to take my time to tell you now.'"

That is one kind of press relations.

Every church editor has his own collection of experiences with non-co-operative clergymen. It doesn't take much pressure to trigger them into repeating them to anyone who will give them a sympathetic ear. They tell these stories with an air of "Now, you are not going to believe this, but I swear it's true."

Newspaper office doors are constantly battered by professional press agents who would do almost anything for a mere mention of their client's name. It is incomprehensible to editors that churchmen as a class are so remiss in taking advantage of the exceptionally generous attitude of editors in relaxing their rigid definition of "news" in their consideration of the churches.

Dwight Marvin, long editor of the *Troy (New York) Record*, was talking to fellow editors at the annual meeting in New York. He had sought to line up one hundred ministers in his readership area to provide him on Thursday, according to a prearranged schedule, a seven hundred-world "cameo" sermon to be featured on the Saturday church page. In response to one hundred requests he received seventeen acceptances.

"Almost never," he said, "were any of them on time. Because I gave this page my personal attention, I would phone the preachers, listen to their excuses, set a new deadline, and even then they wouldn't show up. Finally I gave up. I am a Presbyterian elder. I decided it was easier to write these sermonettes myself than to pry them out of the preachers."

It is difficult to understand why dedicated pastors would pass by default an opportunity to preach through the printed page to as many persons as they reach during an entire year in their congregations.

You may think this is an exception and that Marvin's approach or reminder system was inadequate. The same type of story, however, comes frequently from many directions.

In a Minnesota press seminar James Borman, news chief of station WCCO, told of his desire to close the broadcast day during Lent with a one-minute prayer, read reverently by the announcer and credited to the preacher-author. He wrote forty letters, asking each minister to furnish such a prayer—a service with which he might be expected to be sympathetic.

Borman was compelled to write forty more follow-up letters. He never received forty replies. The project could finally be carried out only by repeating a number of the prayers.

"When anyone says he will call or bring something in, ministers as a whole can be depended on least." This remark or its equivalent has been voiced by editors several times and in various sections of the country.

During World War II Captain Hartzell Spence was the officer-editor of *Yank*, the overseas service periodical. He had come from the United Press into the Army, having written two novels relating to his parsonage background, *One Foot in Heaven* and *Get Thee Behind Me*. It had occurred to him that for some reason a disproportionately large number of chaplain news stories and pictures centered around the brave and unselfish services of Roman Catholic priests.

Because he felt that Protestants might not realize there were even more of their own ministers in uniform, Captain Spence addressed letters to fifty-five Protestant chaplains on duty in the European and Mediterranean theaters of operation. He asked them to supply him with incidents and experiences in their ministry to fighting men on battlefields, in hospitals, in rest camps, and in training centers.

Captan Spence wanted to balance up the chaplaincy picture by weaving this material into the magazine. He knew many of these Protestant chaplains had probably wondered among themselves why their Catholic colleagues seemed to be accorded preponderant attention. He naturally expected the fullest co-operation from them.

But he waited for replies in vain. He received just one. This letter gave him a name and address. "If you ask this man," a chaplain wrote, "I think he may be able to give you some help."

Of course not every minister fails the press, and those who let them down do so only occasionally. Undoubtedly editors generalize on a relatively few disappointing experiences, and most of them, once out of the complaining mood, will speak with enthusiasm about clergy friends who are all a newsman could desire.

However, unfavorable reactions are sufficiently numerous and widespread to indicate that church and press co-operation is not always ideal. These incidents are reported here to point up the problem of co-operation and to help in making the first steps toward the improvement of relations between religion and the press.

News Tips

You can build editorial friendship, especially in a small town, by serving as a news source in other than immediate church matters. Perhaps more than any other professional man, you as a minister have wide personal contacts.

In the course of a week you are in many offices, business places, and homes. In conversation with many of these people frequently the germ of a news story may pop up. Of course you will preserve confidences, but there will be many items of varying degrees of interest to the public.

You can phone in the main items to your reporter friend. Others will need development and follow-up. These you should bring to the attention of the city editor.

A good "tip-off" is a sure way to improve your reputation for co-operation with the press.

When It's Bad News

The business of the newspaper is to print, not to suppress news. When something happens that for the good of the church or for the sake of the persons involved you wish could pass without mention in the press, it may be necessary to co-operate with a reporter or editor, painful though this may be.

Your first inclination may be to confer with the editor, asking him to withhold the story. Watch your step. If editors were to yield to the pressures of everyone to whom certain news might be distasteful, their pages would be a distorted and misleading mirror of life.

Sometimes, particularly in a one-paper town, an editor may be persuaded not to print a story. This will not happen often. It will never happen if there is the slightest attempt to coerce the editor into killing the story.

Where two or more papers are concerned, suppression of news is even less likely, although on rare occasions editors have been known to agree mutually to withhold a story. They definitely do not like to do this, and you would be unwise to attempt it except under the most extreme circumstances. Even in such a case the chances are slim that you could persuade them.

You are not under any compulsion to rush to a newspaper with tidings you would much prefer not to see printed. When there is bad news and you are approached by reporters, however, you will be wise to co-operate fully. The alternative evasion and "no comment" can only do harm.

If the reporter is blocked by your attitude, he will find another news source, perhaps less well informed and perhaps unsympathetic. His story in all likelihood will be distorted, inaccurate, and unfriendly because you have irritated him by your non-co-operation.

Reply to all the reporter's questions, good and bad, pointing out of course whatever extenuating circumstances there may be. Don't try to whitewash the unpleasant aspects. The newswriter will appreciate your co-operation and will be keenly aware of what it is costing you. His story will be likely to give you the benefit of any doubt.

Fighting the Evil, Not the Editor

Now and then editors and preachers actually feud. Usually the minister feels that his position is backed by scriptural precepts, while the editor stands on the constitutional guarantees of the freedom of the press. There is not much hope of compromise in any controversy with such substantial support on both sides.

Editorial positions taken by newspapers often give rise to these animosities and misunderstandings. The editor may advocate bingo for charity or a relaxation of what he calls "blue laws."

The minister's indignation mounts. He lets the editor have it from his pulpit on Sunday. How could any right-thinking person hold such an opinion honestly? He must have hidden motives for supporting the program he advocates!

"He's being paid off by those who stand to gain from the changes he urges." "The newspaper hopes for paid advertising from the bingo promoters." "The editor is bidding for the approval of churches and organizations which will take advantage of the change."

The minister is not wrong in speaking out against the evil. His error is in attacking the editor and his paper. In our system of private enterprise newspapers are under public control only to the degree that they might violate laws of libel or common decency.

Both the pulpit and the press have long and precious traditions of freedom. Both the preacher and the publisher have their own forums. The editor has his editorial columns; the preacher has his pulpit.

Both the preacher and the publisher possess the right to stand for or against anything they please, short of advocating overthrow of the government by force and violence. Both the pulpit and the press have been extremely useful institutions in our democracy, and both will continue to be so. Much of their value has been in their freedom in controversial questions to take whatever side they feel to be for the public welfare.

Some preachers regard it as a personal affront when an editor exercises his right to advocate a cause which the ministers believe is contrary to the traditions and regulations of the church. They forget that an editor has the same right to an opinion and to the expression of that opinion through his medium as the minister has.

It is not necessary to compromise. You can be as much of a social prophet and reformer as your convictions, your judgment, and your congregation permit you to be.

If bingo is the issue, you can preach on the social, moral, and economic consequences of this form of gambling. You may even write a letter to the editor, courteously pointing out wherein you believe the newspaper's arguments to be wrong. Your position may not be accepted by the editor, but on this level it will be respected.

The trouble begins when the personality of the editor is attacked, when his motives are questioned, and when his right to his opinion is assailed. The preacher who does this has gone too far.

A Hollywood columnist some time ago wrote a highly critical, if not insulting, comment about Frank Sinatra. A few days later the singer saw the offending critic on the stairway of a restaurant. Suddenly enraged by the memory of what had been written, Sinatra drew back his fist and let go. The columnist was taken off balance and rolled to the foot of the stairs.

Other columnists described the incident the next day. "Frankie, you shouldn't have done it," one wrote. Another said, "Frankie, we didn't know you had it in you!" Billy Rose in his column "Pitching Horseshoes" had the last word: "Frankie, take it from a showman of thirty years' experience, socking a newspaperman never got nobody nothing, no time, nowhere."

Socking newsmen and attacking editors for their views won't help build understanding between the church and the press. If you are conscience bound to oppose an evil, do so. But respect the right of every American to express his opinion, even if it varies completely from your own. Fight the evil, not the editor!

DEALING WITH EDITORS AND REPORTERS

Saying "Thank You"

Don't ever leave a newspaper in doubt as to whether the space given to church news or the personal services of editors and reporters are appreciated.

A former president of the American Society of Newspaper Editors found it necessary during the newsprint rationing in the war years to reduce his church page, leaving only a corner for condensed church service announcements. During the many years that the page had run, the editor had received only four mentions of this important contribution to that city's church life.

Three of these mentions, he said, were criticisms. One letter that started out with a word of praise was from a woman. The second paragraph read, "If you should have occasion to print my name again on your church page, please remember that my first name is spelled 'Katherine,' not 'Catherine.'"

This fourth letter, the editor felt, canceled out, leaving him with nothing but adverse comments.

Then came the Monday morning after the first diminished Saturday church page. The preachers held an indignation meeting. They appointed a committee to visit the editor and to voice their protests.

It was probably necessary to cut down on the space of the church section, but one wonders whether in the long run an earlier delegation from the ministerium, thanking the editor on behalf of the city's churchgoers for his attention to their interest, would have been more influential in obtaining maximum space for the churches than the unpleasant and negative approach that was made.

Never forget that a newspaper is a private enterprise. Most people believe that by its nature it has a responsibility to operate in the public interest, convenience, and necessity; but unlike a radio or television station, there is no formal requirement or commitment to do so. A newspaper is not licensed by any public authority, and beyond keeping within the law and ordinary standards of decency and good taste, the news it prints and the services it renders are decided upon by the owners and no one else.

Church people believe that full publication of church news not only is beneficial to the churches and the public but is likewise in the interest and to the profit of the publisher. No doubt the publication of church news does build loyalty to the paper, increase good will, and make friends. But this should not deprive him of the gratitude of the community. No law or power compels him to include church news in his paper.

The churches benefit by the newspaper's policy also, and they should express their gratitude. No annual church meeting should adjourn without a written expression of appreciation to the newspapers and broadcasting stations for their co-operation with the churches during the year. These acknowledgments should not be items lost in a blanket resolution but should be separate resolutions expressing thanks so that it is specific and individual enough to be published by an editor or submitted by a newscaster to his station manager or board of directors in his report.

Remember, too, that it is not necessary to wait till the year's end to say thank you. A word of support for a courageous editorial, of praise for some graphic reporting, or of admiration for a dramatic newsphoto to the usually overlooked photographer is always in order.

Such letters of appreciation do not really call for a reply; but if you write some out of a genuinely grateful heart, you will be interested to find that you often will receive a response from the editor. He will probably tell you that your note was a welcome relief from the grumbling and the gripes that always fill editors' trays.

CHAPTER VI

Camera in the Service of the Church

HERE IS A CHAPTER ON NEWS AND FEATURE PHOTOGRAPHS THAT will quote no Chinese proverbs nor estimate the verbal equivalent of a picture. This is not to sell pictures short. The current emphasis upon pictures is not overdone despite criticism from some quarters. The real difficulty is not with photos per se but with pictures which have nothing to say.

The public demands pictures. They are the speediest medium which has yet been devised for the transmission of an idea or impression. In one immeasurable fraction of a second a live news picture can tell you what has happened and can also answer in some detail several of your questions, even before you ask them.

Surveys show that pictures are the top attention winners in any publication. Any reader of a page of type and pictures will first scan the illustrations before he reads a line. There are natural psychological reasons that make people picture conscious. In addition they have been schooled increasingly to learn through this medium. The long popularity of motion pictures as a form of entertainment has been continued and further developed by television.

The picture magazines and the tremendous advance of amateur photography have contributed to the public's interest. People want pictures, and because they do newspapers and TV stations seek them out.

Ideas Conveyed Quickly from Good Pictures

Telephoto for the metropolitan papers can bring faraway happenings to the front pages in minutes. Scan-a-gravers make possible speedy reproduction of photos for small-circulation papers. These magic devices help answer the demand for pictures.

But while it has become easier to publish photos, the standards of both publishers and the public of what makes a good news or feature picture have been going up. Not just any old picture will do. Every third touring vacationer is necklaced with a camera, usually an expensive precision instrument. Supply houses for shutterbugs are almost as numerous as grocery stores, and each one is a veritable school of photography. Critical faculties have been keenly sharpened.

There has never been a greater willingness on the part of newspapers and magazines to publish photographs of church activities. At the same time, standards have never been so exacting. The art editor wants "something to stick in your eye," he will tell you.

One of the major news-picture magazines had two, and part of the time three, staff members shooting at a world conference of the denominations for a total of thirteen man-days. They then decided not to use the story, although it had almost everything from lay standards. In a later picture-story they used two of the several hundred pictures they had taken at such enormous expense. In order to be used, church-life photos must rank with other pictures in interest, or surpass them.

Another magazine of the same general character passed up 200,000 negatives of a denomination's round-the-world activities, many of which would have illustrated satisfactorily the article in preparation. At a cost probably of two thousand dollars the editor sent two staffers to states in the Northwest and Southwest to shoot for themselves what they felt would be better "art." To them the difference was worth its cost.

Working with News Photographers

There are, of course, two ways to get pictures of your church activities into the press. One is to get the papers to take them. The other is to provide them yourself.

Talk with the city editor about the picture possibilities of the event you have in mind. If he sees it your way, he will assign a photographer to cover it. In this case you need only aid the cameraman when he comes and help him get away as quickly as possible. He will always be in a hurry.

News photographers are about the most self-confident and self-sufficient persons who meet the public. Don't make the mistake of telling them how to take the picture, how to pose the group, or even who should be included unless they ask you.

Usually the photographer will come with instructions. You will be wasting your time if you try to get him to do something else before he gets the picture he came to take. This will be true even though very much more newsworthy persons have put in an appearance and even though their instructions seem to you to miss the point.

While the photographer is taking his picture, note the order in which the subjects are lined up. Be ready with the "left-to-right" identification, with home towns if they are visitors or street addresses if they are local residents. Prepare this as he works and have it ready in clear and legible form, together with brief data about the occasion. Better print all names.

A newspaper will publish a photo with more than four or five persons only under the most unusual circumstances. Do not try to crowd more into the picture. Large groups result in faces so tiny that the picture is of no interest except to the subjects and their next of kin. Ask yourself how much attention you would give to a group picture of thirty visiting morticians and you will get the point.

You have doubtless noticed how a good news photographer will crowd you a little unnaturally if he is taking you with a couple of other persons. The reason is that the editor will want to make the faces and figures as large as possible. To do this he must not waste his precious space reproducing the wall in gaps between his subjects. If you have anything to do with the trite but still prevalent check-passing and hand-shaking poses, co-operate in keeping the principals as close to each other as you can.

The news cameraman will also avoid, if he can, the kind of picture which cries out loudly, "Here we are, all lined up to have our pictures taken!" The smaller cameras which many photographers now use, with their finer lenses and high-speed film, make possible more relaxed and more natural pictures.

Every photography manual instructs us that there is far more interest in the pictures we take of our children if we can catch them when they are absorbed in doing something. This avoids the frozen, self-conscious expressions so common when people "sit" for a picture.

If we prefer "action" in pictures of our own offspring, toward whom we are favorably predisposed, how much more "live" must a picture be to attract the favorable attention of an editor. Your suggestion will have a double chance of acceptance if it involves activity on the part of your subjects or if it includes a little touch of drama.

What It Takes to Make a Photo Click

The obviously widespread interest in pretty girls needs no demonstration. They are featured as attention-getters both to enliven news pages and to advertise products. The hucksters use them even when the presence of the beauty has no conceivable connection with the commodity being sold.

There are aspects of this factor in picture appeal which no one in church circles would care to appropriate, but there is certainly no reason why this interest needs to be ignored completely. The attractiveness of Christian youth ought to be exploited for all that it is worth.

A few years ago a Miss America journeyed to a northern city from her southern home. She traveled on a crowded special train to attend the quadrennial youth conference of her denomination. A Sunday school teacher, an active worker in her young people's society, and a member of the choir, she was a "natural" for a photo story.

There was nothing forced or artificial about the photographs a national picture magazine published of this young woman's activities as a delegate. She came because she believed in the program and because

CAMERA IN THE SERVICE OF THE CHURCH

she loved her church. Her character and her Christian attainments matched the physical and cultural qualities that made her Miss America. Her willingness to co-operate with the picture magazine made possible a new understanding of the interests and concerns of church youth on the part of millions of readers.

Next to pretty girl pictures, photos of babies and children rank high in attracting readers' eyes, say art editors. Test this out on yourself. Pictures showing animals are next in interest. Obviously one that pictures a curly-haired toddler making friends with some puppies has a double attraction.

Adding the pretty kindergarten teacher may triple the appeal, but there is a danger of dividing the attention of the reader. The best news and magazine photographers try to catch or pose a picture which has a single center of interest. They say the simplest photos are often the most dramatic.

There is such a thing as getting too much into a picture. Make the story of your photo unmistakable. Keep out elements that scatter the viewer's attention.

Study your own reaction to pictures. As you read newspapers and magazines, maintain an inquiring mood. When you find that your eye has been drawn to a particular picture on a page, try to define its magnetism.

Why did you look at one particular picture before letting your eyes rest on another equally in sight? What was its appeal? Was it beauty, human interest, pathos, humor, danger, conflict? And negatively, as you turn pages, what is it that leads you to dismiss many pictures with slightly less than a glance?

Of course part of your answers will be in your personal tastes, but the remainder will be what you hold in common with readers in general. Not all that you learn in this self-examination will be applicable to your use of the camera to interpret the church. You can, however, teach yourself much about what makes a good news picture.

When you think you have a possibility, call the city editor. If your idea does not appeal sufficiently to him to send a photographer, or if he tells you that his cameramen are tied up, ask him if he would be willing to look at a print if you got it for him. The editor is likely to say Yes, but he will make it clear that this is not to be understood as a promise to use it.

You may turn in a good picture and still have it rejected. There are a number of good reasons. The editor may not have the space. The pictures printed on a given day are selected because of their reader interest. Only a certain number can be used. Yours may not be bad, but others may be better.

Your picture may duplicate with different persons and setting a similar picture from another church.

The editor may decide that your picture will not reproduce well, that it will lack general interest, that it is too "posed," or that it has no story to tell.

Appointing an Official Church Photographer

It is a good policy to have one or more official or semiofficial church photographers so that you know where to turn when need arises. A professional may agree to give you prompt and reasonable service, or there may be highly capable photographic hobbyists in your church.

If you have a choice between the arty kind of photographer with great technical know-how but little comprehension of speed in getting the prints out and a less finished cameraman with an interest in *news* photography, by all means choose the latter. He will know that news pictures must often be taken before the event happens; and that if they are not, they must be developed and printed within three or four hours to be of maximum value.

Sometimes, if such an arrangement has been approved by the proper editor and your subjects are of great interest, the photographer may rush his undeveloped film directly to the newspaper darkroom. With the newspaper's equipment, rapid routine, and speedy print dryers, this procedure can often prevent a picture's being too late to be news.

Occasionally ministers develop their shutterbug hobby to professional standards. A number of these have been conscripted eventually by the audio-visual departments of their denominations. Others are engaged from time to time as free lancers for occasional picture-story expeditions to home or foreign missionary projects.

Still others dedicate their cameras at home to the interpretation of the churches they serve. Their photographs not only tell their stories to readers of newspapers and denominational magazines but also appear in church view books and other printed matter, on bulletin boards, and on the silver screen on a variety of occasions.

A particularly fruitful use of slides is at the annual budget presentation. Telling the story graphically of "where the money goes" is one of the best ways of building church pride and morale, not to mention of increasing pledges. Dedicated cameras in the hands of master photographers, laymen, and ministers are a blessing to many churches.

Some Warnings and Some Hints

To those who have arrived at the status of photographic expert these suggestions are superfluous. These hints and cautions are for others just starting or for those who as public relations chairmen are directing professional or amateur photographers.

When events are taking place at your church which are of historic importance and of which you want a photographic record, it is well not to depend solely upon the newspaper photographer, even if the editor has indicated that he has made such an assignment. Something of interest to every reader may suddenly occur which will change the editor's plans and leave you without a cameraman.

It is always well to protect yourself against such a contingency by having your faithful amateur on the job. It is possible that the newspaper will be glad to accept coverage from you. Policy differs from paper to paper. You will at least have a picture for your own uses.

Except for head-and-shoulders portraits, do not submit prints smaller than 8 x 10 inches. This is the size picture editors ordinarily handle.

Occasionally, when a publicity man or a free-lance photographer has an especially good picture, he submits an 11 x 14 print. It would be hard to prove, and the picture editor would probably deny it, but there is a prevalent conviction that large prints are likely to be marked for larger space.

Of course a photograph can be reduced or enlarged in an engraving shop in the process of making the necessary halftone cut, but there is one exception to this rule. In small city and larger weekly papers a machine called a Scan-a-graver is widely used. This is a cheaper and quicker process of photoengraving. A small percentage of Scan-a-gravers can enlarge or reduce a photo, but the great majority produce plates exactly the size of the original photographs. If you are working with a newspaper which uses this process, ask the editor to explain the operation and size requirements to you so that you can co-operate.

In setting up a picture, use every square inch of the negative area to the best possible advantage. Most amateur shots are taken too far from the subjects. If an action that you are photographing is moving toward one side or the other, when you aim your camera allow a little extra room at the side toward which the subject is moving.

When you are posing a particular group of leaders whom you have selected for reasons of your own, one of your subjects may invite a friend or associate standing by to come and get into the picture.

If this is likely to ruin the picture for your purposes, there are two ways to handle the situation. One is to take the group with the newcomer in it, then say you want a shot with "the new officers only," or "tonight's program participants only." It is worth the film and a flash bulb to keep everyone happy.

If you don't have enough supplies or the time to handle the unwanted person this way, put the one who does not belong in the picture on one side or the other so that he can be cropped off with the editor's shears or by the engraver.

Be sure to keep your subjects well to the front of your pictures. If your photo comes out with an unimportant foreground, cut it off to get closer to the center of interest.

Unless you have an irreplaceable print of historic worth, such as one taken by Brady, the Civil War photographer, don't ask an editor to return your photo. If he prints it, the space given you would be worth at advertising rates many times the cost of a print. If he doesn't publish it, he is much more likely to use your next entry if he does not get the opinion that you are a small-minded amateur in press relations. Let him know that you understand routine newspaper procedures. Returning a photo involves much more trouble than one might suppose. By the time it could be retrieved from the engraving department, the staff would be working on the next issue.

At this point it might be well to inquire of preacher readers, "How long has it been since you have had a formal photograph made of yourself?" An unbelievably large number of forty-year-old ministers are still sending out their college graduation photos when the program chairman in a city where they are booked to speak asks for one.

Such an impostor has only himself to blame if he is unrecognized by the assemblage as the man whose picture was in the paper!

The next time you go to the studio, be sure to tell the photographer that you want a portrait in sharp focus for newspaper and magazine reproduction. Have the ones for the press printed on glossy paper of course. The artistic poses for your wife and for posterity are your own business, even if you are almost lost in fleecy clouds and vague outline, but for your publicity shots insist on crisp glossies.

If you supply a considerable number of prints to newspapers in the places where you are asked to speak, it may save you money to have copy prints made by a specialist after having given the original photographer enough business to provide a fair profit. A 5 x 7 or 8 x 10 copy negative is made by these production-line firms. From it they produce contact prints in quantity for a very small fraction of the dollar or two you must pay for glossy enlargements from the original negative.

It is true that exacting magazine art editors note a loss in print quality in the process. Entertainment personalities quite generally use these copy prints for newspapers. However, it is perfectly true that to illustrate an article in a slick paper magazine original prints should be furnished.

If you do expect to use copy prints, be careful to avoid the kind of high-priced name photographers who copyright their portraits. Even though it is your face, even though you have paid plentifully for the photographer's services and amply for his prints, he has a proprietary relation to it. He will insist that it cannot be published without his credit line and that under no circumstances can it be copied.

Apparently your only right in the picture is the privilege of buying some more prints at a fancy price. It is your picture only in one sense of the word—it is of you.

Photographers who follow this practice are usually excellent; and if you can afford to pay high prices for glossy prints, they are to be recommended. On the other hand, if you need many glossies and if you wish to keep the cost down, use a photographer whose print you can have copied.

Watching Your Backgrounds

Whether you are taking the picture yourself, directing an amateur, or accompanying even a professional, always keep a watchful eye on backgrounds. They can make or break your photo.

The best photographer can easily become so absorbed in lighting, composition, and special effects that he overlooks this important factor. A cameraman in New York, long experienced in the exacting requirements of the entertainment world, photographed an international churchman in conference with the lady who supervises CBS religious programs. Doubtless captivated by the charm of his subject (a former British actress), he did not notice a mural decoration directly behind her.

The finished picture showed her more like Pocahontas than like herself. The design on the wall formed a circle of radiating feathers protruding from her head, like the chief's headdress on the Indian penny. It was almost impossible to believe she was not in costume. The photo was an interesting novelty but was completely useless.

Often objects unfortunately placed in the background will photograph in the most grotesque relationships to the subject's clothing or body. A lamp shade can become a not-too-becoming hat, or a light fixture can appear to be a horn or other protuberance.

The wild patterns of drapery and wallpaper chosen for hotel private dining rooms by interior decorators often distract the attention completely from the subject in a photo, yet they may not be noticeably obtrusive in their setting. You may have to go to the trouble and expense of having such "too-busy" backgrounds air brushed out of the print before you can use it. Try to avoid this if you possibly can, for the extra time involved may prevent your picture's publication.

Some expert photographers throw a too-cluttered or too-conspicuous background out of focus by opening the aperture of the camera and reducing the depth of field. If you can control the background itself, pick one which contrasts with the clothing, face, and hair color of your subject. Also keep your subjects far enough from the wall in back of them to avoid conspicuous shadows.

While you are watching your backgrounds, guard against possible reflections entering your lens from mirrors, windows, or picture glass. Enameled or metal Venetian blinds or highly polished wood surfaces can also give you unwanted burned-out spots.

Observe at what angle eyeglasses reflect light. They often cause the owner to appear with white patches over his eyes. Avoid this by asking the subject to tilt his head just enough so that the reflection will not be picked up by the lens.

In a positive way backgrounds can help locate the action or the persons shown. They can contribute to the telling of the story by furnishing some of the facts that otherwise would have to be included in the cut lines to satisfy the readers' interest.

A bulldozer in the background of the picture of the ground-breaking ceremonies for the Interchurch Center in New York told the viewer that the excavation was about to be made. A table loaded with food, with a floral centerpiece in the foreground, states as plainly as words, "We are at a banquet." Ecclesiastical furnishings or architectural features in the background provide a mood for many church-related news photos.

Bulletin boards, entrances, cornerstones, windows, pulpits, baptismal fonts, altar rails, and carved pew ends are only a few of the handy props that quickly locate and interpret religious action pictures. Be sure of course that this identifying background feature is close to the center of interest of the picture, not off to one side. Otherwise when the art editor crops the print to bring up the size of the faces, it may be lost.

Backgrounds and settings of summer camp pictures can help orient the viewer. If you want to locate visitors as being in a metropolis, a photo taken on a roof top or against street crowds or moving traffic will do it.

Captions and Cut Lines

Cut lines for news pictures are written in present tense. Keep your caption short, but do not omit any facts pertinent to the understanding of the photo. Include the names, titles, and home towns of the people shown and locate the action and tell what is being done unless this is obvious. Accuracy is of cardinal importance where names and titles are concerned.

It is usually best to identify the principal person first, if possible. Otherwise use "left to right" indications. Sometimes you can avoid this: for example, "Bishop Chester Jones of Boston, here to preside at the Maine Conference, smiles as little Annie Martin of Falmouth presents his wife with a welcoming corsage." In a case like this there is no chance for confusion. With two men and a woman you need locate but one man by using the word (left), (right), or (center) following his name.

It may not stick, but writing a catchy, amusing or curiosity-arousing caption when suitable may help "sell" your picture. Even if it is rewritten, as it probably will be, it is worth trying your hand at it. Be sure as always to include all the necessary facts.

Don't write the caption on the back of the print. In fact, don't write anything on the back of a photo if you can avoid it. Type your lines on a sheet of paper no wider than the print. Begin two or three inches from the top, leaving room to apply paste to the top portion. Stick this top section to the back of the bottom of the print so that as you look at the photo you can read the caption hanging below it. If you mail the print or put it in an envelope, fold the caption up and over the print.

The danger in using the back of the photograph is that it is easy to mar the glossy finish. Use a soft pencil and a light touch on a hard smooth surface, if you must.

If you use a rubber stamp on the back, be sure it is applied opposite a dark portion of the print and near the edge. If imprints are behind the face or behind light-colored objects, they often will show through under the powerful lamps of the engraver's camera. Be careful, too, not to endanger a glossy print by using paper clips.

The picture editor will wish to know the source of the photo and how to get in touch with you if he needs further information. Put a typewriter line under the caption. Then, below this line, on the left side, give your name, address, telephone number, the institution you represent, and your relationship to it (pastor, publicity chairman, church secretary, and others). On the right side, still under the line, note the release date, if any. If this is unimportant, write "Release at Will." Because so many amateur photographers submit photographs to editors with the expectation of being paid if they are used, you can avoid any possible misunderstanding by writing a space or two under the release information, "Photo Gratis."

This is not strictly necessary but will make misunderstanding impossible. If you have identified yourself as having a public relations responsibility, though, the editor will assume that you not expecting compensation.

CHAPTER VII

How to Make News When There Isn't Any

SOME YEARS AGO THE PHONE RANG IN THE OFFICE OF THE WEEKLY paper in Callander, Ontario. A somewhat shaken but excited voice asked in French, "How much would it cost to put a little notice in the paper?"

The editor hedged, "How long is it? What is it about?"

"Just a few lines," the voice replied. "My wife gave birth to five baby girls last night and we wanted our friends to know."

Papa Dionne had under his roof the biggest news story of the year, but he didn't recognize it as such. Within hours reporters and photographers from wire services and dailies all over the continent crowded the town, eager for every detail of an event the father was willing to pay for having mentioned in the village paper, if it didn't cost too much.

"There's no news at our church" is a frequent pastoral lament. The preacher may be right or wrong about this. It may be that a pastor has a five-star news or feature story right under his nose, like the astonished French Canadian. If that is the case, the next step is to smell it out. Reference to the chapter "What Makes News 'News'" should be helpful.

Every journalism professor tells of the cub reporter who was assigned to cover a wedding. He returned to the newsroom dejected. "Where's your story?" asked the city editor.

"There isn't any," the reporter moaned. "They didn't hold the wedding."

"Why not?" the editor snapped.

"The bride's former boy friend showed up. He started a fight, socked the groom in the jaw, and they had to take him to the hospital."

The paper hired another reporter. This one was hopeless.

First, then, be quite certain that there is no news. It may be a bit under cover, but it's probably there. Here are some places to look for it when all seems quiet on the news front.

Anniversaries

One of the wisest investments of time for a pastor in the early days on a new appointment is to spend some time with the old church records. Read and master the history of the church. You will usually find that someone compiled it from original sources for the seventy-fifth anniversary or the centennial. In this case your job will be easy.

The first value that this research will have is to identify you with the congregation. In your sermons and in visiting you will be able to make reference to earlier events and sainted leaders of the past. It will speed up the congregation's recognition of you as one of them.

While you are studying the early days, note some beginning dates. When was the first Protestant preaching done in your community? Was it by a minister of your faith? If not, when was the first sermon preached by a pioneer of your own denomination? When was the first society organized? When was the first church built? When did the present church open for worship? When was the first Sunday school held, the first young people's group instituted, the first woman's

HOW TO MAKE NEWS WHEN THERE ISN'T ANY

society organized? When was the first marriage? Also, when was the first one performed in the present church?

For some reason, most churches celebrate only one anniversary. Usually these observances are at least twenty-five years apart. How are the people to relate themselves to the church's traditions with such long lapses between historical emphases? These festivals of loyalty can be built around not just one but a number of beginnings.

Newspapers are particularly generous in their coverage of anniversaries. Somewhere in your researches you will find a founding event that will soon be rounding out one of those symmetrical figures that call for an anniversary celebration.

Such occasions not only will make news "when there isn't any," but as all well-planned anniversaries do, will renew and strengthen loyalty.

A study of the old church records will reveal some usable facts for personal anniversaries. Most of the names will be meaningless, but here and there will appear familiar names of current veterans. Note on your desk calendar the dates of their joining the church, then carry dates forward from year to year until you come to a fiftieth, sixtieth, or even a seventy-fifth anniversary. Make the member a guest of honor at a service, with a special chair in the chancel.

If he is senior member, honor him as such. Preach on church loyalty. If you are receiving new members that day, ask the oldest member to help you extend the right hand of fellowship. Compile a list of all those who have belonged to the church fifty years or more. Recognize the group annually at a Founder's Day Service. Deck them with suitable flowers or present appropriate souvenirs.

Perhaps you will find that on a given day of the month a hundred years ago the first marriage on record was performed in your church or parish. Possibly your present building is now about fifty years old. Find the date when the first couple marched down its aisle. Hold a Family Life Service on such an anniversary. Invite all the couples who were married in the church or by its pastors to attend.

You might at an anniversary of the first marriage in the pastoral charge find descendants who could be invited to the service. They might even have tintypes of that first couple. None of this would in itself be very important, but it could center attention on a service in which the values of a church-blessed, church-centered home would be stressed.

Interest in Notable Numbers

Another twist that could be given to such observances is news interest that centers in certain given numbers. As an example, during World War II, in order to call attention to the large number of chaplains The Methodist Church was sending into the armed forces, the denomination's public relations office waited for the approaching one thousandth chaplain to be inducted. Then, with photographs taken with the Chief of Chaplains of the Army and the bishop who headed the Commission on Chaplains, the releases went out. While the chaplain happened to be a colorful Texan and a crack pistol shot, the real story was in the fact that the denomination had furnished the armed forces with the equivalent of four annual conferences of ministers. It was the magic figure of one thousand that carried the story.

In this same way a tally of baptisms, marriages, and members received since the church was organized might show that soon your church will be approaching one of those notable numbers.

The congregation—and in all but the largest cities the newspapers—will be interested in the five thousandth baby to be baptized or in the one thousandth couple to be married or the ten thousandth member to be received. Here again the significance is in the use made of the occasion. The number gimmick serves simply as a flag to call attention to the occasion.

Someone for Honors

No one would attribute a ceremony at the Vatican where Al Smith and Jim Farley were made papal knights of St. Gregory to a desire on the part of the pontiff for a good news story. On the other hand, no one would deny that a substantial by-product of such an investiture is world-wide publicity both for His Holiness, the donor of the honor, and for the distinguished recipients.

For a minister to select someone from his congregation for honors and for him to build the occasion into newsworthy proportions simply for the sake of a headline would rightfully open him to accusations of exploitation, dubious ethics, and a warped sense of values.

It does not follow, however, that a church should therefore refrain from honoring those who have served it with marked fidelity through the years. Those who have rendered it some special notable services and who have blessed it with generous benefactions rate more recognition than they often receive.

There are several reasons why this should be done. First, it is a way of saying "thank you." The words are as appropriate today as they were in Bible times: "Well done, good and faithful servant; thou hast been faithful . . . ."

A pastor in Dallas had found the services of a retired Sunday school superintendent of immense aid to him, inspiring, planning, promoting, financing, and supervising the erection of an educational wing to the sanctuary. Impelled by a love for children and a devotion to his church, the layman gave as generously as he could and devoted a large share of his time to the project.

When the building was nearing completion, the minister recognized that it simply would never come to pass without the interest of this man. The church was deeply in his debt. Never, he thought, was a "thank you" more in order. The pastor therefore announced that the church would confer upon this benefactor "The Captain Webb Award."

A dinner was planned. Grateful parents whose children's lives would be enriched by the new church school filled the dining hall. A framed parchment testimonial and citation was presented.

For the benefit of twentieth-century Texans unfamiliar with the eighteenth-century British soldier, the minister described Captain Webb. He recounted how, when the first little Methodist society in New York was meeting for devotion and fellowship in a sail loft in Horse and Cart Lane, they were startled by the opening of the door in the midst of their "season of prayer."

In strode an immense red-coated British officer with a patch over an injured eye. His sword clanged as he took a seat. They feared that he was there to break up their meeting and decided that the best policy was to continue in prayer.

When one devout worshiper closed his fervent appeal for divine guidance and protection and a break came, the stranger's voice took up the prayer. A comfortable feeling returned to the little company when the soldier's petition fell into the phrases of the Methodist revival in England. Their visitor was obviously one of them.

Fresh from John Wesley's class meetings in England, this soldier, on duty for George III, had sought out this little band of American Methodists both for fellowship and to help them. It was he who contributed heavily himself and circulated the subscription paper that produced three hundred pounds with which the first Methodist church in America was started. It was on John Street in Lower Manhattan, where a successor church still stands among the skyscrapers of the financial district. This was not the only church which Captain Webb helped to organize and to house.

With fine imagination and a sense of gratitude this Dallas minister helped a congregation to say a deserved "thank you." The occasion gave him an opportunity to recount an inspiring bit of church history. It also provided the recipient an occasion, in his response, to make his own testimony on the joy of Christian service: "Such work for the church is not a burden. It has given me more satisfaction than anything else I have ever done in my life." Words like these are important for younger people to hear.

Incidental to all these advantages of the "Captain Webb Award," but not to be ignored or undervalued, was the publicity. The event made news when otherwise there would have been none. There was the photograph of the minister and the president of the board as they honored the recipient of the award. The news story also reported progress on the building and announced the target date for its opening. It left an impression with the parents that this church was fitting itself better to help them build the character of their children.

Honor the oldest member of your church. Many annual conferences provide a cane that is ceremoniously committed to the lifetime custody of the oldest member. Engraved on a silver plate are the names and dates of its proud succession of holders. Each presentation of the conference cane makes an appealing news photo of the bishop and the beloved conference patriarch.

Any local church could do the same. Perhaps a vase or a loving cup could be substituted for the cane. One side could be appropriately engraved at each transfer. The presentation would make the difference between an ordinary and a notable church service.

If your senior member is a shut-in, the news picture will be even more interesting with the presentation made in the home and the aged man or woman in a wheel chair or propped up against the pillows. Back at the church, you would describe to the congregation the recipient's pleasure in having been honored as custodian of the senior-member loving cup.

Against such a background your exposition of your text will have greater warmth and pertinence: "With long life will I satisfy him, and shew him my salvation." Geriatrics more and more is a pulpit theme as larger and larger proportions of every congregation are in the older age brackets. The special problems of these folks can be brought to the community's attention by such an honoring service.

The elderly are not the only ones to honor. A young man from your church may have been ordained or a young woman commissioned as a missionary. Make the most of a visit to the home church, not simply to glorify the individual but to make real to young people the desperate need of the church for life service recruits.

Except in the largest cities, the return of the home-town boy or girl for such recognition would be news.

On some appropriate Sunday honor the church treasurer and the financial secretary. No church worker is less thanked or appreciated. They spend unimagined hours at the dullest drudgery, slitting envelopes, counting, then recounting to make sure, balancing accounts, and then doing it all over again because of a fugitive five cents.

They write checks and they pay bills. Often because they know of creditors who are nearing the limit of patience, they worry much about delinquent church subscribers who in turn do not worry enough about the state of their accounts. Who but the most devoted would accept these offices?

On occasion laymen might quite appropriately honor their minister. When the anniversary of his ordination draws near, the official board might suggest that he speak on "Twenty-five Years in the Pulpit." Without an invitation the pastor might hesitate to bring his own career into the pulpit as a sermon subject, but the board's invitation would convince him that the occasion was of more than personal interest. Almost any clergyman would be glad under such circumstances to review the high spots of his ministry. The ordination dates will be available to the laymen in the pastor's record section of the conference minutes or the denominational directory.

Similarly, when a pastor rounds out a five- or ten- or fifteen-year pastorate, thoughtful officials could properly initiate a suitable observance. It would lift the minister's spirits, increase his dedication, and at the same time provide a fresh news story that would bring both the church and the minister to favorable public attention.

Don't forget former pastors now retired. How honored one would be at a time when he was beginning to feel forgotten to receive an invitation to come back and preach at his old church on the fiftieth anniversary of the first sermon he ever preached!

Unlike bishops of some other denominations who have a home cathedral, Methodist bishops do not possess a church to which they have a close personal relationship, such as they had to the churches which they served as pastors in earlier days. Their approach to almost every occasion is official.

If you are a Methodist, look up your bishop's biography in *Who's Who*. Take some notes. Then when a suitable personal anniversary approaches—of his birth, of his ordination, or of his election to the episcopacy—honor him with an invitation to celebrate it in your church. Hold the service at a time when Methodists from round about can share in it. Follow the sermon with a reception.

If you think that the bishop won't accept your invitation, try it! Rarely are his services requested as a person; almost always it is in his role as the holder of an office. If you tell him that First Church would like the privilege of helping him observe this personal occasion of his, he will be sure to respond. He will not have had too many requests of this kind before.

Be sure, however, that you issue your invitation far ahead of the date. Bishops are booked long in advance.

Doing Something Differently

Some important church procedures that once made page one have become so routine and hackneyed that the papers now do no more than mention them. Do them differently and editors' interest will climb. A little imagination will enlarge inches to columns.

Take ground-breaking ceremonies as an example. Before you arrive on the scene, you know exactly what is going to happen. After appropriate scriptures and devotions and several half-hour speeches that were scheduled on the timetable for ten minutes, the nickel-plated shovels are going to be handed out. The pompous-looking persons, strategically selected on the basis of office held or as potential contributors, receive these tools a little awkwardly, in some cases giving the impression of uncertainty as to which is the business end. If the committee chairman is experienced, the ground they are symbolically to break has been already well spaded so that the photos of these amateur diggers will actually show some displaced earth.

When this drama was first enacted for reporters and news cameras, it made a rather good show, if only because of the incongruity of seeing bankers, politicians, and clerics wielding the implements of manual labor. But repeated without variation again and again, the news interest survives only because of the importance of the future edifice and of the persons involved.

The Rev. Dr. John Clinton of Des Moines, never one to do anything in conventional fashion, found his church building project ready for a ground breaking during a state-wide observance of the centennial of Iowa. What could be more appropriate than to break ground the way it would have been done a hundred years before?

Clinton scoured the country until he found a pair of oxen. He borrowed a century-old plow from an agricultural museum. Then at the proper moment, garbed in doctor's gown and scarlet divinity hood to fit the occasion into its modern ecclesiastical context, he grasped the plow handles, shouted the bovine equivalent of "Forward, march!" and plowed a furrow to mark the future outer walls of the sanctuary. It won't surprise you to be told that Wirephoto carried this picture not only to all Iowa dailies but from coast to coast and that Clinton's denominational weekly, which could not possibly picture all the routine ground breakings, had no difficulty in finding space for this eye catching picture.

If shovels must be used at a ground breaking, could not they be little ones of the kind used with sand pails on the beach? Could they for a change be placed in the hands not of dignitaries but of every child in the beginners' and the primary departments? Let these small folk make the first move in the erection of the church into whose membership they will soon be received and in which one day they may be married and in due time bring their own children for baptism and for nurture.

Such a rite might lack the formality of the conventional procedure, but it could be that it might have values in endearing the institution to the section of its constituency most important to its future. The significance of the participation in such rites of little boys and girls would not be lost by their parents. From the standpoint of publicity value and public relations results, present and future, is there any doubt that doing it differently would pay off?

Another place where interest might be multiplied by a variation from the outworn routine is in mortgage burnings.

Recently there has been issued a widely published warning against this custom of publicly assigning to the flames these ominous documents when their threat has been removed by the bank's stamp "*Paid in Full.*" While it would undoubtedly be wise to seek legal advice before destroying such primary evidence, as state laws and mortgage forms differ, actually the possession of the canceled note and the record of the discharge of the mortgage in the courthouse would in most places be sufficient guarantee against any impairment of the title. Should there be legal advice against destroying the mortgage, a certified photostatic copy could be made and retained for the record and the original document burned for ceremonial purposes. If counsel were insistent, the congregation might be just as well satisfied to see the photostat go up in smoke.

The important switch in the mortgage-burning rite is that the persons who have been painfully paying off the debt should share more intimately in the pleasure than they are usually permitted to do. Ordinarily the minister, the church treasurer, and the president of the board of trustees have all the fun, and the congregation looks on a little enviously from a distance. Suppose instead that the cancelled mortgages were to be sliced on a print trimmer into several hundred little strips as needed.

Upon arrival at the service the ushers would give to each attendant one of these strips of the mortgage with the words, "Keep this and you will be told what to do with it later."

At the point in the service when the mortgage is to be burned, the congregation, directed by the ushers, would file out of their pews and pass down to the front. Here at a stand with a tray of burning votive candles protected by glasses or into a charcoal brazier they would consign their several fragments until the evidence of any debt upon their church had disappeared. With the choir singing the great hymns that extol the church as the mortgage burning progressed, the simple ceremony could be followed by a most meaningful interpretation from the pulpit.

Don't think the people who helped to pay off the mortgage wouldn't enjoy or long remember the good feeling that came over them as they burned a strip of the mortgage that symbolized what they had contributed toward paying it off. And don't think that they would fail to tell their neighbors or to write to their distant friends about their participation in this colorful rite. That any departure from the ordinary mortgage-burning routine would add to an editor's interest is fairly obvious.

Tying in with Current News Events

Perhaps the best understanding of how to create news by taking advantage of what is currently in the public mind can be conveyed by citing a few examples.

This first one had little if any importance to the Kingdom, but it produced several million smiles. It was one of those timely, bright items that editors often make conspicuous by enclosing with a border, or "boxing" it, to use their vernacular.

One of the wire services picked it up from a Philadelphia daily and offered it to its member papers across the country. Few of them passed it up. The Rev. Dr. Charles D. Brodhead had announced for his text the day before Roosevelt was to be reinaugurated in 1941 a verse from the Epistles: "Behold, I come again unto you for the third time."

During the Kefauver investigations in New Jersey a group of ministers in their Monday morning preachers' meeting passed a resolution in which they used language from Ephesians which described exactly what the Senator's inquiry had been uncovering, "spiritual wickedness in high places." They prayed that their fellow citizens might be "able to stand against the wiles of the devil" and to "wrestle . . . against principalities, against powers . . . of darkness." Because this resolution tied in with the news, it was published. Without this relationship it would never have made it.

Soon after the war ended, President Truman addressed American Protestant leaders in a Columbus, Ohio, hotel. Advance copies of his address revealed that he would summon the churches to organize for a nationwide revival of religion. Bishop J. Ralph Magee of Chicago, who headed the Methodists' "Crusade for Christ," when informed of this, immediately dispatched a message to the President telling him that his denomination shared his concern over the country's postwar spiritual hunger, that it already had launched in line with his challenge a nationwide effort to win a million new members within the year. Copies of the bishop's telegram were handed the President's press corps while they were still at work in their special pressroom. Several reporters and one wire service mentioned Bishop Magee's quick comeback.

News Interest Magnified by Dramatizing

There is nothing new about drama. Archaeologists unearth ancient theaters about as often as they do ancient temples. The miracle plays of the Middle Ages brought drama and religion together.

Interest in the dramatic is universal. Perhaps one of the reasons why a certain percentage of men seem to enjoy attending their lodges more than listening to sermons is that the lodges dramatize the truths they teach while the churches depend upon more abstract communication. To dramatize a spoken message is just as logical and serves the same purpose as to illustrate printed words with photographs or drawings.

When Cecil B. deMille's *The Ten Commandments* opened with great fanfare in Washington, D.C., the Rev. Dr. Theodore H. Palmquist, seizing upon the revived interest in this ancient code, encouraged the dramatic club of Foundry Church to write scripts and produce brief dramatizations of the central idea of each of these historic precepts. Enacted as prefaces to his sermons on the commandments these playlets produced a crowded church twice each Sunday morning for ten weeks. Not only did local newspapers carry the story, but it was reported also in one of the nation's news weeklies.

This is related here not as advocacy of giving every sermon a dramatic prelude, but first to re-emphasize the importance of tying in with what is in the public mind, and second to stress the value of the occasional introduction into church activity of a dramatic element. Until this becomes more common than it now is, doing so will continue to be news.

When Bishop Cushman retired, a Methodist Jurisdictional Conference divided his much-too-big episcopal area into two areas and assigned two new bishops to administer the territory once administered by one bishop. One bishop was now to supervise the Dakotas, the other Minnesota. To help the news story make this action clear, a news picture was posed and sent out in mat form to the smaller dailies and larger weeklies of the three states.

This photo told the story at a glance and in a way no one could forget. An outline map of the three states, about five feet in length, was prepared. Then it was cut into two along the borderline between the Dakotas and Minnesota. Bishop Cushman, who was giving over all three states to the care of his two successors, was posed in the center holding with his right hand the top inner corner of the

HOW TO MAKE NEWS WHEN THERE ISN'T ANY

Dakotas and with his left the corner of Minnesota. To his right Bishop Voigt supported the other corner of the Dakotas section, and to his left Bishop Coors held the map of his new Minnesota Area. The picture scarcely needed a cut line except for identifications. The drama of the torn map told the story.

Augustana Lutherans voted in their annual synod to authorize a new style of vestment for their clergy. News of this could, of course, have been conveyed in type. However, they chose to dramatize this change. Their public relations man hunted out the latest pastor to have been ordained. He arrayed him in the newly designed robe. Then he sought and found the oldest pastor present. Suitably he was asked to model the vestments which he had been using through his career. Obviously newspapers were interested in a photo of the two together. Readers grasped the fact and the nature of the change instantly.

On the fifteenth anniversary of an important church merger a commemorative plaque was designed and presented for the wall of the building in which the union had been consummated.

To the group that gathered for the presentation of this marker to the city manager, the years since the merger seem very few. To enable them as well as those who were to see the photographs of the ceremony to comprehend this time lapse, a fifteen-year-old boy was found who had been born while the uniting conference was in session. The participation of this full-grown lad dramatized the passage of the years.

When the goal of a million new members was set by one denomination, a two-column mat release was sent to two thousand small dailies and larger weeklies answering the question "How many is a million?" by dramatized drawings. One was of Washington Monument, 555 feet high. Beside it was an imaginary stack of index cards, on each of which it might be imagined was written a new member's name. Piled one hundred to the inch, the stack of a million cards would reach as high as the famous monument, then mount up above the capstone half as high again.

Another drawing showed the birth of Christ against a background of calendars of the years since. The caption stated that there have not been a million days since that first Christmas, nor will there be until the year 2740. After arousing interest in these dramatizations of a million, it was simple to explain in the few lines of type under

101

the line drawings why these church workers were interested in how many is a million.

I have provided you with six general principles which will guide you in developing news-making occasions in your church. They are capable of endless applications and variations. Nor are they the only ways that news is made.

Don't let your imagination drowse when you read your newspapers and the church press. When you notice an activity of another church or organization, keep asking yourself, "Does this have values for us?" If there is an idea that appeals, yet is not quite right, don't discard it until you have turned it over in your mind. "Can it be adapted to our use?" "What does it lack to make it workable?"

So there's no news in your church! I doubt it. But if at the moment you are right, at least the makings of news are all there.

CHAPTER VIII

Covering Conferences and Conventions

THE NEWS HAPPENINGS AT RELIGIOUS CONFERENCES ARE LIKELY to mirror the emphases that are currently interesting the pastors and members of the local churches involved.

For this reason it is important to take full advantage of the willingness of newspapers and the broadcasting media to help interpret to the public important issues that have brought the visitors to town.

When this is fully accomplished, not only has the conference been publicized to outsiders, but something has been done for the church's own adherents including the delegates themselves. It gives the attendants the feeling that they have been a part of something sufficiently important to be mentioned by the newspapers and the commentators. And if the convention has launched its constituency on some new enterprise or has embarked on some forward movement as conventions should, the fact that these destinations have been declared before the public is an important step toward their attainment.

Conventions in the News

But there are other reasons for squeezing every possible publicity value out of a conference. Gatherings of this kind, because of their infrequency, because they bring together people from distant places, because they attract crowds, and because they feature high church officials and speakers of renown, possess in large measure the elements that make news.

The identical things said and done within the setting of a local church without the conspicuous background of a convention would probably rate little news attention. It would seem to the press as just so much of the routine curriculum of the church. Because on the city desk there exists the presumption that where there is a convention there must be news, conventions offer the publicity chairman one of his best opportunities.

The convention program, reported in its more newsworthy aspects, will reveal to the nonchurchgoing reader much information concerning the interests and concerns of present-day Christians. There is no doubt that the typical religiously indifferent citizen who thinks that he has outgrown the church, who feels that it is an anachronism in this mid-twentieth century, would be compelled to revise his opinions were he to sit for even a day in a general conference or in a general assembly of one of the major denominations. Since in this free country no one is inclined to coerce him into an observer's seat, the best chance to show him that church conferences deal with vital, contemporary problems is through news pages and newscasts.

The editor knows that the readership of church convention stories is not confined to the adherents of the denomination currently in session. The realm held in common by the several Protestant bodies is much larger than the trifling area of their differences. In consequence leaders of all bodies, lay and ministerial, have a deep interest in how their colleagues are handling problems and programs that are essentially the same as their own. Even those of radically different religious traditions will not be totally oblivious to reports of what

COVERING CONFERENCES AND CONVENTIONS

goes on in the councils of Protestantism. To the degree that news of conferences and conventions helps toward mutual understanding, it is a contribution to ecumenical progress.

While only a public relations man would have such a thought, it is possible that church conventions and conferences are worth what they cost in labor and money, if only to provide news hooks for photos and exhibitions of the diverse activities of the church and a sounding board for the denomination's pronouncements.

There are three stages to the full news coverage of conventions and conferences: what you do in advance of its dates, procedures during the conference, and the follow-up.

Preparing for Convention Coverage

First steps should be taken several months before the delegates leave their homes. Begin by drawing up a schedule of what is to be done and when. It makes for efficiency and reduces worry. Your list should include:

Consult with Convention Officials
Prepare Timetable for Advance Releases
Make Personal Contacts with Media
Pressroom: Preparation and Equipment
Arrange for Press Tables in Auditorium
Provide Photos and Biographies of Principals
Request Advance Copies of Speeches
Obtain Directories of Delegates
Procure Reports and Documents for Distribution to Press
Prepare Fact Sheet for Reporters

PRESS RELATIONS ASPECTS OF PROGRAM PLANNING—A PR director doesn't like to concede it, but he really is aware that the primary purpose of conventions and conferences is not to make news. He is annoyed, however, when programs are planned so thoughtlessly that one might think the purpose of the committee was to suppress news. Often meetings are scheduled without the slightest consideration of how the newsmaking highpoints will work out for reporters and newscasters. Timing is of the utmost importance.

If you are handling convention press relations, see to it, if you can, that you are included on the program committee either as a member or as a consultant. Try to be present when the big features are being scheduled.

As the program is being made up, guard the major events that are important enough in themselves to make headlines from competition with one another for news space. Often one evening bills two or three stars, any one of whom would provide an adequate story. This is bad planning because the reporters usually have only space enough to do a good story on one, and they will be compelled to play down, if not ignore, the others.

Another mistake in scheduling is to plan a strong late afternoon feature, followed by a news-making evening event. Both of these break for the morning paper. The result again is that one may receive worthy treatment while the other gets the barest mention.

It is bad enough to make your newsworthy events fight each other for space, but it is even worse to allow the scheduling of sessions entirely devoid of any news elements. Nothing can lose your press quicker than dull spots in the program. It is hard to revive the interest of city editors once they have called reporters off a story.

Of course an entire convention program cannot be planned for the convenience of the press. There is a logical succession of events. Noted speakers are not always available for the ideal spot. Granted that your committee, in building the program, cannot give the interests of the press right of way at every intersection, it should keep in mind that the convention will be reaching thousands through the press, radio, and TV, even though briefly, for every hundred it will touch in person. The rights of this portion of your own constituency as well as thousands of Christian friends in other communions, you must champion in the program-making process.

ADVANCE STORIES TO PRESS—The first temptation when dates and place and general details have begun to take form is to give the newspaper all the data you have. Such enthusiasm is understandable but far from wise. If you release all the facts at first, there probably will not be enough new material to justify a second advance story.

Divide the total amount of advance news about the convention into a logical and reasonable number of releases. Spread these out so that you have a fresh story every week or two until the big event begins. You will reach many more readers with several briefer releases than with one fully detailed advance story. But don't, in your eagerness to multiply references to the coming conference, try to make something out of nothing.

COVERING CONFERENCES AND CONVENTIONS

The nature and content of your meeting will suggest advance stories to you. Here are some possibilities.

The original announcement of the choice of your town and church as the convention meeting place is news. Include in this first story only the most essential details such as dates and meeting place; what official, body, or committee made the decision; any special factors that influenced the choice; whether the convention had ever met in your town before; frequency of meetings of this body, and where the last session was held.

Your next story might be released in connection with the appointment or first meeting of the general or local committee on the conference. The committee will doubtless appoint subcommittees. Since names make news, these should be included.

Another story can grow out of the committee on local arrangements. Tell how many guests are expected. Will they be ministers or lay persons? From what counties, sections, or states will they come? Will they be entertained in homes or in hotels? Where will meals be served?

The program committee is good for another story. Who are to be the presiding officers, the secretary, the speakers? Now is the time for photo mats and brief biographies. Exploit name personalities. Build up the reputations of those less widely known.

Local or imported musical organizations will be singing for the convention. Perhaps a historical pageant or other dramatic program is planned. Will there be exhibits, teaching, or documentary films? Wrap up these cultural aspects of the conference into a special story if the facts warrant. Perhaps there are angles for the woman's or society pages. Do not overlook this possibility.

Are visiting clergymen to be invited to fill neighborhood pulpits? One town and country conference meeting on a state university campus assigned nearly all its two thousand delegates to Sunday morning service up to a hundred miles from the conference center. Hundreds of individualized advance stories went out to weeklies and smaller dailies, each with a home-town angle. Every release described the nature and extent of the conference, as well as announcing Sunday's pulpit guests.

Publicize your coming convention through feature stories too. If the meeting is of the state or sectional body of your denomination, the church editor may use an illustrated historical roundup the week end before the conference. Be sure to call the attention of the press to any institutions, educational or philanthropic, conducted by your denomination within the bounds of the convention's constituency.

The committee preparing the printed program will doubtless have asked the mayor for a brief word of welcome. Release this to the press just before the conference opens.

A short statement from the bishop, moderator, or president of the convention, acknowledging the hospitality of the community and telling the public in a few words the purpose and goals of the session, could also be given to the papers. If you want such a statement, here is the way to get it: your presiding officer will tell you that he is too cramped for time to write anything. Before you ask him, prepare a paragraph that might serve the purpose. Then say, "I realized you would be hard pressed, so I wrote out something that might be used with a little editing on your part."

Hand him what you have written, with an extra sheet of paper and a pencil. He will either accept your statement, modify it, or discard it entirely and hastily write something he is more willing to have published over his signature. In any case, you are getting what you want.

Previous meetings of this body in your town are possible subjects for feature stories. Turn up someone who attended a similar convention forty or fifty years ago. Let your reporters know about this. One of them might like to do a "then and now" interview.

MAKING CONTACT WITH MEDIA—Early advance stories are not enough if the coming conference is an important one. Talk personally about the coming session with the newspaper editors, wire service representatives, and radio-TV newscasters and program directors. Explain that you will be set up with a fully equipped pressroom and press staff to aid reporters. Tell what the major stories will be and what the photo possibilities are.

Such contact will get the event on the editors' assignment books. It will also increase hospitality for the advance stories you will be supplying them.

Write letters to editors of newspapers in nearby towns, alerting them to the coming conference. If enough delegates from a neighboring city are planning to attend, the editor may assign a reporter to

COVERING CONFERENCES AND CONVENTIONS

cover the event, majoring attention upon the activity of the delegates from his own town.

Sometimes editors ask a local minister who is attending a conference in another city to send back his own interpretive story. You might suggest to the editors in the more important cities in your convention territory that if they cannot spare a reporter they might consider naming a qualified delegate to represent them. Explain that upon request you will grant such a person press credentials and full assistance.

PREPARING AND EQUIPPING THE PRESSROOM—How much space and equipment you will need for a pressroom depends upon the importance and the length of the convention, and the number of reporters it will be required to serve.

It is rare that either an auditorium or a church will contain a room which meets all of your requirements. The room must be easily accessible but far enough from the platform and delegates so that the noise will not disturb the meeting.

Place directional signs at each entrance so that reporters can locate it without difficulty and label it "Pressroom" conspicuously.

Your pressroom must have telephone service available. This is the most necessary specification. Some churches have a single line with several extensions. This setup is definitely not satisfactory. When a convention is in progress, church phones are in incessant demand. Long distance calls for delegates come in. Young mothers working in the kitchen call home to see if their children are surviving without them. Dinner chairmen frantically call the dairy for more coffee cream. In a situation like this it would be a miracle if a reporter found the line free when he needed it.

In order to include last minute happenings, reporters naturally wait until the last possible moment before phoning in afternoon stories. They cannot wait for phones. They must be instantly available.

Temporary phone installations are a rather heavy expense but are worth it. If the budget makes this impossible or it is a very short convention, try to arrange for the use of telephones in nearby friendly homes.

You will want in your pressroom table space, chairs, and typewriters for at least half as many reporters as you think are likely to register.

There may be reporters whose coverage of your conference will be only one of several assignments for the day. These will simply drop in, take your handouts, ask some questions, and move on.

When they get back to their desks to do their stories, some items may not be clear to them. Be easy to reach. This is another reason for a private line into the pressroom.

Keep each table supplied with 8½ x 11 inch paper. At a central place have the following supplies available: No. 10 envelopes, stamps, postal scale, carbon paper, typewriter erasers, soft lead pencils, a pencil sharpener, a bottle of ink, large shears, paper clips, rubber cement or a paste pot, scotch tape, manila envelopes to hold 8 x 10 inch photos and card stiffeners, dictionary, Bible, hymnal, *Editor & Publisher Yearbook* or Ayers or other newspaper directory, and copies of the minutes or journal of last year's convention.

Reporters greatly appreciate the provision of some kind of individual desk tray, cardboard box, or mailbox that can be clearly marked with their own names and names of their papers. These trays can be arranged in alphabetical order on shelving. Into each one is placed every news handout as it is released, together with all the booklets, reports, and directories of the conference. The reporter uses his box as a locker, leaving his own notes and partially completed materials in it when he is away temporarily. Messages for the newsmen may also be left in their boxes.

Pressrooms that do not make this arrangement usually have a table covered with piles of releases. Because they look so much alike, this is confusing. A reporter comes in and picks up a release to see if it's a new one. "No, I've had that," he says after a glance. Maybe he will eventually find the fresh releases. Often he doesn't because the piles become mixed up. With individual trays or mailboxes there is certainty that each reporter promptly has an available copy of each release.

In general, a mimeograph is indispensable in a pressroom. For brief conventions, lasting only a day or two, you can do your mimeographing in advance, provided the speakers are co-operative. Be prepared, however, for the unexpected. If you have no duplicating machine on hand, know where you can take unexpected stencils for quick service.

During major conferences and conventions of a legislative character, where resolutions are presented and debated, the mimeo drum is rotating most of the time. Be sure there is someone on your pressroom staff who can cut a clear stencil quickly and who is on friendly terms with the whirling dervish.

Your preconvention contacts with the press will determine how much table space you will need for reporters at the front of the auditorium. Requisition from the committee on local arrangements press tables and enough chairs. Be sure to make provision in all your plans for representatives of your own denominational press, other religious editors, and the representative of Religious News Service.

Do not provide too much press table space in the auditorium. If it is not fully occupied, delegates, not familiar with how reporters work, may feel that the press is letting you down. With good press service it is not necessary for reporters to attend certain sessions. A good public relations director will provide advance copies of the addresses. Before the session itself is under way in the evening, reporters will be pounding out stories for their morning papers, either in your pressroom or at their own offices. Should the unexpected happen, reporters know that the press director will make immediate contact with the city rooms.

PREPARING PHOTOS, "BIOGS," ADVANCE ON SPEECHES—While local newspapers usually prefer to take their own photographs of big meetings, they will often use "mug shots" of the officers and visiting celebrities before and on the day the convention is to open. Occasionally, too, if they fail to connect with a late-arriving speaker they may use a column half tone along with the story on his address.

Therefore, provide yourself with photos of the principals and in smaller cities with mats. Reporters from nearby places may want them for their papers too.

Newspapers now rarely give as much space to the life history of speakers and officials as they once did. Still it is well to have available brief "biogs" of the leading participants. Usually if Who's Who does not provide the needed data, an inquiry from the speaker's office will bring a full, mimeographed biography. From it you can select the data you want and prepare your own sketch.

If important officers are to be elected, be prepared with photos and "biogs" of the persons who are likely to be conspicuous in the balloting. If there is a nominating committee, keep in touch with the chairman. Help him to see that you can do a much better job in servicing the press when the time comes if he lets you know confidentially in what direction the wind is blowing.

EXTRACTING ADVANCE COPIES OF MANUSCRIPT—The most disheartening task is obtaining copies of the speakers' manuscripts. Persons addressing your conference are accustomed to receiving such requests, but your first letter usually arrives long before they have given this particular occasion thought.

Your speaker doubtless will have to get several other occasions off his chest before he can give yours attention. If you do get back a manuscript promptly, you can almost take it for granted that it's from the barrel. In case your distinguished visitor is preparing a new speech, you will probably have to send someone out to meet his plane or to his hotel room to get it. There are, of course, occasional refreshing exceptions to this generalization.

Begin your request for a manuscript by apologizing for laying this extra burden on the speaker. Then quickly say you wish his address to receive the best possible treatment by newspapers, wire services, and radio-TV newscasters. Tell him that you are sure he has long ago discovered that newspapers are so short staffed that they rarely send a reporter to cover an evening event, and that even if they did, morning papers are on the street so soon that by the time a reporter could write a story and the paper publish it, it would make only the last editions.

You don't know what the papers will do with any particular speech, but you can tell him that the chances of its being used are greatly increased if you can have his manuscript in advance. He may not be a speaker who writes out his addresses. In that case ask for a one- or two-page abstract or some typical quotations bearing on important emphases of his speech.

You may need to explain why you need his "advance" several days before the conference opens. Remind him of how many are on the program. He will realize that all of these addresses cannot possibly be processed properly at the last minute. As an extreme example, a world conference of one of the denominations listened in its two-week session to sixty-five formal addresses.

PROVIDING PRESS WITH WORKING TOOLS OF DELEGATES—Any handbooks, reports, directories, rules of order, or manuals which are to be supplied the delegates should be procured for distribution in the pressroom. Without having in their hands the same documents as the delegates, the reporters will be lost. Accurate reporting will be impossible. This material should be obtained in advance from committee chairmen or conference secretaries. Go over the program in advance with the secretary before the convention session by session. You may uncover features on which you might otherwise be unprepared.

At one national interchurch event the secretary read a message from the President of the United States. Reporters rushed to the pressroom for copies of the text. The director knew nothing about it. When he chided the convention secretary after finding that the message had been in his possession, the secretary said, "It just never occurred to me that you would want it."

FACT SHEET FOR EDITORS—About a week before the conference opens, alert editors again by sending out a fact sheet. Enough extra copies should be made to supply the reporters' trays in your pressroom. This fact sheet may run to several pages. It must answer all the questions an editor or reporter might ask. It may be arranged in question and answer form, as an outline, or in any style you choose, as long as it is easy for reference. Leave plenty of white space.

State the nature and purpose of the convention, the dates, the meeting place, the most interesting items on the agenda, names and identification of celebrities on the program, the number of delegates, their classification as to ministers or laymen, men, women, youth, or where applicable, racial and national distribution.

Be sure to indicate the territory represented by the conference. Give statistics of the area represented. Include some statement of the body's relationship to its larger organization. If a "Who's Who" of the program participants is not part of the printed program, it should be included in the fact sheet.

Coverage at the Convention

What you have done in preparation for the press relations of the conference will make for a smooth, unruffled operation during the sessions.

Be in the pressroom early on the opening day so that phone callers and visiting pressmen will not have even a moment's doubt that there is someone at hand who can give assistance. Normally, church reporters are assigned to cover important conventions, but often these events are handled instead by reporters from the city staff. The person who draws this assignment may never have covered a church gathering before. He or she may have a totally different religious background from yours or none at all.

Often reporters, blasé as they seem, approach such assignments with dread. To discover that there is someone available to answer questions, to keep them from blunders, and to provide advance manuscripts or abstracts of the scheduled addresses will be most reassuring to them.

ACCREDITING REPORTERS—It is well to register the reporters who put in an appearance. Blanks can be provided for this if several newsmen are expected. Note their local addresses, telephone numbers, city or managing editors (you'll need this later), and the name of the paper they represent.

If this is a convention where admittance to the floor of the conference is restricted to badge wearers, be sure that you, your press staff, and the reporters who are covering are provided with some kind of visible press credentials. This is particularly desirable if space at the press tables is likely to be at a premium.

There are in every large convention gate crashers who are looking for special privileges. Often this takes the form of a demand for a seat at the press tables. Some of these have proper claims, which you will be glad to honor if you can. Among these are former officers or retired church editors who do not now have official status.

Other less deserving visitors, after scanning the distant balcony seats, try to talk themselves into a press seat so they won't have to climb the long ramp. They will tell you that they are planning to send back to their hometown editors some news of the convention.

If you consent, always make a provision that the working press has right of way and that in case there are insufficient seats, the "honorary" press-table guests must vacate in favor of those for whom the facilities are provided.

At some of the meetings of the great national church bodies the job of separating the legitimate reporters from the phonies is the director's worst headache. His desire is naturally for the widest possible coverage. Like most people, he finds it easier and pleasanter to say Yes than to say No. But the press relations director is obligated to provide the best possible working conditions for the news writers who are paid by newspapers and wire services to cover the event. Cluttering up the pressroom and overcrowding the press tables with persons who have no logical claim to be there tends to demoralize the service to the legitimate newsmen.

To enforce the principle of limiting the pressroom admissions to bona fide reporters, a public relations chairman has to be painfully hard-boiled even with his best friends. One method is to refuse anyone who does not have a letter or other credentials from a newspaper. Even this does not always work. Plenty of editors are "good fellows" and will write a note to the pressroom director requesting accreditation for a minister friend, even though they have no expectation of printing any other news of the conference than that the preacher attended.

PRESS BRIEFING LUNCHEON—If yours is a convention where several representatives of the church press, daily papers, and radio-TV newsrooms are on hand, one of the most rewarding and hospitable services you can render is to give a luncheon or dinner for the press on the eve of the conference. Include on your invitation list not only the church editors of the local papers but managing editors and station managers themselves. Often if Mr. Big cannot attend, he will send a city editor or someone of similar importance to represent him.

Secure the presence of the top men of your organization. Following the meal, call upon your leaders to greet the press and to outline briefly what the conference hopes to accomplish, where the news high spots are likely to be, and the meaning of procedures that are likely to baffle reporters attending for the first time. Have them explain any peculiarities of your denominational nomenclature.

Of course an overzealous church official can cancel out the benefit of a press dinner by launching into a too-detailed history of his denomination or a verbose defense of its doctrinal positions. Guard against this. Keep the program brief, informal, practical, and pleasant.

PURSUING SPEAKERS FOR MANUSCRIPTS—An early duty of the pressroom director as the conference begins is obtaining manuscripts, abstracts, or quotes from the speakers with whom earlier efforts have failed. Locating these speech makers will require all the sleuthing methods of a missing persons bureau. If when found the speaker has nothing on paper, get him to write out or dictate a summary of the most newsworthy parts of what he plans to say.

A HANDBOOK OF CHURCH PUBLIC RELATIONS

A member of the pressroom staff should always be present at the press tables to serve as host, to answer questions, and to supply needed information. Reporters may need full names, initials, and home towns of delegates who take the floor. Often these are announced only partially or not clearly.

You and your staff must be a jump ahead of whatever is happening. The host at the press tables should keep on the alert for any changes made in the agenda or in the established orders of the day, and for any special announcements involving readjustments in the program. Conferences have a way of suddenly altering their schedules. When this is done, the changes should be reported immediately to the pressroom so that incorrect information will not be given out.

At all but the smallest press relations operations, you as director will find yourself unable to remain in the auditorium. A capable observer must be there to represent you at all times.

Reaching Outlets Not Represented

After the convention has opened, check your list of representatives of newspapers, wire services, and broadcasters as soon as you find time. If some who were expected have not appeared, contact them by telephone. The conference may have been overlooked or the news agency may be short staffed. A city editor may be underestimating the news importance of the meeting.

In any case, remind the editor courteously of the nature of the occasion, of the people who are present, of the area the conference covers, of the timely issues that are to be discussed, and of the interest that many of the readers will have in what is taking place. Offer to deliver the releases, reports, and other documents to his desk or to phone in the news to a rewrite man at such hours as he may suggest. Often this extra help will make the difference between the convention's being bypassed and its receiving reasonably good coverage.

One of the major nationwide wire services at a denominational conference was shorthanded because of illness. All the news it dispatched to its member papers throughout the two-week session came to it through regular phone calls from a pressroom staff associate. Have sufficient pressroom helpers to enable you to meet any need for special service that news editors may require.

REFRESHMENTS FOR BUSY REPORTERS—News writers usually pound out their stories while delegates are eating. Because of pressing dead-

COVERING CONFERENCES AND CONVENTIONS

lines there may not be time enough to go out. Provide coffee and light refreshments in or near the pressroom if the working patterns of the visiting reporters indicate that this hospitality would be appreciated. Local reporters usually prefer to return to the familiarity of their own desks and typewriters between sessions where, if they are near a deadline, they can pass in part of their copy before the story is fully written.

Even if the reporters do not use the pressroom during lunch and dinner hours, they are accustomed to occasional "coffee breaks." They will enjoy a hot or cold drink, as the season indicates, and a cruller, sweet roll, or sandwich when they return to the pressroom at recess times.

PHOTO ASSIGNMENT POSSIBILITIES—During the conference be watchful for feature-story and photo-assignment possibilities. As these ideas occur to you, prepare memoranda to tip off the reporters. Put the memos in their release boxes so that you are not playing favorites. This way your suggestion becomes available to all simultaneously.

First, run over in your mind the list of visiting speakers. Sometimes they are from distant countries or have had contacts with world figures or movements. In your memo state briefly the experiences, adventures, or special knowledge that such a person possesses which would make him a likely subject for a lively story. Tell the reporters that if they see possibilities for a feature story, you will set up an interview.

Never push or overurge a reporter to see anyone. Give the facts as alluringly as they warrant but do it casually. Let the reporter take the initiative in asking to see your lion. Sometimes the newsman will not seem to give your suggestion much attention. He may bypass your offer of help, then hunt up the important visitor himself. Reporters like to bring in to their editors stories they have personally unearthed. Sometimes it is best to drop the hint as effectively, yet as unobtrusively, as you can. Then see what happens.

ABOUT PRESS CONFERENCES—Now, about press conferences—arrange these, of course, any time two reporters or more ask for one. Be cautious in calling them when they are not sought. Most reporters would rather do their quizzing privately. The reporter who interviews his subject alone has an "exclusive," even though rival newsmen may also interview the same celebrity.

Press conferences help beginning reporters and the less resourceful and imaginative ones. They benefit from the more skillful inquiries of the experts. For this very reason, old-time reporters don't take to press conferences too well.

There are occasions where a press conference is a necessity. Should you have an Albert Schweitzer on your program, every reporter would demand a personal interview. The only way to avoid such an imposition on the great man would be to hold a press conference. But there are not many Dr. Schweitzers.

You can do yourself irreparable harm by building up the expectations of reporter friends, then disappointing them with a dud at a press conference. Don't call a conference unless you are positive from your own experience or observation, or by trusted testimony, that you have a newsworthy person who has something new, interesting, different, and important to say.

Don't ever take it for granted that a V.I.P. will come through at a press conference just because he has been elected moderator or stated clerk or bishop or ruling elder, chancellor, or president general. With all respect for high-ranking church officials, they differ greatly in gifts. Some simply do not have what it takes to produce a fruitful press conference. When in doubt about calling a press conference, don't.

At one important church convention, an overseas delegate was for good reasons unable to hold a much-desired press conference. He obliged newspapermen another way. The reporters submitted their questions in writing to the pressroom director. The visitor dictated his replies to a stenographer after taking an evening to ponder the queries. The questions and answers were mimeographed and given to the press. Perhaps this suggests a method by which a high official or a visiting celebrity who prefers to frame his replies carefully and to be quoted exactly can provide the makings of an interview story.

HELPING FEATURE WRITERS—Feature writers can approach a convention from many directions. What part do women take in the meeting and in the work of the body it represents? Are there women preachers? What proportion of the delegates are women? Have women always been allowed to sit as delegates in this assembly? How did they first break the taboo? What are the occupations and attainments of the

COVERING CONFERENCES AND CONVENTIONS

women delegates? Who are some of the better-known people present? Similar data about the growing participation of laymen and the part taken by young people will provide readable stories.

Don't forget the old stand-bys: photos and feature stories in which the oldest and the youngest official delegates are brought together; fathers and sons or twins among the delegates; the delegate from farthest away with the one whose home is nearest the auditorium. Related to these human interest stories is one on the churchman who had been a delegate the greatest number of times. His answers to how the emphases and procedures have changed since the first convention he attended may interest readers.

Point out to your reporters the possibility of a feature picture story centering on the conference exhibits. Book displays are likely to be in the custody of high-level personnel from the denomination's publishing house. Such an official might be interviewed on current reading habits and the future of books in the television age. (The dean of the Liverpool Cathedral prophesies that audio-visual processes may eventually displace books.)

Experts in church architecture are often present at conventions in connection with church extension exhibits. They will be glad to be interviewed on current trends in church building. Few readers realize the degree to which church design has gone modern. These authorities can provide photos to illustrate such an interview.

Another good feature-story possibility at conferences where there are audio-visual exhibits would be an interview with the expert in charge. It is generally known that churches are producing recordings for classroom and radio use and films for church and television use, but the public is still only slightly aware of the progress that is being made in this field. There are timely, informative features to be written in this area.

IF THERE ARE PASTORAL APPOINTMENTS—Assignments of ministers for the following year are made at the annual conferences of several denominations. These appointments are subject to last-minute change and may be difficult to obtain before being officially read.

If you can get such a list in advance, when you give it to each reporter, be sure he understands: (1) that it is confidential, (2) that it may not be final in its present form, and (3) that it must not be released in whole or in part until it has actually been read and thus made official by the proper officer.

If you are unable to get an advance list, prepare work sheets to facilitate the reporters' getting the facts with the least possible delay. List the appointments in the order they will be read, using double or triple spacing. Opposite each church and its location, name the ministerial incumbent. Leave adequate blank space below the pastor's name or to the right. Where changes are made, the reporters can easily write in the names of the new appointees as they are read. There is no room to do this on printed lists. Send advance copies of these work sheets to newspapers to aid them in recording the changes when you report them later by telephone.

EXHIBITING YOUR CLIPPINGS—Post clippings the conference is producing in a conspicuous place. Passing delegates should be sure to see them. A corridor or lobby near the pressroom is often a good location.

Many convention delegates will not have time for newspapers. Others will find that the hotel newsstands quickly sell out. Delegates will be glad to stop for a moment and glance at your exhibit.

Be sure to include stories that were published before the convention opened. Then display current clippings as they appear. A modest card on the exhibit board may state that the press service of the conference is being given by your committee. This not only will give credit where it belongs but will help gain support for your next year's public relations budget.

Remember that reporters are interested in such exhibits too. If two or more newspapers are covering the meeting, staple each paper's masthead at the top of one of the display panels. Mount clippings from each paper under the name of the paper that published them. If you display the clippings in this way, it will be apparent how much attention is being given the conference by the several papers. If one is lagging, the reporter will notice it. Often the inactive paper will spur its efforts and give more space to the convention news, features, and photos. Editors may not admit it, but they are often influenced in their judgment of news value by what the competition is doing.

Circulation departments of local newspapers often will set up a table and take orders for a package deal on the papers published during the conference, mailing them to the homes of attendants and their friends. These issues, containing a record of what happened during the conference, are valuable to delegates when they have to make reports.

Commercial agreements of this kind when permitted are not usually made by the public relations director. However, it will be to his advantage to encourage such an arrangement unless there are special reasons to the contrary. Such a package sale spreads news of your convention much further than would be possible otherwise. It also is likely to influence the paper's editorial department. If the editors and reporters know that the circulation department has sold several hundred or several thousand mail copies because they will contain a full report of the conference, they will do their part to fulfill the expectation. Such a plan is to everyone's advantage.

After Conference Chores

"MOP-UP" AND OTHER WINDUP STORIES—As the convention comes to an end, a "mop-up," or summarizing story, is in order. Lead off with any commanding accomplishments of the delegates. Without too much repetition bring together and organize the more memorable and permanently significant accomplishments. Introduce again any new leaders who have been elected to places of prominence. Repeat briefly the essentials necessary for an understanding of the nature and scope of the gathering. Include the date and place of the next convention, if it has been decided. Perhaps you will wish to summarize the accomplishments, if they have been numerous enough, in a series of short statements near the beginning of the story.

Write your "mop-up" so that a person who has not read anything about the conference will have a well-proportioned comprehension of it. Be careful, on the other hand, to do this quickly and with a fresh touch. Avoid boring the readers who have been following the convention news.

You may wish to make copies of this final story available to delegates as they leave. Some will think they can persuade their home-town editors to publish it, although this is unlikely. Others will find the story helpful in preparing reports for their constituencies. Still others, somewhat bewildered by all that has been happening, will find in it a perspective on the conference and will be helped to see it whole.

Another postconference task is to send out specially written stories to the home-town papers of persons who have been elected to office or who have been otherwise honored. Ordinarily, during the session there will not have been time for this. Now, before you leave and before it ceases to be news, supply to the home friends and personal constituencies of these new officers an interpretation of the duties, responsibilities, and magnitude of the offices to which their townsmen have been elected.

FINISHING THE JOB—Too often the volunteer press relations chairmen have sacrificed so many hours in preparation for a conference and throughout its sessions that when the final gavel falls, they rush home to take up their own neglected duties. If you are tempted to do this, keep remembering that one final lapse, after days of perfect public relations, can undo much of the positive good will which you have been building up.

There is the job of dismantling the pressroom, paying for rented equipment, and arranging for its return. It would hardly be fair to lay these responsibilities on the local committee, if they are still breathing. Return the borrowed articles to their owners and restore the rearranged furniture of your pressroom to its original position. Your weary conference host will call you blessed.

REGISTERING GRATITUDE—But more important than all this, don't leave without thanking those connected with the media that have made your press room operation so successful. Without them your efforts would have been invisible and inaudible. It must seem odd to publishers and station managers that the services which were so ardently courted by the PR committee previous to the conference now that they have been granted do not seem worth a grateful word.

If you can do so during the closing hours, secure a separate action from the body thanking each newspaper and each broadcasting station for its co-operation in bringing the program of the convention to a vastly enlarged public. Try to avoid having the only reference to these important allies appear in the blanket "thank-you" resolution. The newspaper may want to publish the convention's grateful expression in its "Letters" column. The radio-TV manager will find a ready place for your appreciation in the file he carries to the Federal Communications Commission when his license is up for renewal. It will help him prove that he has been operating in "the public interest, convenience, and necessity."

COVERING CONFERENCES AND CONVENTIONS

If the chairman of your main body rules against such specifically aimed expressions of appreciation, get them voted by the executive committee, the local committee, or your own public relations committee. A newspaper or station will appreciate your resolution far more if it specifically identifies the individual medium and cites the specific service that has been rendered. Mention reporters and newscasters by name. Don't forget the cameramen. They are often overlooked.

Your other "thank you's" can wait until you are back home, if necessary. The sooner they are written, though, the more genuinely they will convey your appreciation and the less likely you are to forget them when you discover what has accumulated on your desk during your absence.

It is almost pathetic to learn from replies we have received to deeply felt words to publishers and broadcasters that their great contributions to the success of conferences and conventions, not to mention other church activities, go largely unacknowledged.

Handling the press relations of a convention is a wearying and sometimes nerve-racking task. It has its rewards, however, not only in clippings and radio-TV program schedules, but in some much deeper satisfactions. You will have helped the delegates themselves to an enlarged sense of the significance of their labors. They will have been impressed as they read of their own actions or listen to newscasters quoting striking passages from addresses they have heard. To see in print the actions they have taken and the resolutions they have passed gives a sense of reality to it all. The announcement of the goals they have set will start them on the way to their achievement.

You will find no little satisfaction also in the knowledge that you have helped to dissipate the vague clouds that in the minds of many strangers to its purposes have been obscuring the church. You pray that your efforts may have changed hostility into open-mindedness toward the church and indifference to friendliness.

PART TWO

RADIO AND TELEVISION SERVING THE CHURCH

CHAPTER IX

You, Your Church, and the Networks

"MIRANDA PRORSUS" WERE THE WORDS WITH WHICH POPE Pius XII opened his encyclical dated September 8, 1957.

The key words, translated "remarkable inventions," were followed by instructions to bishops all over the world to set up committees on radio, television, and films. In addition to interest in the religious utilization of these media the pontiff indicated a desire for studies leading to their moral evaluation.

Protestant bodies on their own and in co-operation have along with those of other faiths made a certain amount of use of these "remarkable inventions" from their earliest days. There is, however, a general feeling that, compared with the high percentage of people to whom religion is a most important interest, the portion of time devoted by broadcasting stations to religion is small.

Obligation of Churches to Broadcasters

Most reasonable people do realize that, before the industry can be blamed for this condition, the churches must be prepared to furnish networks and local stations with programs consistent with their standards in content, production, and audience interest. Anything less than this is an imposition on the station, not only because it discredits its reputation for program quality, but also because it affects the salability of broadcast periods immediately following.

Regardless of the excellence of programs provided by the churches, stations are bound to lose a portion of their audience due to the disinterest of many people in religious programs of any kind or quality.

On general principles it is a duty of churches to encourage watching or hearing all acceptable programs for their educational, inspirational, and evangelistic values. Programs can supplement the preaching and teaching of the church. Their promotion is justified on the same grounds that the church supports and facilitates the reading of religious books and magazines.

Churches which are the recipients of sustaining broadcast time have an added moral obligation. Out of a sense of justice and as a way of registering appreciation to the station which is losing listeners by "airing" religious programs, all churchmen should, by special promotion of such programs, seek to replace those who dial out with a new and sympathetic audience.

Many churches list in their Sunday bulletins the recommended religious radio and TV programs of the coming week and announce them in services or in class and group meetings. If this were done generally across the nation, the results would be immense. Parishioners would benefit from the programs themselves, and good will between the churches and the industry would be built.

Influence on Network Broadcasting

Radio and television, with their multitudinous audiences, operate on such a colossal scale that individual units—personal or local churches—feel they are helpless to make any contribution toward increasing and improving religious programs. Do not think that because you live in a community which has no broadcasting station, there is nothing you can do to influence the situation.

First, you can help build up the listening audiences for local and network religious programs. You can write the station managers from time to time, telling them of your appreciation for their presenting them. Tell them also that you are doing all you can to promote listeners, by word of mouth, by pulpit or church society announcements, in church calendars, and in parish papers. Even a very few letters like this, arriving at the right time, could make the difference between the cancellation and the continuation of a program.

None of the various types of audience-measuring methods indicates very large audiences for religious programs, compared with the size other kinds of programs attract. Station managers and network officials are always asking if it is worth contributing to religion time that could otherwise profit the stockholders, when apparently so few listeners are interested. Your letters of thanks and your evidences of support for these programs, multiplied by similar assurances from other sections of the listening area, may easily be the decisive factor in shaping the attitude of the program director toward religious broadcasts.

On the positive side, you can be a very helpful influence through making and stimulating requests to nearby stations with network affiliations to "air" the religious programs that the network makes available to them.

The only reason stations do not give their audiences the benefit of world-renowned preachers, religious drama, discussion programs, and inspiring church music is because too few people in the listening area indicate an interest in them. Each network's sustaining (non-sponsored) programs are available to its affiliates at the flip of a switch. If a local program has been scheduled at the same time, the program director can easily record the network religious broadcast when it comes on the network, then present it at a later hour. In the case of television it is currently common, when a locally scheduled show prevents the station's carrying the network program "live," for them to present it on film at another hour a week or two later.

Equipment will eventually be in all local television studios that will make it possible to broadcast delayed network telecasts on the same day.

Fewer than half of the local affiliated stations carry network religious programs. Not enough people show interest. Church members in America could double the number of listeners to network Protestant radio and TV programs within the next three months if they really want to.

All they need to do is to ask the stations not now carrying the excellent network sustaining programs to do so. When enough church people make such a request, the programs will be scheduled. It is that simple.

CHAPTER X

If You Want Air Time

APPRAISALS OF THE MANNER IN WHICH RADIO AND TELEVISION have influenced modern life make interesting reading. But churchmen need no findings from survey investigators. They are aware of the main facts from their own observations.

Figures concerning the number of radio and television stations, the census of receiving sets in use compared with the total dwelling units, and statistics on listening habits are never more than approximately correct. By the time reports are compiled and published, they are out of date. Changes are that rapid.

Everyone knows that the potential coverage of the country is practically an accomplishment. The saturation point is nearly here. These media are making their contribution. People are better informed.

By a twist of a dial cultural opportunities are available to millions to whom they would otherwise be forever denied. The voices and the faces of the key personalities in world politics are almost as familiar as those of one's neighbors. Radio (still powerful) and television need no one to plead their cause.

Why Time Is Hard to Get

It is therefore understandable that ministers and church officials, reading the reports of the number of hours that radio and TV sets are turned on, covet access to these waiting ears for the purpose of communicating the gospel news and interpreting the noble services of the church. "Here," they reason, "is a ready-made audience. Unless we can get broadcast time, these people are entirely out of reach of our message."

Actually, of course, it isn't quite that simple. The so-called "unseen" audience out there is probably not mourning the absence of any preacher's program on the air. They are not just waiting to be taken over.

Those millions with tuned-in receivers have at their command a simple rotating device by which they can instantaneously escape from a distasteful program. No one can compel attention, least of all a broadcasting station. Its only lures are programs people like.

Even when a listener is hospitable toward a church program, no one can guarantee his continued attention. In every household there are competitive possibilities—the door buzzer and unexpected visitors, a long-winded telephone caller, children's mishaps, or a summons for the parental disciplinarian. Remember the disadvantage of radio and television, compared with letters, magazines, books, or newspapers: you can't return to it after an interruption. What you missed isn't there any more.

These somewhat negative comments are included simply as a reminder that while it is highly laudable to secure and utilize air time for the propagation of the faith, obtaining the opportunity to do so is not necessarily the consummation. It is possible in the heat of enthusiasm to get the idea that if some broadcasting time could only be commanded, all would be well.

Program managers are not hard to crack because of any ill will they

IF YOU WANT AIR TIME

have toward churches or other organizations which request public service time. On the contrary, most stations have a desire to devote time to "the public interest, convenience, and necessity" quite apart from the Federal Communications Commission's demands.

Then why is it so hard to break into radio or television? The broadcasting business is one of the most highly competitive of enterprises. It has its eyes and ears at all times directed to what the competition is doing. Readers may buy rival magazines—but listeners can choose only one broadcast at one time. For this reason, in allocating free time the programing officials feel compelled to schedule what they believe will draw the maximum audience.

Hints That May Help

Now for some suggestions that may help you get that broadcasting opportunity you want.

First, get to know the station personnel. Go to the stations with which you are likely to have future relations. Later, when you propose a program or nominate a guest, you won't be a stranger.

Next, become familiar with their programs and schedules. For example, it might not be fatal to your relations, but it would not be helpful to them if you congratulate the station manager on a program broadcast by a rival station.

In making a proposal to the station, give it as broad a base as possible. If your request is simply as the representative of a local church, the station manager will calculate mentally the number of local churches in his listening area, wondering what he would say if the pastor or top official of each one came around with a similar petition.

Try to get the endorsement of the local ministerial association or the radio-TV committee of your city or county council of churches for your proposed program. Take one of these officials along so that the manager will know that in granting your request a service is being rendered to the Protestant churches as a whole.

If you can't secure their co-operation, at least obtain the backing of the churches of your own denomination within the market of the station. Include with the other material you put in the station's hands some written indication of this general endorsement. Emphasize the number of churches and church members represented.

Never under any circumstances base your request upon the fact that someone else of some other church has been given some time and that you think it is now your turn. Programs are accepted on their own merits and because of the probable audience interest. Any implication to the contrary is unwise. Almost without exception it is also untrue.

Have a strong program idea. Work up an arresting title. Make it short enough to go on one line in the newspapers' program listings. Tell the program director what you hope to accomplish by the program. Describe the audience on which it will be focused.

If you propose a series, give your general title, then the titles of the several periodic installments. For radio programs, record a sample program on tape. Leave it for the station to audition. Leave television scripts to be read.

In the very first discussion of a program possibility give facts enough for a clear picture of what you have in mind but don't load in details until later.

With a plausible program idea before him that promises to attract and hold listeners, the station manager will want to know what you and your church associates are prepared to do toward building an audience. Your promotion plan is as important to the decision as the program itself. Stations are always interested in new listeners.

A Strong Promotion Plan

Don't miss out at the point of promotion. You must not rely for audience on the persons who may be tuned in by chance. You are getting the time free. The least you can do is obtain a promotion budget.

Outline the publicity steps you have in mind. You might include: advance announcements from pulpits and in Sunday church calendars; releases to newspapers in the listening area; a story in the sectional denominational papers that cover your territory; posters for church bulletin boards, inside and outside; envelope stuffers to be used by willing business people and by church members in their personal correspondence; post-card announcements to be mailed from church offices and by church members to their friends; and an organized campaign on the day before the program starts to remind listeners by telephone. You may plan listening groups which will discuss the program after each broadcast.

Other ways to promote the program, depending upon its nature, will occur to you. Be sure to give the station full credit in all publicity.

If you do all this and there is time available, the chances are that you will get your program. But if the station manager says, "Sorry, no!" under no circumstances start high-pressure tactics. Never try to bring personal influence to bear. This can fix you and your church for good.

Relations with Stations

Accept the station's decision as pleasantly as your disappointment permits. Then come up with a better idea next time.

In dealing with station managers and program directors, you may want to follow this miscellaneous counsel:

Don't take their co-operation for granted. Let them know they are appreciated. Share with the station officials any favorable reactions to the program that you receive, particularly those that mention the station's part.

Ask the professional advice of the station personnel on any decisions that need to be made on the technical production of a program. Then follow it.

If you are broadcasting, be sure not only to be on time but to be in the studio sufficiently in advance to prevent jitters over your possible nonarrival. Studio personnel always have an eye on the sweep hand of the clock. Their sense of time is better developed than that of most other mortals. It's a black demerit on your page in their book if you put them through any agonies.

If you have arranged with a station or with an M.C. of a particular program for a guest to appear, make it your personal business to see that he gets there and that he arrives ahead of time. If they are counting on him and he doesn't show, you are the one they will hold guilty.

Be careful on any program on which you appear or for which you have a responsibility that nothing that can be construed as a financial appeal is voiced, no matter how indirect it may seem. If you do want to do this, take it up with the station manager. He may give you permission, although many stations have strict rules against it.

In seeking to interest a station in covering some special event outside its studio, such as a cornerstone ceremony or a convention, approach the program director as far in advance as possible. Remember that programs are shaped months ahead.

Your chances are much better if you can plant your occasion in their thinking as soon as you know about it. Much valuable radio and television co-operation is lost to churches because they come up with their invitations after schedules are in final, inflexible form and time is not available.

If your special event is scheduled, you will, of course, punctiliously control the timing, as the broadcast could easily be marred if your event is not ready to begin at pick-up time or if you or your speaker does not conclude on the dot. This is your responsibility.

CHAPTER XI

Program Formats Are Many

EVER SINCE KDKA, ONE OF THE PIONEER STATIONS, FIRST PUT church services on the air, the practice has continued. While there are still many pickups directly from sanctuaries, the trend has been more and more toward church services under the controlled conditions of a studio. Particularly is this true among the networks, where the most exacting standards prevail.

Almost the only exceptions to this rule with the networks are the services broadcast from cathedrals on Christmas or New Year's Eve, on other religious festival days, and the on-the-spot pickups of community Easter dawn observances across the nation.

In statistical terms the total listeners to a sermon broadcast would be gratifying when compared with church attendance, but few attempts to gauge the popularity of sermons on the air have ever impressed broadcasting authorities. When tested by the usual audience measurement methods they have often entirely failed to register.

Talks and Sermons

There are, of course, notable exceptions, but leading radio and television experts in the church field have long since sought to capture larger audiences of persons hitherto uninterested by shifting to other types of programing.

This does not mean that the day for radio and television talks and sermons is past. It does mean that the most careful attention to their content and manner of presentation is called for. Anything less is a contribution toward their entire extinction.

Whether delivered within the walls of a church to a dual audience, seen and unseen, or within a studio in the presence of engineer, director, organist, and singers, broadcast sermons must be prepared carefully. Many readers have long been practicing some do's and dont's, which others may find helpful. All of these suggestions apply to *radio* preaching; some, to television as well.

The radio preaching that registers is directed to the solution of some pressing human problem, something that has been puzzling the mind of the listener or burdening his conscience. Whoever it was who described the church as "the greatest institution for answering questions that no one was asking" raised a warning sign for would-be radio preachers.

This is the reason why expository preaching seems to find low acceptance from radio audiences. Such sermons assume that listeners are greatly curious about the history and precise etymology of the words in the day's selected scripture passage.

Such an assumption is appropriate concerning churchgoers (or ought to be). The average radio listener, however, cannot be presumed to be receptive for any information about the Bible which their spiritual teacher chooses to impart.

To catch the listener at all, early in his address the speaker must arrest attention and let it be known that here help is to be offered in overcoming a baffling problem. That's the reason the first couple of minutes are so important. Some say "the first twenty seconds."

This typical listener is not a collegian, much less a seminarian. He is thrown by theological terms. By the law of averages he will not have finished high school. You can give a demonstration of all the sesquipedalians you can pronounce if you don't mind losing him. Words and figures of speech daily used in religious circles may be meaningless to him or may be completely misconstrued.

Keep it simple for another reason. Radio listeners are not always giving concentrated attention. He may be momentarily diverted from your long, involved sentence. "How's that again?" he will ask. He can reread a newspaper paragraph, but a radio sentence is gone forever. By this time your listener may be gone forever.

Good radio preachers hammer one central idea. Too many ideas confuse the listener. Argue the point logically, but do not be afraid of a little emotion in your illustrations.

If you stick exclusively to syllogisms, you'll limit your audience to the relatively small percentage of humanity which lives by logic. "Radio's stage is the imagination," it has been said.

Use words of visual imagery, picture words, words of feeling, and onomatopoetic words (buzz, hiss, soothe, splash). Choose verbs of action. What gestures and facial expression add to your pulpit delivery, try to put into your voice in pauses, phrasing, and animation.

Always keep in mind that the radio audience is not a congregation. It's an individual, or at most two or three persons. You are a guest in their car or their home. Don't be pontifical—this isn't the place for it. Don't shout. Don't harangue. These attitudes would be incongruous with nothing but a coffee table between you (your voice) and your listener. That's why anything but a conversational tone and a conversational style is out of place. Be as personal as you can. Keep relaxed.

The length of your sermon will probably be determined by the occasion and the broadcast period, but don't grieve if it seems too short. It's better to stop before they want you to. The saturation point is quickly reached, particularly with nonchurchgoers, and these are the ones you are out to reach. Think of how much a sponsor pays for a program in order to tell people about his product. Isn't your thirteen minutes to promote your product at no cost to yourself quite a bargain?

When you prepare your script, avoid lengthy quotations. These are apt to sound dull, no matter how brilliant they are. Also, they make trouble for the continuity acceptance department of your station, since no more that fifty words may be quoted from copyrighted prose without permission. Poems need to be similarly watched. For example, van Dyke's will denies radio the use of his poetry.

As you doubtless know, the station will want a copy of your script in advance to check against anything that counters their policy or endangers them legally. Later they will file it with the station's records. Be sure the script carries the call letters of the station, the name of the program, date and hour of broadcast, and full identification of yourself.

Your rehearsal at home will give you a close approximation of the time your sermon will consume. Most speakers find that before a live mike it takes slightly longer. Some broadcasters time their manuscripts page by page. Others backtime the last page or two or final paragraphs. A glance at the studio clock indicates whether they are maintaining the correct rate of delivery.

Interviews

Interviews rank near the top of public service programs in listener and viewer appeal. They are sufficiently popular that many of them are being sponsored. Some, in which large crews turn the homes of celebrities into studios, are pretentious and costly productions.

Nothing is more interesting to people than people. Magazines that tell stories of the experiences of unique personalities, their successes, their failures, their sins, and their redemption, sell millions of copies.

Some control their curiosity better than others; some conceal it better. But few of us do not possess some of the impulses of the eavesdropper.

This natural interest in "overhearing" conversations, our curiosity about other people and how they live and act, our desire to know what others are thinking, are all closely related to the popularity of biography. It probably helps explain the fascination of plays and novels, even though their characters are imaginary. It certainly is related to the enormous following developed for a program which, step by step, reports the high spots in the lives of its heroes.

Radio and television interview programs live on this innate curiosity that we all have about one another.

Churchmen can make good use of the interview type program on both network and local stations. There are possibilities here for you.

First, look for someone with a story. Who in your church has overcome difficulties or completed some incredibly laborious task? Who has had an exciting adventure? Whose unusual hobby is related to religion?

Perhaps there is a collector of old Bibles or of hymnbooks on your church roll. Some other member may have curios from Palestine or from the mission fields. Another may collect crosses of different shapes and materials, each with a story. Television interviews with persons like these could make quite acceptable programs.

Look for "special day" possibilities and use them for all they are worth. Such a tie-in adds to the station's interest in the program. For example, the collection of crosses is a natural for Holy Week or Good Friday.

The collection of Bibles would be appropriate for World Bible Sunday. The program director may be more interested in an interview with the hymnal collector if it is timed to coincide with the birthday of a great hymn writer like Isaac Watts or Charles Wesley. Tying-in with a great personality will allow appropriate lively anecdotes from his career to brighten up the program.

A visiting missionary, educator, or church official may be scheduled to speak at your church. You will wish to share him with that part of the public which will otherwise have no touch with him. A radio or TV interview is the best way to do this if it can be arranged. If you are fortunate enough to schedule this prior to the public meeting he is to address, it will, of course, help your attendance.

Suggestions are made in another section of this chapter on how to approach the program managers of broadcasting stations. You can apply these same principles in attempting to schedule an interview series conducted by you, with the guests supplied by you. You might also propose providing the interviewees for a program conducted by a staff announcer.

Probably the most effective way to get a guest on the air is to make use of a well-established program. A radio or TV personality with a large, ready-made audience may introduce and interview interesting visitors. The time given on the air to your guest on a program of this type will be shorter than if you arranged a special program, but the number of listeners will undoubtedly be larger.

Building an audience takes weeks. One-shot programs in general do not pull anything like the number of listeners that tune in a familiar, well-established interview series.

Approach the broadcaster or a staff member of the show directly when you want to make a nomination to a regularly scheduled master-of-ceremonies type interview program. Use the same methods that you would in making a presentation to the station.

On the network level of radio and television, hundreds of great Christians, well known and little known, from small towns and large cities, from this country and abroad, have appeared as interviewees. Through a perfectly proper process of eavesdropping, millions of people listening in on these conversations have acquired a new knowledge of the church's outreach, of its medical, social, agricultural, and educational services and of its spiritual program.

You can promote interview programs on your local stations. Many of the counseling and pastor's study programs on the air are in this category. They need your support.

Here are a few suggestions if you participate in such programs either as behind-the-scenes producer or as interviewer or guest before the mikes and cameras.

The more conversational and casual the interview the better. But it must be well planned in advance. The general line of questioning must not be left to chance.

The interviewer should know everything relevant about his guest. This information can be gained through a preinterview or through an outline of pertinent facts presented by guest or his sponsor.

The visitor may himself propose questions that will evoke the contributions he is most qualified to make. Of course the interviewer does not agree to ask these questions and these only, but he will ordinarily agree upon request to avoid any areas of questioning that the interviewee finds irrelevant or too personal.

Guests may be overly modest. They may underestimate the public's interest in matters that to them are commonplace. In consequence, famous interview programs go into lengthy preparations to discover the personal accomplishments and unusual backgrounds of guests. Diligence in digging out the most interesting facts pays high dividends.

Don't be afraid to pry. I once helped to place on radio and TV interview programs a woman physician from a village in India frequently isolated by floods. She had just come for a year's study in a U.S. woman's hospital. Here are some of the facts dug up in conversation that made nationally known interviewers eager to have her on their programs.

She had never worn stockings or shoes until the day she started for America. She had never seen an airplane, except high in the sky, until she boarded one. She had not known that there was room for passengers *inside* the plane. She had expected to cross the oceans riding on the outside, as on the back of an elephant. She had been dreading this, fearing she might not be able to hang on for so long a journey.

The largest group of her patients, next to maternity emergencies, were people clawed by tigers. She liked oxcarts for transportation much better than jeeps and buses. "With oxcarts, if you get tired riding you can rest yourself by getting out and walking a while. You can't do this on a bus."

Her chief problem in retraining old-time midwives: "They could understand why they should wash their hands after delivering a baby. It just didn't make sense to do it before."

These almost incredible rejoinders could easily have been missed, if only routine questions had been asked. When the famous M.C.'s heard these answers, all their resistance to putting her on their shows vanished.

Panels

The same interest that leads crowds to gather around two or three soapbox disputants and listen in on their heated debate is responsible for the drawing power of panel programs. In Pershing Square, Los Angeles, in Union Square, New York, and in Hyde Park, London, people love kibitzing.

A chief advantage of the panel discussion is that it lends itself to the presentation of all sides of a controversial question. Sometimes it is written fully in advance, but this is likely to result in a wooden, mechanical performance unless the participants are professional actors. Even then the program may be dull, artificial, or insincere.

Good panel shows are spontaneous. Like the interview program, immense advance preparation is needed, but the moment the audience becomes conscious of this preparation the program slips. Painstaking care must assure that the presentation is fair and balanced and that the content is adequate to reward the listener, but the show itself must appear entirely impromptu.

A preliminary conference can help, just as a preinterview prepares the way for an interview program. The contribution of each participant on the first round can be carefully planned in order that the program may get off to a flying start. Also, each panelist may be asked to frame in advance his closing minute, so that the discussion will terminate neatly in a roundup that is fair to all points of view.

The success of a panel program rests heavily on two factors: a relevant and controversial discussion topic and informed, articulate, and agile panelists whose points of view conflict. The moderator plays another role of primary importance. Whatever his private sentiments, he must maintain a strictly nonpartisan attitude while presiding. The slightest indication of bias on his part will warn the listeners that the discussion is rigged.

The moderator has the duty of stimulating reticent panelists and at the same time of restraining an aggressive brother who insists on more than his share of the fleeting minutes. He must keep the discussion in balanced proportion and pace its movement with his eye on the clock. Often he must tactfully shut off a speaker, even when the contribution being made is germane and interesting. Otherwise the program might close with only one point of view fully developed and the other angles barely touched upon.

The moderator, personally or with the aid of the panel, must pull together the several contributions that have been made, summarizing the discussion but letting the listeners feel that they are making the decisions.

Several important matters must be kept in mind with radio panels. Voices can sound alike. If the subject and general situation permit, panelists of both sexes will be better than all men or all women. The contrast in point of view and the contrast in voice texture will add interest to the discussion.

Let radio participants introduce themselves, stating their own names, occupations, and relationships to the topic. This will help listeners identify panelists when they speak. During the discussion the speakers should refer to each other by name more frequently than in ordinary conversation. If they are strangers, directors often label them with their names either pinned conspicuously on their lapels or on desk signs in front of them.

Another way to help the listener, who knows each participant only as a voice, keep the personalities differentiated is to inject frequent comments, such as, "Dr. Stone, our clergyman panelist, has expressed himself on the increasing divorce rate. Let us hear what Professor Shaw, our sociologist, thinks."

The moderator in this remark not only has helped with the "Who's Who" but also has indicated the general nature of the discussion for the benefit of late tuners-in.

In television there is less possibility for the viewers to mix up panelists since their participation is visible and their positions are usually marked with their names. Neverthless the M.C. will often try to give those who have dialed the program after it started some clue to the theme under discussion.

Panel discussions with important community or national leaders participating can often be used as the basis for group discussion in adult classes or youth fellowships following the broadcast. If the broadcast comes at an inconvenient hour for this purpose, the radio panel can be recorded on tape and played back to the meeting as a discussion self-starter. Television panels can be repeated with borrowed Kinescopes run on a 16 mm. sound projector.

Documentaries

Imparting information not by narration but by letting the characters in a given situation speak for themselves is a frequently favored method in radio and televison.

For radio it can be accomplished with a tape recorder on the scene at little more cost than the travel. Continuity music and sound effects are dubbed in during the editing process. For television, on-the-spot documentaries are much more expensive.

It may not be obvious in the finished product, but usually considerable research goes into this somewhat dramatic form of commentary. The facts thus garnered can, of course, quite easily be made part of the speeches of appropriate characters if a script is used. Without a script, in preliminary warm-ups any desired figures, historical facts, or traditions can be planted without too much difficulty and called forth with the proper questioning.

The quest of the documentary is for findings. Personal, on-the-scene observations of the narrator are recorded. Then live interviews with persons representing every point of view, old-timers and newcomers, the satisfied and the discontented, are held. Usually the opinions of those in authority, who may be either at the scene or elsewhere, are needed to round out the presentation.

Devise a hard-hitting opening. Challenge the listener by setting forth the problem importantly. Capture your listener at once, or it will be too late.

Most documentaries presented by churches and social agencies have a cause to promote or a problem to solve. Often the problem is too vast and too involved to hope for a solution. The program can still result in helping the listener to feel that he must do something about the situation, that it really matters. Be sure the program has time enough to suggest some remedies. Let there be spoken or powerfully implied an appeal for action. Include a clearly stated path which the listener who wants to help may take.

Dramatic Programs

Radio and television drama is for professionals.

Churchmen who want to see the cause of religion promoted by this effective medium will accomplish the most by promoting listeners for the several excellent network programs, by encouraging local stations to use the high-grade religious drama films available, and by helping to raise money for their denominational agencies to produce more and better films.

Tangible support of these professionally written, professionally acted, and professionally produced dramas can help challenge millions of persons otherwise completely out of reach of a religious message with the truths of the gospel.

Drama is the field least developed in the past by denominational and interchurch radio and television departments. It is also the program format which is now receiving the most attention.

The boards, commissions, and departments of the several churches are convinced that while preaching programs have their values, much of the effort that goes into the worship service—sermon broadcast— is "feeding the already fed." Without discounting this service, they see the real evangelistic opportunity in radio and television for getting through to those who know or care little about what the Christian faith has to offer.

"Tell me a story," the little tot pleads. His interest in stories will be lifelong. Radio and TV dramas tell stories. Jesus spoke in parables.

Life stories in the form of religious drama can be packed with soul-probing truths without losing their capacity to hold attention. Through identification there can be real communication.

Stations are growing more and more willing to provide free time for the religious dramatic programs produced by church radio and television agencies. This is true only because their quality is comparable with that of network programs. Program directors know that by showing them they further the public welfare and build good will. If the church agencies can continue to provide excellent programs which meet broadcasting standards, the stations will, by every indication, carry their share of the partnership by providing free time.

Unfortunately, the production of top-grade programs, despite the acceptance of minimum pay scales by interested script writers, actors, and directors, runs into big figures. Actually these costs, figured on a per-viewer basis, are laughably small. But this does not make religious radio-TV budgets any easier to raise.

The men and women who staff the churches' television, radio, and film departments have the ideas, know-how, and consecration. Hundreds of local TV stations welcome their films. The bottleneck in the production of enough strong drama films is insufficient money.

If you believe thoroughly that religious drama can awaken religious impulses and start men on their quest for God, see that your church sends a dollar a member next year and every year to its denominational radio-TV department.

There is another way you can help. Send and inspire letters of appreciation to the networks which not only give sustaining time but pay production costs as well. Let the local stations which carry these network programs know, too, that you are grateful for their part. Now and then a sponsored program dramatizes a powerful religious message. Let these people have the pleasure of knowing your approval.

After saying all this about professional production, it must be conceded that here and there some amateur groups have come up with some excellent dramatic religious programs. In one instance a weekly drama centering on a pastor's service to his community was produced for several years. Eventually it attracted national attention.

A series of these dramas was put on film and under general church sponsorship has been "aired" on several hundred stations. Doubtless other groups, particularly in college drama departments, attain almost professional quality in their productions.

In general, however, the program director takes a dim view of amateur Thespians. As he knows them, they play before quite limited and select audiences composed largely of relatives and friends who, happily and unanimously, leave their critical faculties at home. Everyone comes to the hall favorably predisposed toward the participants. When the final curtain falls, everyone is hearty in approval. Only superlatives can describe the perfection of the performance.

With this kind of jaundiced conception influencing his judgment, the program director is inclined to handle gingerly any proposal to risk his station's reputation by giving time to an amateur group. His shyness is aggravated when it appears that the would-be television actors are from a church, for in this environment, he has observed, standards of critical judgment are on a truly benevolent level.

He may have a little difficulty in persuading the emissary that television listeners, unacquainted with the players and accustomed to the world's best in dramatic art, would probably not applaud the proposed performance quite as wildly as the stacked audience in the church vestry did last Friday night.

There are, as has been indicated, exceptions, and the station manager knows it in spite of his cynicism. You may have a dramatic organization with a really high potential. Tell the station manager about it and try to persuade him to assign a staff member to audition the group.

If this report is favorable, ask the manager if he could recommend an experienced TV dramatic director who for a moderate fee might coach your group for a few weeks in the special techniques of television acting. The interest of this person in your group and his opportunity to judge its progress will be helpful in getting before the cameras when you are really ready.

CHAPTER XII

Broadcasting the News of Religion

THIS CHAPTER WILL APPROACH THE BROADCASTING OF RELIGIOUS news from two directions. First, the placement of your church news in the regular, established general newscasts of your nearby radio and television stations. Second, some suggestions directed to the possibility that you yourself, or someone from your church, may wish to obtain time for a weekly broadcast of religious news.

There should be one program of this type in every broadcasting center, if not on every station. If your favorite station does not offer such a newscast, look into the matter. The station manager may be waiting for your offer to do it.

Newscasters

Don't be uncertain as to which to use—newspapers, radio, or TV—for news of your church. Any story sufficiently important should be given to the newsrooms of both media.

You will know what to expect if you are in a metropolitan center where there are hundreds of churches, in some cases thousands. Obviously only the most exceptional news from a local church can hope to make either the newspapers or the airways. On the other hand, in smaller cities many radio and TV stations are glad to have church news if it qualifies as news.

If they use your story, newspapers are likely to give it in greater detail. This completeness is one of the primary advantages of the press. Consider how long it would take to read an afternoon paper aloud. Compare this figure with the minutes allotted by radio or TV stations to news during the hours the paper is current. You will see why any version of your story on the air is certain to be brief.

The electronic media suffer from this limitation. About all the split seconds permit a newscaster to give are the same unadorned facts that the newspapermen summarize in the first paragraph or two of a story. The style is different for the air—in fact, it is likely to be more entertaining. But if a story is really important to you, you must go out and buy a paper. Neither radio nor TV can supply many details.

On the other hand, broadcast news is immediate. As often as possible it is phrased in the present tense. "I have just been handed a news bulletin," says the newscaster, interrupting himself. One feels he is getting the news as it happens. News pictures received from afar by telephoto are seen on television, and even film clips are shown incredibly soon after the events they portray.

Against all this the city editor claims an element of permanence, at least relatively, as he compares his transient sheet with a broadcast. Your mind wanders; you are called to another room from a newscast. Though you return with all speed, you will miss what the Secretary of State said to the Russian ambassador. But you can pick up a newspaper and go back to where you stopped reading—it's still there. If you don't quite understand a story, you can look back to the headline for help. You can read it again. You can even tear it out, neatly fold it up, and put it in your billfold and two weeks from now wonder how it got there.

The moral is that each medium has its own wonderful capabilities. We in the church will make all possible use of them.

Should you send your story to the local station? Ask yourself whether you would be interested in a similar story from a comparable church of another denomination on the other side of town. If you would be bored, wait until you have a more distinctive story. It must have general appeal.

If you would be interested, by all means get it to the station. If it is a smaller newsroom with staff members who wear several hats, you may want to submit your news in a style in line with their practice.

Remember that most news stories on the air are told in fifty to a hundred words, about as many as in the Lord's Prayer (less than seventy). The writing must be for the ear, not for the eye. You cannot begin with dependent clauses, because listeners won't know to what they pertain. They might even confuse them with the commercial if your story should happen to follow it.

Use round numbers. They are easier for the listener to retain. Many newscasters find the formal "quote" and "unquote" inconsistent with the conversational style they seek always to maintain. Instead, a quotation may be introduced by "and these are his words . . . ." A pause and a change of pace indicate the end of the quote. A short quote may be preceded by "what the general called a . . . ."

In typing use triple space. Do not divide words or figures at the end of a line. Do not put two stories or parts of different stories on the same page. Each story must be a unit in itself.

For quick identification of stories type a one-word description at the top of the page. If it goes to an additional page or pages, put the same catchword and the page number at the top of each page.

Use the word "more" at the bottom of any pages where there is more to follow, just as on newspaper releases. Make a long dash, hatch marks, or -30-, or write the word "end" to indicate that there are no more pages.

You as Church Newscaster

Many radio and TV stations carry a regular program which reviews the top interest religious events of the week. Sometimes these are exclusively on the world-wide and nationwide level, local matters entering in only when the happenings are of comparable importance with the other news reported.

Some religious news broadcasts divide the period between general religious events and local church news. Still others center exclusively on what is going on in the churches within the listening or viewing areas.

Your station manager, aware of such programs elsewhere and knowing your interest, may ask you if you bring up the matter to help him experiment with such a broadcast. Many churchmen regularly cover the religious front in this way, and there is room for many more.

Probably the preferable way to schedule this kind of program is to work through the radio-TV committee of your local council of churches or local ministerial association. The support by such a representative group of your request for a religious news program will indicate promise of a broadly based audience. Of course the station manager will need assurance that no church group will receive preferential treatment or use the opportunity to its own advantage.

In communities where the Roman Catholic Church is particularly strong, it may avoid trouble to have a commentator for Protestant news and another for Catholic. However, this is not a necessary requirement.

Objectivity is the goal and pride of every good reporter. On the original "Religion in the News" broadcast, which the N.B.C. network carried for nearly twenty years, the late Dr. Walter W. Van Kirk handled Roman Catholic, Protestant, and Jewish news with such fairness that he was cited by the National Conference of Christians and Jews.

Complaints were rare. When someone did complain, it was quite likely to be a Protestant listener who did not know that the commentator was an ardent Protestant and a national church official. "Your obviously biased Roman Catholic commentator is overloading his broadcast with the news of his own church!"

Of course some weeks are heavy with Protestant news; other weeks are predominately Roman Catholic in news interest. If one is to report impartially the happenings of the week in religion, he must deliver the news as it breaks.

Should you draw the assignment to do a weekly religious news program, or if you are on a radio-TV committee that supervises one, accept the job with a feeling that here lies a service opportunity of inestimable worth.

There are multitudes who have only the vaguest idea of what are the objectives, accomplishments, and satisfactions of church members. Millions of others retain conceptions of church life and emphases which are twenty to fifty years old.

A religious newscast can help interpret the churches and gradually lead disinterested listeners to reappraise the church. Many who would tune out a church service will listen to a "news" broadcast, even if it is about religion.

Another reward for doing a religious news program is that it can narrow the distance between differing groups. The interpretation of the news of several communions is a service to Christian understanding and fellow feeling.

If you prepare the script yourself, you will not find it easy, but it will be rewarding. Your own appreciation of what is going on in the church world will be greatly enhanced if you read world news with your mind magnetized for material for the coming broadcast. You will be compelled, now that you in a sense are setting yourself up as a source of information, to do considerable background study which has hitherto been crowded out.

Incidentally, you will have to go through a vast amount of material each week. Preparing a script is a selective process. For every story you use, you will consider and discard another dozen. You will need to keep your broadcast as representative and balanced as the flow of news permits.

There are two ways of providing the script. One is to write it yourself. The other is to subscribe to a news-script service. Of course it is possible to combine these methods. Use your weekly ready-made script as basic material. Then substitute here and there commentary or stories that your own researches have developed which seem to you have greater interest or significance.

If you decide to do your own script, you will first probably wish to expand the list of magazines that are coming to your study. The ones you receive are apt to reflect closely your own point of view and your own interests. Now you are to be the objective spokesman of all trends of doctrine and churchmanship. Include in your subscription list the most representative magazine of every major denomination and faith and several that represent interdenominational interests.

Next, you will need to write to the national and regional public relations offices of the several major groups whose news you intend to report. Get their names and addresses from ministerial colleagues.

Tell the directors about your newscast and ask to be placed on their mailing lists either for all of their releases or for such as might have general interest.

Much of what goes out from these church public relations offices is institutional, intended purely for denominational consumption. However, even this material is often usable. If you note that the boards of missions, as an example, of several denominations seem to be issuing similar news stories, this may indicate an interesting trend. What would not be significant coming from one church alone may be of value when used in combination.

You will also want releases from the councils of churches on all levels and from other interdenominational agencies. These often carry denominational news as well as news of their own organizational activities.

News services of the churches are glad to list you for their mailings if there is some real prospect of your using a story now and then. However, these lists have a way of building up fast. Postage, paper, and labor are more costly now than ever. If you find you are not making use of releases that are being sent or if you discontinue your broadcast, you will demonstrate your thoughtful understanding by requesting that your name be dropped.

On the other hand, if you make use of the releases from time to time, it is much appreciated by the PR offices if you tell them so. Send them once in a while a marked copy of a script in which you did rather well by one of their stories.

At least once a year tell each PR office that you appreciate their releases. Ask them to keep sending them and tell them that you are able quite often to make use of them. This not only is proper gratitude, but it is also assurance that your name will remain when the inevitable house cleaning is done on the mailing lists.

Another source of news which would involve considerable work is the constant stream that flows via the teleprinter from one or another of the wire services into the newsrooms of the radio and television stations. Going through this material, most of which has no bearing on religion, is possible but would be burdensome. Perhaps an arrangement could be made with a staff member to segregate it as it comes in.

Incidentally, Associated Press and United Press in particular give increasingly excellent service in the reporting of religious news and in providing useful week-end religious feature material.

Newspapers like the New York Times and the Christian Science Monitor are of great value to religious newscasters because of their full coverage of national church occasions and their custom of publishing important speeches and documents, often in full.

In preparing your script keep in mind the need for an informal conversational approach. Refer also to other suggestions elsewhere in this chapter on the points that distinguish writing for radio from writing for newspapers. The same principles that apply to sermon delivery can be applied to newscasting.

Remember that your appeal is to the ear. Keep reading aloud what you have written. Does it flow smoothly? Are there any "successful thistle sifter" phrases that are easy to read but hard to say? If your sentences are complex and require close listening to be understood, simplify them.

If you must use statistics, try to make them vivid by translating them into dramatic comparisons. Make your presentation in human terms, not in abstractions. Maintain to the end the same enthusiasm with which you begin your broadcast.

You must be interested yourself in the news you are reporting. See that you project this interest to your listeners. Be original and imaginative in your news treatment. Don't hesitate to be entertaining.

All of the principles of accuracy, objectivity, and fairness contained in the chapters of this book having to do with newspaper reporting apply equally in straight newscasting.

However, if the program director's request should be for a commentary on the religious events of the week, the stricture on editorializing would be off. In this case you are free to introduce your opinions. This may seem more enjoyable and more creative, but religion being the touchy subject that it is, your career on the air is likely to be longer if you tell what happens each week on the religious news front without comment or interpretation.

This disinterested attitude is a particularly difficult one to maintain, particularly for one trained to homiletics. However, events have a way of speaking quite effectively for themselves, and this kind of program is well worth doing.

On the other hand, if you are given freedom to point out the meaning of the news of the week in the light of generally accepted religious principles and against the background of Christian history, there is undoubtedly and intelligent audience which is waiting for it.

PART THREE

YOUR CHURCH MEETS ITS PUBLIC

CHAPTER XIII

Buildings Can Invite or Repel

THE FIRST IMPRESSION A PERSON OBTAINS OF A CHURCH IS FROM its building and its grounds. Sometimes this is the only impression.

If you are blessed with a church plant so designed that it is a public relations asset, be grateful. You are off to a running start. All you need to do is to keep everything else up to the standards set by the building.

This isn't always easy. If your organization falls short of perfection at any point, the very effectiveness of the building throws into sharper contrast the defects in the total picture of your institution. Public relations operates on the principle that "unto whomsoever much is given, of him shall be much required."

If your architecture is a public relations liability, you usually can't do much about the building, after cleaning and painting. If this is your case, perhaps by majoring in landscaping (if there is sufficient land to be "scaped") you may produce such attractive results that attention will be diverted from the unimpressive building.

Even if your building is most unpromising, you may be able to capitalize on its better points. Perhaps you are the fortunate owner of a well-designed tower or an attractive entrance or a lovely window.

Where the building as a whole is not artistic, try to trade on one of these features. Illuminate it by night and make it a kind of trademark by day. From photographs or drawings have halftones or linecuts made. Use these on Sunday calendars, church leaflets, stationery, and in newspaper advertising.

Landscaping and Lighting

Each problem has a solution if you look for it. For example, should your church be awkwardly perched on a steep, sloping plot where on one side or the other it is impossible to maintain a lawn, organize your horticulturalists into a green thumb club. Put them to work on your problem plot. Presently people will begin talking about "the church with the rock garden."

Meanwhile, capitalize your odd site by pointing out that elderly persons do not need to climb stairs. They can enter various sections of the church from the street on two or three levels, choosing the lower entrance for parlor or social hall and the upper door for the sanctuary or the office.

Attractive, wellgroomed landscaping conveys the instant impression that the church is beloved of its members. It also lifts the church in the esteem of the community because it is one of the town's beauty assets.

Where the budget is adequate, your landscape plans will be carried out by professionals or by church employees. Where this is impossible, the alternative is not to let the lawn grow into an unkempt jungle. In every church are highly skilled amateur gardeners who, with the proper encouragement, organization, and recognition, will make your church grounds look like part of paradise. If you turn the job over to them, be sure to give them a free hand.

You have probably already thought of illuminating your church or at least some feature of it. Traditionally when the sun sets, churches have been outclassed in gloominess only by cemeteries. This melancholy alliance with darkness is happily coming to an end. Trustees today are more obedient to the injunction, "Let there be light!"

If you contemplate floodlighting, consult your power and light company both for rates and for current and technical advice.

Whether or not you go into illumination in a big way, see to it that all entrances are well lighted. If all the nice old ladies who have broken their ankles on church steps were brought together, they would fill St. Swithin's Home for the Crippled ten times.

Often the entrance lamps or lanterns are so placed that they are satisfactory when no one is present, but their rays are shut off and the steps dangerously shadowed whenever a number of persons are entering or emerging. While you do not need the illumination of a theater marquee, there should be enough light to provide safety and a cheerful atmosphere.

Another way to keep your sanctuary from looking like a mausoleum during the evening hours is to illuminate a window from within. For maximum effect be sure you are using strong enough bulbs and a parabolic reflector. It takes more wattage to bring out the rich color in stained glass than you may think.

Giving passers-by the inspiration that comes from a picture or a rose window each night is making it pay dividends perhaps for the first time. Since these windows are fashioned to reveal their beauty exclusively to those within the church when the sun is shining, their uplifting service is limited to a single hour or so on Sunday morning. Often the most inspiring window in the church is the one on the street elevation. When such a window is located behind the seated congregation the worshipers scarcely have an opportunity to notice it. To illuminate it for three or four hours each evening multiplies by twenty-five the hours when it can sing and teach and preach.

Left dark, your window ministers only to your congregation at best. Illuminated, it communicates with thousands who will never enter your church.

A broad Tiffany window which pictures the whole nativity story in its five bays is the proud possession of a Vermont church. It is located across the street from the small city's largest hotel. Beautifully illumined each night in a way that makes the star in the East glow again over the ancient city, it has inspired scores of thank-you notes from the hotel guests. Many arrived weary and disheartened. They turned out their lights, and looking out they found themselves in the peace of Bethlehem.

Angel choirs sang them to sleep, and the message of good will among men straightened out their thinking. This is what they have written.

Adequate Parking Provisions

Parking provisions are part of good church public relations. A modern church cannot just welcome a man and his family and offer him a comfortable pew. It must welcome his car, too, and provide a place for it while the family worships or enjoys the social life of the church.

After a driver has unloaded his family at the church door, he will work himself into quite a stew if he can't find a place to park. As he circles block after block hunting for a place big enough to tuck the family bus into, he is saying to himself, "I don't care if Mabel's grandfather *was* one of the founders of this church, I'm not going to keep coming down here just to cruise around until church is out. We'll transfer out to the Heights church where they have a two-acre parking lot."

Don't think he doesn't mean it. Some downtown churches do not have this problem because parking rules are off on Sundays. This doesn't help churches located in apartment house neighborhoods. Here thousands of people in big cities keep their cars in what they call the "mayor's parking lot"—on the street where there is never an open space for longer than a few minutes.

Some of these churches have been able to arrange with nearby supermarkets for the use of their parking spaces for parishioners. Blanket, low-cost commercial arrangements have been made by other churches with parking-lot owners whose Sunday business is small.

There are no solutions here for this vexatious problem. Every pastor and his board of trustees who face it are wrestling with it. The advice these churchmen would give with regard to parking problems is, first, to those soon to build new churches, "Be sure you buy enough land!" And then to others, "Better purchase that old building next door to the church before the price goes higher. They know you'll have to have it sometime or disband."

BUILDINGS CAN INVITE OR REPEL

Signs of the Times

In an age which so obviously believes in signs, it is surprising to be able to find many churches completely without identification. On the other hand, quite as many churches have accepted the neon age and have gone the whole way in letting the public know what they are and where they are.

In between are thousands of churches which have equipped themselves with signs of one kind or another but which do not evidence much concern in whether they are deriving full value from them. The most common fault is in the position of the sign. If the sign itself doesn't actually date back to pedestrian and horse and buggy days, the thinking that located it is that dated.

Probably your own signs are satisfactory, but take a look anyway. Observe the building through the eyes of a stranger, from every possible direction. At what distance are your signs legible? Have shrubs grown up and shrouded once-visible signboards?

Look at the formal informational tablets or plaques which may be against the wall next to the main doors. Do the doors cover them when open? Are the names and facts about time for services up-to-date? Does the lettering need regilding?

If the church is on a corner, is it as well identified for visitors approaching from one street as for those on the other? Make a quick traffic survey. Do more people pass your church by bus and automobile than on foot? If so, are your signs aware of this?

Most signs on church lawns ought to be set at right angles to the street and designed so that they do business on both sides. Anyone riding in a car can read only a word or two of a sign that is parallel to the street. The driver can catch nothing without imperiling the public.

Place your sign near the sidewalk. Design it with the motorist in mind. It can be easily read from the driver's seat if it is in the normal range of the eyes as the car is approaching. Don't use too much copy. Note how few words there are even on the huge twenty-four-sheet roadside billboards.

Outdoor changeable-letter bulletin boards are deservedly popular. They are dignified and adapt themselves well to the needs of churches. While designed primarily for pedestrian readers, they can sometimes be placed advantageously at an angle on a corner. Here, if there is a stop light, they can be read by motorists as well. Occasionally on a corner they are used in pairs at right angles to each other.

Many churches, instead of using the usual pipe uprights and brackets to mount their boards, design and build bases and supporting wings from the same stone or brick of which the sanctuary is constructed. Then the bulletin board is set into place. The harmony which is achieved keeps the sign from seeming in any way obtrusive.

Pastors often enter the church through the side or rear door near the place for parking. They are not then in a position to observe a common abuse of the bulletin board. If they did notice it, it would be corrected, as it is the poorest public relations. This too prevalent offense is their leaving displayed announcements of events which have already taken place. The public quickly loses confidence and interest in a bulletin board that advertises falsely.

A really alert church publicist will remove the copy board as soon as the last of the morning services begins. He will display a new message centering on further services of the day or events of the coming week.

A fresh, timely message on the board as the congregation emerges gives the impression that someone is on the job. You can purchase extra copy boards quite reasonably from the manufacturer of your board. The second message can be prepared during the week, and the sexton or a publicity committee member can make the change quickly.

An empty copy board is an eyesore. Some churches leave the bulletin bare from Monday morning, when Sunday's announcements are removed, until late in the week when the minister decides on his coming sermon topic. Nothing looks as lonesome as an attractive, eye-pulling bulletin of this type with nothing in it to read. It seems to shout, "Nobody home! House cleaning time! We've gone out of business!"

Anyone can avoid these demerits which passers-by give for ill-used bulletin boards. If you have an extra copy board, make a "wayside pulpit" of it. Set up a motto, a slogan, a short verse of scripture, or a word of invitation. It will fill the emptiness and set its readers thinking in the interval between the removal of one Sunday's announcement and the display of the next Sunday's subjects.

Here is an alternative: Engage a sign painter to cut a sheet of stiff building board the size of your copy board. Then have him paint on it a simulated letter, something like this:

> To the Stranger
> Within Our Gates:
>
> Grace Church extends to you
> the hospitality of its worship and
> fellowship.
>
> (in script) Pastor's Name
> Pastor

Park it in the frame if there's room behind the changeable part of the sign. When the copy board comes out for its new lettering, your personal invitation is right there ready to go to work inviting people to church.

The letters on some older changeable signs have a tendency to rust and discolor. Investigate yours. Perhaps a new set is indicated. Aluminum ones won't give you that trouble again. If the price isn't in the budget, the right person in your church has the ability to re-enamel the ones you have. A coat of varnish over the enamel will prolong their usefulness.

Read your copy twice before you turn it over for someone to set up on the bulletin board. A Middle West church leader came to a church where he was to preach on Good Friday. He was dismayed to find on the bulletin board:

> Dr. Raines Preaching
> MY GOD, WHY?

More striking and eye-catching than changeable boards are large hand-lettered signs that churches in central locations occasionally use. They are expensive, but the cost on an annual contract basis is less than the cost of one-time orders. Now and then a minister finds a talented and willing member of his congregation who will take on this responsibility as his service.

One of the best of this type of signboard is the immense one on First Methodist Church, Los Angeles. It is horizontal and at least fifteen feet long. Tremont Temple (Baptist) and Park Street Church (Congregational), both of Boston, for many years have used huge upright painted signs.

The illumination of outdoor signs adds materially to the hours of their service. In addition, against a contrasting background of darkness it draws attention that would not be given in daylight. If your signs have not been lighted and you are thinking about doing so, a time switch which will automatically control the hours the signboard is illuminated costs much less than you might think—around ten dollars.

Courtesies can be extended through bulletin boards. Marble Collegiate Church in New York on Rosh Hashana, the Jewish New Year, carried on its boards, passed by thousands of that faith each day, the following good-will greeting: "This church extends Holy-Day greetings to its Jewish neighbors and friends." When a conference of another faith or a convention of a civic or patriotic group is visiting your city, the visitors will gratefully note a friendly, hospitable sentence addressed to them on your bulletin board.

Look over your church plant to discover any architectural feature that may frame a sign. The Protestant Episcopal Cathedral in St. Louis, when it built adjacent community center and parish house, made one of the pairs of double doors to the sanctuary unnecessary as an entrance. The doors, framed by a Gothic stone arch, were covered over, and a beautifully designed sign in dark red and gold was painted. It was artistic and completely in keeping with the rest of the building and served to identify the church and to announce service hours.

Directional road markers serve a useful purpose in any location, but particularly if your church is somewhat off the beaten path. They can, of course, be made locally from your own design. However, the denominational houses are prepared to supply them at prices that would be hard to match. They are usually heavy rust-proofed steel finished in a baked enamel that stands all weather. They can be purchased blank or lettered. Those that are visible clearly both night and day are also available but at considerably higher cost. With their luminous lettering at night they make an almost irresistible claim to be read.

Immaculate Housekeeping

A church does not need expensive furnishings and decoration to be attractive.

Is it clean? Is it orderly? Is it in good repair? These are the questions that the eyes of visitors are answering.

BUILDINGS CAN INVITE OR REPEL

Good housekeeping is one of the most persuasive influences in creating a favorable response on the part of newcomers. And good housekeeping keeps the regular members happy and proud too. Something happens to the aplomb of a church official who at the moment of greeting a stranger notices cobwebs or a torn curtain or a dirty door jamb.

Members feel a sense of possession toward their church—"my church," "our church," they say, emphasizing the adjective. Because of this most churches are well kept. We speak of "our church home." No woman wants one standard of housekeeping for her own home and another for her church home.

The occasional church that is found dirty and run down is usually one that is having a financial struggle. There is not room in the budget to provide an able-bodied, active janitor. For a pittance some feeble person with failing eyesight is chosen.

Little by little the untidiness develops but not fast enough for the congregation to notice the change from Sunday to Sunday. It is possible gradually to become accustomed to environments which, were we to see them as strangers, would fill us with dismay.

Dull, dingy walls, the colors originally chosen not for their beauty or good cheer but for their dirt-proof qualities, are typical of many older churches. When you repaint (make it soon!), be sure that a committee of young-marrieds chooses the tints, not the senior trustees.

One of the problems of church housekeeping is the lack of storage space. In consequence piles of hymnbooks are often found on pianos, left over literature from church boards is stacked on back pews, and "lost and found" articles are awaiting their owners on window sills.

Suitable closets, file drawers, and cabinets would make it possible to keep things shipshape for a while, but the trouble with church storage facilities is that everyone puts things in and no one ever removes anything. When the cupboards and the cabinets are full, we are back where we started.

In many thoughtfully planned churches built years ago there were adequate storage rooms, but they are useless now. They are so full you can't push the door open. The Japanese lanterns used at the ground breaking are still there somewhere. This explains why some people who ought to weep when their church burns down are able to restrain their tears.

There ought to be a statute of limitations on how long junk can be allowed to remain in church cabinets and closets, under stairs, and in storage rooms. Good housekeeping demands a judgment day and a dump truck now and then.

Equipped for Worship, Training, and Service

Congregations are equipping their plants to meet many special needs, all of which contribute to and supplement the primary purposes of the church. Many of these projects have public relations values as well as building the spiritual, educational, inspirational, and cultural life of the parish. Through them people are enabled to understand the interests and concerns of Christians and in many instances are drawn into the fellowship.

A small, intimate chapel was once rarely included in Protestant churches. Now one is part of the layout of a large percentage of newer buildings. The chapel is suitable for weddings, funerals, and other services where small numbers are expected. It also provides a place where a pastor may go for prayer with someone with whom he has been counseling.

The chapel contributes to the mood of private devotions. The first awakening of an interest which may lead to Christian decision and church affiliation may take place here.

Some very small chapels have been electronically equipped to provide private ministrations fitted to the visitor's special need. They are furnished as worshipfully as possible. An adaptation of the automatic record player makes available a choice of recordings made by the minister of kind and understanding words of counsel, Scriptural passages, prayers, and blessings. The chapel visitor simply selects a button, such as "Word to the Sorrowing," "Help for the Tempted," "A Blessing on your Newly Founded Home," or "For Those Facing Parenthood." Other recordings are of great religious music, choral and organ, and of Bible readings chosen for particular moods and needs.

In one such chapel the amplifier was placed in the altar, hidden by a loose fabric that screened the opening. Above the altar on which was always kept a bowl of flowers was a spotlighted Sallman *Head of Christ*. This pastor had prepared a special recording which he asked the bride and groom to share privately immediately following the wedding, if this was convenient.

Another use of recorded messages is the widely practiced "Dial-a-Prayer" plan. A one-minute recording, changed every day, may be

BUILDINGS CAN INVITE OR REPEL

heard by dialing a well-publicized telephone number. Printed post cards are available at the church which worshipers may address and mail to friends they think might be helped by these devotional minutes.

It is good Christianity and good public relations as well for the church to evidence understanding of the problems and state of mind of young parents. Any show of interest in the little newcomer is immensely appreciated, and any provision for him in the church plant is regarded as real co-operation. Don't allow anyone to persuade you to trim your building plans at the point of the nursery. Here is a most important gateway into the church, not only for the members of the cradle roll themselves but for their proud fathers and mothers too.

Some churches have gone so far as to build the nursery at a balcony level at the back of the sanctuary, shutting it off acoustically from the congregation with insulated, soundproof glass. The effect is somewhat like a control room in a radio or TV station. The mothers bring their babies and tiny tots to this room. The music and sermon are picked up by microphones and reproduced in the nursery.

The worshiping congregation is quite unaware of the presence of the parents and children behind and above them. Those in the nursery can see and hear the service. This architectural arrangement may not be particularly desirable, nor is it being recommended. It does, however, "set the child in the midst" and is in keeping with the words, "let the children come to me."

Whether this plan is totally worth while, its purpose of recognizing young parents' problems and of making provision for their babies is one that it is wise to consider in one way or another. Few investments are more productive than those which tie families to the church.

To further family life, one Southern California church built a most imposing barbecue fireplace and patio behind the building. Church groups use it, and church families may sign up for it on evenings when it isn't scheduled for neighborhood family parties.

Indoor bulletin boards serve several useful purposes in churches. They must be well located and changed frequently to be effective. Unless something new appears every week, however, or the arrangement is changed, the board will quickly fade into its surroundings.

Much information can be conveyed and institutional loyalty developed through bulletin boards when displayed in hallways, reception rooms, near church offices, and in meeting rooms of organized groups. Some appropriate person should be given responsibility for each board with instructions to keep it attractive, current, and helpful.

As well as notices and announcements, photographs of church activities and attractive, quick-reading cuttings from religious periodicals and promotional literature can be posted. Some churches exhibit on the bulletin boards near the church office all the clippings from local newspapers relating to the church and its members and to denominational activities in the surrounding area.

A bulletin board devoted to photos, clippings, and short excerpts from letters from missionaries or national workers whom the church is helping to support will greatly aid such projects.

How Comfortable Are Thy Dwelling Places?

What are the discomforts in your church? There may be some which worshipers have accepted, thinking nothing can be done about them. Others may be staying away from church for reasons of which you are unaware.

The minister may easily not know of unpleasant conditions because of his unique role. He has his own seat. He does not see things as the worshiper does. He faces the opposite direction.

Perhaps no general inquiry is necessary, but a minister might emulate Ezekiel once in a while. He sat "where they sat." At the service hour but on a weekday, let him sit down in a pew, first in one part of the church and then in another. Have the lights on as they are during the worship.

He should stay in one pew long enough to let it make an impression. Perhaps the cushions are lumpy and hard. Possibly there are none. This is a soft generation. Compare the comfort of your members when they are on buses, airplanes, trains or in theaters, or in their offices with what the church offers them. Are your pews like park benches?

Remember anyone can leave a park bench when it gets uncomfortable and look for a softer one. In church one has to stay until the benediction. Perhaps it is time for airfoam cushions if not new pews.

The Puritan tradition notwithstanding, there is no virtue in making churchgoers any more uncomfortable than necessary. Or is there? Are we not enjoined in II Timothy to "endure hardness"?

Watch for light in one's eyes. The lectern or pulpit reading lamp may show through chinks in its construction. A slight readjustment, a simply constructed blockade, or an added flange will make it pleasanter for certain worshipers.

Light from the organ console lamp sometimes is a similar offender. If there is a balcony, it is often easier on the eyes of those who sit there if certain hanging fixtures are turned off before the sermon.

Because of the relation of the church to the points of the compass there may be times on sunny days when light pours into the faces of the worshipers in unpleasant amounts. Consider the installation of a pull curtain that will either shut out or diffuse the light.

On the other hand if the church belongs to the "dim, religious light" tradition, the minister ought to satisfy himself that there is sufficient illumination to read the hymns and the responses. If doing so puts a strain on those with normal vision, the inability of those with less than normal to participate is sufficiently depressing to cancel out much of the help that might otherwise have been theirs.

Other discomfort may come from lack of ventilation. Such difficulty can usually be handled by providing the janitor with a short course in the virtues of ozone. You might explain that the reason Eutychus fell asleep while listening to so great a preacher as the apostle Paul was that the open lamps and the crowd had exhausted the oxygen.

Many churches in the parts of the country where the climate is oppressive have air-conditioned their sanctuaries. The cost of doing this, in view of the few hours a church auditorium is used each week, is heavy. However, churches which have installed cooling systems and others which are building them into new churches never seem to regret doing so. They regard such equipment as a top-level public relations investment.

CHAPTER XIV

Public Relations and the Church School

IT WAS A MASTER STROKE OF GOOD PUBLIC RELATIONS WHEN the church first established Sunday schools and programs of weekday youth activities. To be sure, providing one more public relations channel was not the motive, but this fact does not deny that a rich by-product of church schools is their capacity to interpret the church both to the current generation and to coming ones.

Nothing is as precious to parents as their offspring. When a group of officers and teachers indicate their willingness to share with a mother and father their impressive responsibility for the spiritual nurture of a child, most parents respond with grateful appreciation of the sponsoring church.

Many of the most ardent friends and supporters of churches have become such because of the interest these institutions have taken in their children. It could be proved, if it were not offensive to educators to have their services described in these terms, that the contributions made by the church school, directly and indirectly, constitute a church's most effective and most appreciated public relations impact.

Keen Sense of Public Relations Values

Further, church schools, in developing their patterns and practices through the last half century, have demonstrated a keener sense of public relations values than any other department of church life. Many methods traditional and commonplace now were innovations when they were introduced. They often reveal a true knowledge of human nature on the part of their creators.

In a day when reading matter for children was scanty, "story" papers appeared. Sunday school libraries were developed. The introduction decades ago of colored lesson pictures, poster size and pocket size, was the forerunner of the artistically illustrated curriculum materials of today and also of current successful experiments in transferring the curriculum to film.

Pupil participation in special-day programs both provided personal recognition, resulting in the child's development, and had favorable effects on proud relatives.

Appointed stork watchers were ready with suitable cradle-roll procedures when a new baby arrived. Few other organizations, if any, start recruitment before their candidates for future membership are released from the hospital nursery.

Church school Christmas entertainments, summer-time picnics, class parties, and all the many attendance-stimulating awards, advised or ill-advised, lie in the loyalty-building and, therefore, public relations category.

The interest in children's birthdays, promotion certificates and ceremonies, and solicitous absentee cards, whatever else their purposes, certainly help to make friends, and making friends for the church is good public relations.

Valuable, also, are the parent-teacher relationships fostered by the church school. These benefit all—parent, teacher, child.

Neglecting to Use Press

Doubtless there are many exceptions, but the most general point at which the church school falls down is in its failure to make full use of the press.

The small town and country church has a great advantage over the one in the metropolis here. In the smaller community in which there is but a limited number of schools, a much larger percentage of a newspaper's readers is interested in news of any particular one.

In a city where there are several hundred Sunday schools, only a fraction of one per cent of the readers will be interested in activities in any particular school. To the editor this means that it isn't news.

Occasionally a church school story has sufficient novelty or appeal to interest a considerable body of readers. Then it is not difficult to get it published regardless of the size of the paper. But we must remember in using a medium that belongs to someone else to be content to accept without complaint the editor's decision on what is or is not news.

We cannot control what is or is not published in our secular daily and weekly newspapers, but we can come closer to doing so in the publications of a church in which we have some official relationship. A survey of the content of parish papers and church bulletins would certainly show that church school news is given scant attention in proportion to the number of persons concerned and the extent of their involvement. There are, of course, exceptions to this rather general situation.

This absence of news of the church school is the more unfortunate since in major cities parish publications are about the only places where very much information about the church school can be expected.

Many weekly local church publications go for months without any reference to the church school other than a brief mention of time and place, and an occasional announcement of a meeting of officers and teachers. Such a situation can usually be correctel by calling the attention of the editor of the church paper to the fact and making arrangements to provide him with suitable and regular news items.

One frequently overlooked news medium for larger-city churches is the neighborhood "throwaway" shopping paper. Their editors are chiefly interested in the advertising revenue which is the paper's only source of income, but they are often hospitable to any news of local concern that adds to the reader interest of their publications.

Plenty to Publicize

It is true that in the church school, just as in the public school, most of what takes place is so routine that it has long since ceased to be news.

This should not lead the superintendent to the discouraged conclusion that he has *nothing* to publicize. Many happenings each year in themselves are newsworthy—more than at first he might think. Then there is always the opportunity when "there isn't any news" to make some.

What are the ever-present news stories? Here are a few suggestions, some with good picture possibilities:

Elections of new general and departmental superintendents and other officers.

Statistical stories reported in terms more human than mathematical. If the average attendance has increased by fifty during the year, isn't it more interesting to say: "One more than the week before was the gain in attendance each Sunday of 1959"?

Teacher training items. Let it be known when your teachers enroll in winter training courses and summer assemblies or attend conventions. It is a credit to your school, and such teachers themselves deserve the mention.

Physical improvements. These may be on a grand scale as when the school moves into a new education building, or more modest as when classrooms are enlarged, readjusted, or newly equipped. This would include, of course, the announcement of new facilities like the modern nursery that the old storage room has become, or the new Scout room the men and boys have built in the coalbin since the oil burner was installed. In these cases "before and after" pictures are interesting.

Educational advances, told interestingly and supported by quotes from authorities. The regrading of your school, a change to improved lesson materials, or a reorganization of departments are all news. The introduction of new audio or visual methods of instruction makes a good story, as do interesting teaching projects.

Installation of officers and teachers. It may not be possible for larger newspapers to publish names of officers and teachers at the time of their annual public installation. These names ought to be listed somewhere in full for the congregation.

Full listing of officers' and teachers' names often goes undone because there is insufficient space on the church bulletin. This is not sufficient reason to justify overlooking the enormous contribution of time and nervous energy made by these devoted persons.

Additional pages should be added to the bulletin if necessary to inform the congregation of the identity of those who represent them in this needed service. The least that should be done is to insert a mimeographed roster of church school officers and teachers in the installation Sunday calendar.

Creating News

You can stimulate newsworthy happenings and occasions, such as these:

Service projects. Because a baby is at the heart of Christmas, one church school organized its junior carolers to go from one baby's home to another singing Christmas Eve lullabies. A toy-repair and repainting shop can be set up in the church to provide gifts for children who will otherwise not have them. Organize volunteer baby-sitting on young couples' club nights. Start something that fills a need. Then tell the world about it.

Honor Someone. Who is the oldest regular attendant at your church school? Who has a long teaching record? Plan a recognition. Make it an occasion. Have a child of eight present flowers to the patriarch of eighty. Be sure recognition is given to retiring staff members.

Observe Founders' Day. Find in your church records the date when the first Sunday school session was held. Commemorate it with an annual Founders' Day. Is the first superintendent or teacher buried locally? If so, could not a youth delegation carry flowers from the church to the grave?

Learning by doing. Such projects not only are pedagogically valuable, they also generate the publicity of personal witness. Children go home and talk about them. Example: Beginners plant bulbs alongside the church in the fall, then watch their emergence and flowering in the spring. Doubtless your classes are carrying on many interesting enterprises that deserve to be publicized.

PUBLIC RELATIONS AND THE CHURCH SCHOOL

Still and Motion Pictures

In almost every church there is a "shutterbug." He may have brought back from Germany or Japan a fine camera with which he loves to take Kodachromes. Is his hobby 8 or 16 mm. motion pictures?

Get him interested in making a "documentary" of your school. If he needs the money, provide the film. Help him edit it. If you announce that it will be shown at some general social occasion, you will have a crowd. People love to see themselves and their children on the screen.

Perhaps the film could be scheduled in connection with the church school superintendent's annual report. It will then serve a useful purpose in bringing some new information and impressions to that often substantial proportion of the church fathers who know little or nothing about the church school.

Handling News

If your church school can find someone who now has or once had professional contact with newspapers, it is best to make that person the press relations representative. He or she should, however, work closely with the chairman of your church press relations committee.

It is a great advantage to the newspapers to have one rather than a number of contacts with the church. Also, when the secretaries or press chairmen clear through one person, a schedule of timing releases can be set up which avoids the possible competition of a story from one organization in your church with one from another unit.

If an experienced person is lacking, the task may fall to the church school superintendent, the church secretary, the pastor, or the pastor's secretary. The person, of course, should make every effort to learn the rudiments of good press relations through some of the helpful books on the subject or through pamphlets that your denomination's public relations department will gladly supply.

Teachers

When a church school teacher's better self overcomes his original hesitancy and he accepts the job, he becomes not only a teacher but at the same moment an important public relations representative of the church school.

"Public relations begins in the classroom." This is almost an axiom in the teaching profession. "As the child thinks of the teacher, so the home thinks of the school," it is said.

It is almost frightening to realize that one ill-tempered outburst, one thoughtless, belittling word, one inconsistent act, can cancel out what it may have taken weeks to implant.

There is much that can be done to supplement the objectives and ideals of the church school through direct mail, parish publications, the public press, and radio-TV. These media should be used in full measure. But every public relations man would agree that the most desirable and most influential publicity is "word of mouth."

Good teachers and good teaching are the best public relations assets a church school can have. Happy-hearted and faith-filled children are its best publicity agents.

CHAPTER XV

The Parish Paper in the Public Relations Program

It is desirable, of course, to have both an attractively printed Sunday bulletin and a parish paper. However, should the budget compel a choice between the two, there are good reasons why a public relations committee might choose a Saturday newssheet distributed under a second-class mailing permit in preference to a Sunday calendar.

Even the most attractive church calendar has three drawbacks: it reaches only that fraction of the constituency which chances to be at church; it has no prepublicity value, at least for the morning service; and a good one is expensive.

More and more churches are avoiding these difficulties and at the same time are gaining advantages by the publication of a weekly church newspaper.

Public Relations Values in Parish Papers

Parish papers go into every home in the parish, carrying information concerning the program of the morrow, thus stimulating attendance. At the same time such a paper becomes an economy, requiring a smaller appropriation from the treasury, since part of its way may be paid by subscriptions and by advertising. There is further saving due to the fact that the exact number needed may be ordered, while with the customary bulletin a guess is made which is invariably too high or too low, with resultant waste or embarrassment.

A typical weekly newssheet is at first glance not unlike a four page church calendar, although the two vary greatly in page size and in format.

That parish papers are appreciated is attested by the experience of one minister-editor. By mistake one whole Addressograph tray was run through twice, and another similar tray was omitted entirely. In consequence two hundred families were delivered two copies each and two hundred others received none. Dismayed at first, the pastor was ultimately glad that the mistake was made, for the stream of inquiries as to what had happened to the *Messenger* assured him beyond a doubt that the little paper had become an essential.

Among the advantages of the weekly newspaper over the old calendar is the fact that it is much easier to keep in touch with absent members. As many as can be located are put on the mailing list, often through the kindness of old friends. To one New England church at Christmas time came a huge crate of holly and mistletoe from a former member living in North Carolina who had been kept in friendly awareness of the church through the weekly visits of the parish paper.

During a benevolent campaign a member living in another part of the state sent one hundred dollars to help her church meet its quota. She learned about it through the parish paper.

The announcement of memorial flowers in one issue was followed by a gift of one hundred gladioli and a permanent pulpit floral basket from a nonresident who noticed it.

In many churches the result of a weekly church paper has been that at the season of the every-member canvass the budget has been fully subscribed or even oversubscribed for the first time. The connection between this and the parish paper is not always recognized, but it is probably there.

In every church there are numerous people on the fringes. They rarely attend services, and they make no regular pledge to the church. They are the type who say, "I never hear from the church except when they are after money." To this person the weekly parish paper arriving Saturday morning is in a sense a call from the church. Only rarely does it ask for money. It disarms this person of his complaint. He still receives the letters from the finance committee, but every week he is reminded that indifferent as he has been, the folks at the church still think of him as belonging to the family. This is a helpful background for church visitors whether they come to the home on friendly calls, on evangelistic visitations, or on the every-member canvass.

Another reason why the parish paper is an ally of the church canvasser is that its issues prior to the canvass have been building up an understanding of the budget items—local, connectional, and world wide. The greatest obstacle to generosity toward the church is not stinginess; it is ignorance—ignorance of why money is needed and of how and where it is disbursed. The parish paper, going into every home from week to week, replaces this ignorance with knowledge.

The minister finds the weekly newspaper a personal aid. Through it he speaks each week to his entire constituency, and the visit of the printed messenger to the home is often more to the point than an actual pastoral visit with its distractions. Opportunities are given to express appreciation for service rendered and for praise of worthy accomplishments or organizations. Every pastor knows that each such mention is an inspiration for future effectiveness.

Financing the Paper

The chief satisfaction of having the advantage of a paper delivered every Friday or Saturday morning by Uncle Sam's carriers is that, instead of costing the church more, it may actually be less expensive than the usual Sunday calendar. The difference is derived from advertising income and from a nominal subscription price.

Commercial advertising printed on a Sunday bulletin passed out in the sanctuary would seem to most worshipers out of place. This ban need not hold in the case of a weekly periodical mailed to homes. Of course no objectionable advertising would be accepted.

It is as logical for a parish paper to be aided by advertisers who find its columns useful as for an official denominational journal to do so. But there is a point where serious objection to advertising in a church periodical should be voiced: when advertisers have been subjected to a pressure that leaves them wondering whether they have been hijacked or blackmailed. A church with any sense of self-respect (not to mention good public relations or ethics) will never extort money from unwilling businessmen under the guise of selling them an advertisement which they do not want in a medium that has no real advertising value for them.

This admonition does not apply to legitimate advertisements at reasonable rates in a well-read weekly or monthly parish paper. Such advertising should be solicited completely without pressure. Explain to the prospect that if the proposal does not appear to him to promise a reasonable return for his investment, you would much prefer not to have his order. With this presentation you will have no difficulty finding advertisers in the community who will welcome the opportunity of having their names and their messages carried weekly into your church homes.

Many parish papers, of course, prefer to devote all their space to the news of their churches and to the general promotion of Christian culture. If the church treasury can cover the total publication costs, this is the simplest way. Such an investment will prove the most productive of all the items in the budget.

What such a paper may be able to do for your church is easily worth the sacrifice of making up a budgetary deficit occasionally. The following illustration is drawn from the general church level, but it may be paralleled in your own church in proportionally smaller terms.

In 1881 *The Christian Advocate*, published in New York, pointed out that there was not a single Methodist hospital in all America. The editor soundly chided a church that purported to follow the Great Physician for this omission.

Over in Brooklyn a layman, George I. Seney, read the editorial. The next day he called on Dr. James M. Buckley, the editor. "I have

$100,000 that will be available soon, which I am going to donate for a hospital. I think some of my friends will help, too."

The editorial sparked a movement that produced not just one hospital in Brooklyn but a chain of seventy-two hospitals across the nation with assets above $220,000,000 and which every year are rendering more than $5,000,000 worth of free service.

What difference does it make whether that church weekly finished the year in the red or in the black?

You can charge a small subscription price to help finance the paper. You may include a special envelope in the church members' packets of weekly offering envelopes, placing similar envelopes in the pew racks.

Sometimes a list of subscribers is needed for the second-class mailing permit. A sentence printed above the signature on the annual pledge card used in the every-member canvass can cover this need. The wording can be an authorization to send the parish paper to the undersigned and a promise to pay the dollar (or whatever the price may be). If the budget carries all the cost of the publications and no request for an amount above the regular pledge is made upon the members for their papers, any postal requirement for a bona fide list of paid-up subscribers can be met in this way: print in small type on the pledge card something like, "My signature on this card is authorization for the first dollar (or fifty cents) paid on this pledge to be used to meet the cost of one year's subscription to the *South Church Herald*."

The requirements for a permit for second-class mailing are changed from time to time. Get the current information from your postmaster. The privileges vary with the periodicity of the publication, being in general more favorable in postal rates to weeklies than to papers of less frequency.

Rural churches enjoy special provisions and are entitled under certain conditions to the "free-in-county" mailing privileges traditionally granted to weekly newspapers. Requirements for the maintenance of a list of subscribers are in some situations waived as in the case of papers that do not carry miscellaneous advertising.

Second-class mail is defined in postal regulations as "printed matter." Only publications done by offset process or on letter press (from type) are admitted. Mimeographed papers are definitely excluded from the low pound rates which a second-class permit makes possible.

In launching a new periodical or in revamping an old one, consult the local postal officials. If your periodical conforms or can be made to conform, application blanks will be furnished. Since regulations are complex and many postmasters have infrequent occasion to become familiar with them, it is sometimes wise to write to the Division of Mail Classification, Post Office Department, Washington 25, D.C.

The difference between mailing costs under second-class (bulk) mailing and stamped mail (third-class) is sometimes as much as the cost of printing a modest paper. Do not overlook this great benefit which the government makes possible.

Thousands of dollars are being wasted by churches who mail at third-class rates. A little effort and some adjustments could make publications conform to requirements for a rate of postage so low that it is almost negligible.

Editing the Parish Paper

In most churches someone, who may now be doing something else, once worked on a newspaper, edited his college weekly, or has been in some phase of the publishing or advertising business. Such a person may be glad to take over the editorship of the church paper as a Christian service. If it seems the thing to do, his or her services may properly be compensated.

Working newsmen or teachers of journalism in high schools and colleges are well qualified for such assignments. In case such a person is available, his services should by all means be utilized, leaving the minister free for other duties.

However, it may be difficult in some cases to find such a person, and the job will fall to the minister and his secretary (and in the great majority of churches where there is no secretary, to the minister himself). In some instances if he has a flair for it, the minister may welcome the job as a hobby.

Unless he is well tutored or experienced in journalism, the minister-editor will want first of all to read two or three of the scores of excellent books in this field. The chapter on "How to Write News" in this book should be helpful. This will not only help him with news writing and make-up but will also enable him to understand what the printer means when he uses the vocabulary of his craft.

He will want at once to get on the exchange list of his fellow parish paper editors. Here he will find that there is much he can learn and much that he can borrow from other papers with due credit.

Because he will want to be more than parochial in planning his paper's contents, he will ask to be put on the mailing list of the press relations departments of his own denomination and of such interdenominational associations with which it may be affiliated.

A parish paper will thrive on news. Make it straight factual reporting without embellishments. Keep in mind that the use of action verbs gives a sense of movement and vitality. Go easy with adjectives.

In addition to announcements of your program events, include news made by new members of the church and of the church staff. Stories of church members' unusual experiences or capacities are interesting. The constant parade of personal events should be recorded —births, marriages, deaths, well-known members moving from the city, and others coming to take their places. News of students in college, young people in military service, and beloved former members encourages fellowship by correspondence.

Church papers render a useful service when they publish a full schedule of the week's religious radio and TV programs. Occasionally a motion picture or a new book or an article in a popular magazine, is of such character that it deserves mention.

All of the organizations of the church that do newsworthy things should be covered. It is easy to overlook some whose activities may not concern the editor. Remember that although you may not rate the news of the church bowling league very high, it is of interest to the participants.

If you have the space, do not be too parochial. You can help make well-informed, broad-visioned Christians. Include brief items on what is happening in other churches of your denomination. Cover the great general agencies and the national councils of your church. Help your readers to know, in brief at least, what is stirring in the Christian world at large.

If you are editing a paper for the first time, you will quickly discover the need of "fillers." These are short items that are set up in advance (on Linotype slugs if you use letter press) or kept on file until needed. They are what is called "time copy" and may be used at any time. Collect such brief statements of fact, quotations, wise counsel, couplets, quatrains, or humor. Keep a supply ahead, as your printer will need them to fill out short columns. In the aggregate they can supply considerable inspiration and information if you select them wisely.[1]

In all your writing try to use the simplest, most interesting style. Keep it readable and lively but remember that a church periodical, even as informal as a parish paper, is not the place for flippancy. Don't whoop it up for causes in the manner of class secretaries trying to lure you back to your college reunion. In an effort to avoid being stuffy it is easy to become too chatty. Within the limits of dignity and good taste use as vital and as fresh a vocabulary as you can.

Most of us are not gifted with too much originality, but we can avoid the opposite effect in our writing by straining out the wearisome clichés that sneak into our phrases if we are not on guard. Here are some: "point with pride," "view with alarm," "a good time was had by all," "pure and simple," "ripe old age," "go over the top," "put our shoulders to the wheel," "each and every one." There are hundreds.

If you decide on an editorial column, give the laymen a break. The pulpit is the minister's forum. Let the church officials express themselves now and then.

Here's a short course in editorial writing:

Treat just one subject at a time.

First, introduce your theme as interestingly as you can.

Second, state in a sentence or two what it is that you believe or what you deplore or what you wish to see changed or accomplished.

Third, present your arguments one by one, briefly, forcefully, and supported by evidence or authorities.

Fourth, tie up what you have said, in a logical, clearly stated conclusion.

Keep up the tone of your editorial column. Don't scold. Don't admonish. Don't express despondency and discouragement. Don't plead pitifully for co-operation.

If you want to build attendance at an occasion, you will interest many more readers by writing about it so alluringly that the reader becomes eager to attend than if you beg and cajole.

---

[1] Webb B. Garrison, *Improve Your Church Bulletins* (New Jersey: Fleming H. Revell Co., 1957) is a useful collection of such material.

THE PARISH PAPER IN THE PUBLIC RELATIONS PROGRAM

Don't confine your editorial subjects narrowly. Comment on community problems, world events, educational, social, evangelistic, and missionary progress. Interpret such developments in the light of Christian principles.

Make-up, Layout, and Style

Since your parish paper represents your church and you believe that there is no more important or nobler institution, you will not be content with anything less than the best possible product. This applies first to the appearance of your little magazine or newspaper. Observe periodicals for special methods of getting attention for a poem, a quotation, or a picture. If you like the appearance of a printed page, analyze what it is that makes it attractive. You cannot duplicate the effects professional layout men and artists produce in the slick magazines and Sunday supplements, but you can learn much by studying their methods.

"Boners" are bound to creep in, but make every reasonable effort by careful proofreading to avoid typographical errors and misspelled words. They grate on many readers and tend to discredit both your publication and your church.

One of the most common faults of amateur editors is that of crowding the page. Advertisers know the value of the white space ("air" is what they call it). Very narrow margins and overloaded pages discourage reading. Some papers are so packed, so unimaginatively edited, and so monotonous in appearance that they are less attractive than a page from the telephone directory.

Technical instructions for styling your paper and for its make-up can best be provided by your printer or by an advertising or newspaperman in your congregation. Many page sizes are possible. Decide first whether your publication is to follow newspaper or magazine lines, whether it is to be printed on newsprint or on coated, slick stock. Determine the page size you want and the number of pages which you will normally use.

All these decisions will help to answer other questions, such as column width, the kind of heads to write, the "screen" to use for best reproduction of photos.

In general, narrow columns are easier to read than wide ones. They also save space when the last line of a paragraph consists of a single word (called a "widow"). Narrow columns permit a more varied and more attractive make-up. Sometimes you may wish to break the sameness by doubling your column width for all or part of a story or feature.

Study the various styles of head writing. Some prefer heads that summarize the story. This method is a help to hurried readers who often are satisfied with these few words. Smaller papers such as house magazines often prefer headlines that do not digest the story. Instead, they use the head like bait to a fish. They are teasers that lure the reader to start and then to finish the story. Sometimes they consist of just a single word.

Styles have changed greatly in American newspapers from the days when major stories were headed with several banks of carefully counted words set in inverted pyramids of type in diminishing sizes. Newspapers now, with occasional exceptions, have simplified the head writing. Heads that are flush on the left and come out on the right where they will are very common. Subheads have been almost abandoned by many papers.

Decide on your style. Count your letter spaces carefully and don't send the printer heads that are too wide for your columns. Use Roman type for heads on ordinary news stories and major announcements and italic heads for less important stories and features. This will permit variety and avoid the possibility of having two heads of the same type size and design next to each other. (This gives an odd, undesirable effect which in newsrooms is called tombstoning. It can be avoided when you have three columns by putting a shorter story with an italic head between the two similar ones.)

A much-repeated mistake in local church papers is taking pains with page one, so that it may present a pleasing effect, then letting the printer throw the remaining type on his galleys into the succeeding pages with no thought of design or effect. Usually this is compounded by jumping lengthy stories from one page to another with no new catch-line headings to identify them.

Church editors are often responsible for dull-looking pages due to inconspicuous one-line heads in boldface type of the same size as the text. These are suitable for short items at the bottom of columns, but longer stories need to be set off by heads appropriate to their size and importance.

While there is a great "do it yourself" satisfaction in editing, publishing, and circulating your parish paper right in your own community, there is another way to do it which greatly lessens the labor and considerably reduces the cost.

There are two firms, and doubtless others, which will take your copy, set it up, lay it out, and print it with other pages of suitable religious material which they furnish. The result is a professional-looking weekly newspaper or monthly magazine for your church, particularly churches in the South and Southwest. We suggest, if you are interested, that you write to All Church Press, Tribune Corner, Fort Worth, Texas. Plans are under way to make their service nationwide.

While All Church Press is a privately owned business enterprise, its personnel are devoted Christians who render their service with a sense of vocation. Hundreds of churches which would find a weekly parish newspaper prohibitive in cost are enjoying the benefits of one because of this unique plan.

Another publisher who has pleased many through the years is The National Religious Press, 523 Ottawa Avenue, Grand Rapids, Michigan. Unlike the Fort Worth firm, they supply not newspapers but a magazine type periodical on coated paper, normally printed once a month, although other periodicity can be arranged. Both of these concerns have been serving churches with satisfaction for many years. It is possible that one of them might meet your needs.

CHAPTER XVI

Ushers--Hosts for God

CHURCH USHERS ARE CONSPICUOUS, FIRST-LINE PUBLIC RELATIONS functionaries, equal perhaps to the pastor himself.

While I was a pastor in New England, a recently graduated electrical engineer sent me the previous Sunday's calendar of a New York church. He had just taken his first job but now is a vice-president of the American Telephone and Telegraph Company.

On the first page was the usual picture of the edifice. Under the halftone was a slogan in bold italics, "You're only a stranger once." With his pen my young friend had pointed an arrow toward the slogan, then written in the margin, "*This is the bunk!* I went there this morning and not a soul spoke to me—not even the minister." How often do you think he went back to that church?

In another part of the country, I attended the Sunday morning service of a downtown church. I was about two feet inside the door, pausing to get my bearings, when a feminine voice to my right startled me. A quick glance revealed an earnest-looking woman seated at a small table. I had a swift impression that she was holding out a registration card for me to sign but (shame on me!) I made as if I had not noticed her. I pushed on, hoping to make the sanctuary before the conclusion of the first hymn, already in progress. This was not to be.

An immensely jovial gentleman headed me off. He was clutching a pack of programs in one hand. The other hand was extended with such cordiality and his expression was so radiant that I was certain that somewhere in the past we must have been fast friends. Since I was unable to recall ever having seen the man, I was embarrassed to realize that I was failing to match the enthusiasm of his greeting. I swiftly acknowledged his welcome, then started to move toward the inner door, still hoping to find a seat before my entrance would be too conspicuous.

But again, no.

My exuberant greeter, stopping me by draping his arm over my shoulder, wanted me to meet a fellow usher standing near. This colleague, if we described his sensations accurately, was "more than delighted" to meet me.

The congregation intoned the hymn's "Amen." Meanwhile, the welcomers were plying me with questions. I had not the slightest reason for avoiding these queries, but for some reason, I am ashamed to confess, I found myself clamming up on them. My replies became curt and slightly evasive. My usher friends told me there would be a reception with light refreshments in the church parlors after the service. They hoped I'd be there to meet some of the "swell" people who belonged to their church.

The inner door opened. With the aid of a fraternal slap on the back, I pushed through. I side-stepped the inside guardian and found my own way to the protection of a sequestered pew. For good reason I needed some time to get into the spirit of the service.

An ideal and appropriate expression of hospitality is somewhere between the indifference of the church that gave the deep freeze to the newcomer to New York and the overdone and badly timed welcome I received in another city. How to find it is not simple.

The temperamental differences among people are complicating factors. To the Garbo type who wants to be alone, the privilege of attending divine worship with a minimum of human distraction is ideal. The lonely soul far from home, shriveled and diminished by the impersonality of a metropolis, may require even the exaggerated friendliness of the second church for the restoration of his self-confidence as a human being.

The trick is to pattern the normal greeting procedure to the taste of the average churchgoer, if there is such a person. Techniques must be flexible, and the welcoming staff must be sensitive enough to discern when to increase or decrease the standard dosages of hospitality.

Few or Many Ushers

Should you use one crew of ushers, two sets which serve on alternate Sundays, or several teams serving less frequently? Some public relations aspects must be considered.

Some churches maintain successful ushers' associations which enroll almost every qualified man among the regular attendants. These are divided into teams, each headed by an experienced usher chosen for his qualities of leadership. The chief usher, aided by the sub-chairmen, schedules a rotation. A duty roster is set up so that each usher knows the Sundays on which his team is scheduled for service.

Advantages of this system are obvious. It helps to provide jobs for several times as many men as are required for an unchanging Sunday-after-Sunday group of ushers. This is important because one doesn't really begin thinking of a church as "my church" until he has been given some responsibility. Using many different ushers enlarges the acquaintanceship of all of them with the other members of the congregation.

A man who serves as usher once a month develops a continuing sense of host responsibility that carries over through the other three Sundays when he is in the pews. He enlarges his interest in strangers and his concern for the comfort of those seated near him because of his occasional ushering.

On the negative side, using a small crew makes it possible to be selective and to choose only those who are best suited to the task.

Ushers who are on duty every Sunday can build up contacts with strangers from Sunday to Sunday in a way that is not possible with rotating ushers.

From the standpoint of the newcomers, the church is probably more homelike when the same now-familiar face that smiled a welcome on the first visit is met on succeeding Sunday mornings. There are advantages in both practices.

Appearance

Ushers should present a neat, dignified appearance. Practices vary greatly among churches, but there is no exception to this rule.

At one extreme there are, of course, boards of ushers who for purposes of dignity and uniformity wear cutaways or Oxford gray jackets with striped trousers and identical neckwear. Such formal dress may be indicated in churches where the architecture and the congregation's standards of attire are in keeping. In most churches adopting such a uniform would be overdoing the matter (even without considering the expense to individual ushers).

Contrasted with the ultradignified attire of some ushers are the variegated suits, shirts, socks, shoes, and ties of ushers who never give the matter of their composite appearance the slightest thought. The motley array frequently exhibited in the row of men drawn up before the congregation for the offertory is distracting, if not amusing.

For the same reasons that have dictated almost everywhere the vested choir, ushers should try to create a harmonious effect. The ushers can without undue hardship agree to purchase and to wear when on duty Oxford gray or charcoal suits, white shirts, black shoes, and similar ties. Or they may agree on blue with brown shoes or simply "dark" suits.

In summer they may shift to lighter color and weight materials. The important matter is to maintain sufficient similarity to avoid conspicuous contrasts.

The spirit and manner of ushers are more important than their dress, but attire is worth some thought and perhaps some individual expense. Think how much money is frequently involved in providing the exactly right raiment in which to usher at so transient an occasion as a wedding. Aren't ushers every bit as justified in planning their wardrobes for a harmonious appearance at the weekly worship of God?

Uniformity of dress is not a matter of display. On the contrary, harmonious apparel contributes to the unobtrusiveness of the ushers' services.

Many churches provide a flower or a printed ribbon or badge for their ushers to aid in their being quickly recognized.

"Given to Hospitality"

Pastor and people, the choir, even the sexton—all share with the ushers the responsibilities of hosts in the House of God. Consciously or unconsciously, they combine to set the thermostat—frigid and forbidding, cool and indifferent, or warm and welcoming.

In a special sense the welcoming responsibility is specifically delegated to the ushers. Many a worshiper comes and goes with no personal contact other than with the ushers. The other elements of the service make their respective contributions, but the important first, and (often) last, impressions on visitors are made by ushers.

Ushering is much more than simply a matter of mechanically filling and emptying the sanctuary. Ushers render important services to the church in three ways.

First, the usher affects newcomers, visitors, and occasional attendants—the growing edge of the congregation. Second, he makes the "regulars" feel glad that they have come and that they are sharing the fellowship of like-minded, like-hearted members of the church family.

The third privilege of the usher is to make his contribution to those he serves in such a way that he adds to the total spiritual accomplishment of the church srevice. The welcoming usher should keep constantly in mind the purpose that has brought the churchgoers to the sanctuary and should make all his contacts contribute to that end, in addition to greeting and seating. He may do or say very little, but he should be in every respect helpful to the comforting, uplifting worship experience the person he serves has come to find.

The ideal usher should say constantly to himself: "This is God's house. I am privileged today to be host for him. How can I, in my demeanor, in my bearing, in what I say and do, help these people who are now approaching the church to find the fullest satisfactions in their hour of worship? How can I co-ordinate my service with those of my associates—the minister, the organist, the choir? What can I do that will help to 'usher' the worshipers not only to a seat but into the presence of the Most High as well?"

In this mood the usher cannot fail to be a worthy host for God.

Front and Center

One of New York's most famous church ushers was Sydney Hutchins. A police officer, he stood for forty years at Madison Square in front of the famous old Flatiron Building directing the converging traffic of Broadway, Fifth Avenue, and Twenty-third Street. On Sundays during those same years he was chairman of ushers at Janes Church in Brooklyn.

Churches have their traffic problems too. One principle on which all experienced ushers agree is obvious: fill the front seats first. This not only prevents confusion in the aisles but avoids the distraction to worshipers that is inevitable when people are being seated in front of them.

Filling the church from the front also results in leaving vacant seats in the rear where late-comers can be seated with the minimum disturbance.

With the tendency for shy persons to want to drop into the first seat they reach, it is not always easy to overcome a resistance to being taken forward. An aid in this is the custom of many churches to ribbon off the back pews while those in front are being filled. A weight sewed into the ends of ribbons so used is a help in shifting their positions quickly.

A church in Chicago forty-seven pews deep found filling its front seats a problem. The head usher discovered that in the period before service the stationing of a pair of ushers in each aisle halfway to the front was the solution.

A first usher greets the worshipers in the narthex, then escorts them half the length of the aisle, and transfers them to the waiting ushers. These then take over and lead the guests still farther up the aisle to the front seats. This procedure sufficiently distracts the worshipers that before they know it they are much farther forward than they normally would choose to be. Once they are in these choice pews with the ordeal of getting there safely behind them they are doubtless glad to be in close contact with the minister and the choir.

On those occasions, rare we hope in your church, when the indications are that there will be considerably less than a full house, the ushers have it in their power to help the spirit of the service and the morale of the minister considerably. A hundred persons can be so distributed in a sanctuary holding three hundred as to make it seem either almost empty or semifull.

Distributing the congregation to avoid great open spaces can make the service inspiring rather than depressing. Often shutting off the side sections will help give a small congregation a sense of solidarity.

Courtesy Toward Guests

Despite all that may be said about the desirability of seating people in the front, ushers will do well to respect the wishes of attendants. Often, for reasons of their own, persons will desire to sit in a particular place. An officious usher may succeed once in overruling the visitor's expressed desire but not without resentment.

A close relative remembers unhappily that on the Mother's Day following her mother's accidental death a well-meaning usher forced her to a conspicuous front seat when she preferred to sit back under the balcony in case she found it difficult to control her grief. Another friend, a reserved New Englander who would not care to advertise any eccentricity, experiences severe claustrophobia if she finds herself anywhere but in the aisle near an exit. Forcing her to move into the center of the pew would result in a decision not to return.

Such phobias are not uncommon. Often a worshiper will hold an aisle seat, not necessarily because he is selfish or because he wants to inconvenience others, but because he may be feeling slightly ill and uncertain and wants to be where he can make an exit without disturbing others. He may find it necessary to leave a little early.

Ushers inevitably create ill will and defeat the worship mood of persons they attempt to coerce. The guest is always right.

Some Do's for Ushers

This differs with the locality, but in most cases give a welcoming "good morning" to arriving worshipers rather than a handshake, unless the guest offers his hand. You can make a less formal approach after the service.

Accompany the "good morning" with the visitor's name if you know it.

Try to convey the feeling that the visitor is wanted, that his presence in God's house is appreciated.

Arrive early.

Remain after service as long as is necessary to greet as many as you can of those you have served, particularly strangers.

Relax. Tenseness is "catching."

If you have responsibility for control of lights or ventilation, master these mechanisms in the absence of the congregation. Bumbling, clumsy, noisy operation of such apparatus can ruin a service.

Watch for absences among the "regulars." Learn if there is illness or trouble, and if so, report it to the pastor.

And, of Course, Some Don't's

"Be careful not to place your hands on persons either in persuasion or in familiarity" is a rule of the New York Ushers' Association. People do not like to be handled.

Don't let anything happen that will interfere with the attendant's desire to worship.

Don't counteract the reverant atmosphere of the sanctuary by needless conversation with fellow ushers.

Don't lose your temper regardless of the provocation.

Don't let a guest feel that one person is receiving more attention than another.

Don't slouch. Stand and walk erectly.

Don't rush suddenly down the aisle or make other sudden movements, even in minor emergencies. Such motion disturbs and distracts the congregation.

Don't keep worshipers waiting unnecessarily or without explanation.

Ushers must "not be civic club backslappers with loud voices or mum funeral parlor robots," wrote Raymond Musser in the *Christian Herald*.

Names on the Dotted Line

It is highly desirable to obtain the name and address of the visitor, but any effort to coerce it by what may be regarded as high-pressure methods is likely to be both unsuccessful and resented. The same may be said of attempts to get this information before the guest has been in the building long enough for the sense of strangeness to have worn off.

Such requests, if inadequately explained or prematurely made, are viewed with suspicion by some people. They take it as an invasion of privacy or as a request to sign a contract before reading the fine print. They are not quite sure what obligations they are incurring.

The familiar information-registration card in the pew rack is still probably the most satisfactory method, since this method is entirely voluntary. The cards may be dropped on the offering plate or left with an usher.

These forms often carry spaces for the visitor to check, providing additional information about himself and permitting him to indicate his interest in a pastoral visit or in some specialized or age-group activity. The difficulty with this method is that too often the cards are overlooked or ignored by visitors. It is helpful to mention them and their purpose in the church or even from the pulpit.

Another method frequently employed is the visitors' register. This is usually a large bound book resting on a lectern or small stand-up desk conveniently located in the narthex. Occasional visitors may locate and sign such a guestbook without prompting, but it is usually necessary for an usher or hospitable church greeter to make the suggestion. This is ordinarily effective if one says, "If you have not already done so, we would all feel honored if you would register in our church guestbook."

If the visitor omits his street address, he can be encouraged to include it if you say, "If you would care to include your street number, our office would be able to send you notice of special events in the church," or "—put you on our parish paper mailing list."

Ushers can be particularly useful at this point in watching at the exits for new people they have seated, greeting them, introducing them to others, and tactfully exploring the nature and degree of interest they have in future relations with the church. They should have in their pockets some of the pew cards, so that on any indication of willingness to supply it, the desired information can be obtained.

Filled out by the visitor or by the usher, the cards should be turned in promptly to the church office or given to the minister. Information about newcomers, no matter how skillfully it is gathered, is of no value until it leads to an effective follow-up. After a visitor has given these facts, he has a right to expect to hear from the church in one way or another. If he doesn't, his reaction is likely to be negative.

Many pastors, of whom Dr. Ralph W. Sockman is one, have a secretary who stands near as they greet the departing congregations. All names and other information developed in these church-door conversations are unobtrusively recorded. Later the visitors are followed up with appropriate notes from the minister or with calls by the parish visitor or by member-neighbors who have been informed.

Training Your Ushers

Ushering is a rapidly developing science involving crowd engineering, social psychology, and public relations. More and more churches are providing training for those to whom this important responsibility has been given.

A great university in its adult education programs has prepared a filmstrip with teacher's guide on the subject.[1] Short extension courses are available which can be taken by correspondence.[2] There are inexpensive ushers' manuals available at most denominational bookstores.[3]

All but a few churches need to improve their ushering services. If more formal training cannot be offered, at least informal conferences between pastors and ushers can be scheduled to review present practices in the interest of their betterment.

Groups of churches who desire to combine in sponsoring a school for ushers can arrange for a former dean of the College of Adult Education of the University of Omaha to come and conduct one locally for a reasonable fee.[5]

Few persons are in so privileged a position as an usher to envelope the stranger in a spirit of Christian friendliness and to create a mood that will aid him both in glad participation in the worship and in giving a sympathetic ear to the message.

---

[1] *The Art of Church Ushering*, Bureau of Audio-Visual Instruction, University of Nebraska, Lincoln 8, Nebraska. With teaching guide.

[2] University of Omaha, School of Adult Education.

[3] Willis O. Garrett, *Church Ushers' Manual* (New Jersey: Fleming H. Revell Co.).

[4] P. Lang, *Church Ushering* (St. Louis: Concordia Publishing House). *Principles of Church Ushering*, Protestant Council, 71 West 23rd St., New York 10, New York.

[5] Everett Hosman, address c/o University of Omaha, School of Adult Education.

CHAPTER XVII

Telephone and Post Office Work for the Church

How many times does your church phone ring each day? Whatever the figure, this is the number of opportunities the persons who answer it have to build good will. It also numbers the occasions that are theirs for making negative impressions unless they are constantly on guard.

The person who answers the telephone in the church office or pastor's residence must realize constantly that whenever he does so, he is for the moment a public relations representative of the church.

The ringing of the phone almost always is an interruption. This is particularly true with persons as busy as church secretaries and ministers. The secretary is nearing the bottom of the last row in the addition of a long column of figures. The preacher has just received an inspiration for the phrasing of next Sunday's "thirdly" and is feverishly writing it down before it escapes. This is when the phone rings.

In situations like this pause a moment before taking the phone from its cradle. In those few seconds replace the natural irritation aroused by the interruption with your "voice with a smile."

A smile rightfully belongs at the church end of a telephone line. The persons there are dedicated to Christian service. They find their deepest satisfactions in helping other people. Phone calls should be welcomed with the thought, "Here is a chance to be kind and helpful to someone."

Telephone courtesy is in order everywhere by everybody all the time. Any lack of it is particularly noticed in a church office. One never knows what the call will be. It may come from someone in desperate trouble. It may be a summons for the minister to the bedside of the dying or to a home just reached by the worst possible news.

Callers like this already begin to be comforted and supported when the voice that answers carries overtones of friendliness and the desire to help. This is a further reason why church employees and ministers should guard against the bored, the annoyed, and the indifferent approach to the telephone.

Never think of the phone as a mechanism. It is a connection with a person. In man-to-man encounters the kindly facial expression, the warm handclasp, and the welcoming manner all aid two persons in getting into communication. Over the telephone the voice must do it all. Your only representative is the spoken word.

Haven't you called friends whose answering voices said as clearly as words, "Why in the world (or other suitable expletive) did you have to bother me right now when I was just finding out who dunnit?" Even if the hostility ends and your friend immediately turns on his cordiality the moment he finds out it is you, you cannot at once forget the sting of that first surly answer.

Telephone Manners

Occasionally a church janitor, whose duties do not include answering the telephone, is called by the insistent ringing in the pastor's office from the basement where he is stoking the furnace. Grumbling, he hurries up the stairs, sorting out the key as he goes.

Panting up the stairs, he mutters, "Why can't those crazy people call during office hours?" Irritated at the possibility that the party will hang up after all his trouble, he snatches up the phone and snaps peevishly at the caller.

As the sexton returns to his boiler room, the hotel guest who just called fumes to her husband, "Well! I never heard such a gruff, surly minister in all my life. I wouldn't go to his church if it were the only one left in the world!"

We can understand and sympathize with the harrassed janitor. Unfortunately, he didn't tell who he was when the lady asked for the next day's worship hours. She assumed that the curt voice was the pastor's.

Since this little episode is not imaginary, it is suggested that the church janitor be included in staff briefings on telephone manners. Outsiders often judge a whole establishment by the treatment they receive from just one person.

Compare the gracious courtesy of those who service airline reservation telephones with the traditional boorishness of persons in similar relationships to railroads. If the railroads have learned something from the airlines and are doing better these days, thousands of people don't know it because they no longer give these impatient, unpleasant impersonalities a chance to humiliate and depress them. Almost invariably one left the phone feeling that he had imposed on the railroad agent and wishing he had tried to get the needed information any other way.

One would be silly to suggest that the shift from train to plane travel has been very much influenced by the difference in telephone public relations as practiced by the two transportation media. The other merits and demerits of each are too pronounced. But telephone courtesy is certainly one of the plus values a passenger enjoys in doing business with the airlines. A person accustomed to something else is almost embarrassed when he first experiences the friendly helpfulness of the airline agent.

Here are some suggestions adapted from telephone companies' employee-instruction books and other sources for telephone usage in a church office. Most of these are probably routine practice in the offices and homes of readers, but since gross violations are found frequently in places where they are least expected, they are included.

When the phone rings, it speeds the ensuing conversation if your

TELEPHONE AND POST OFFICE WORK FOR THE CHURCH

answer eliminates what would otherwise be the first two questions. Assure the caller that he is connected with the desired number and identify yourself: "First Presbyterian—Charlotte O'Neal speaking."

If the church secretary answers and the minister is wanted, the worst thing is to say, as so often is heard, "Who is it?" or "Who is calling?" or "What is the call about?" or "I'll have someone else help you."

If she has to protect the pastor (warning: too much protection is often a boomerang), she would do better to say, "I'm sorry. Dr. Marsh will not be able to receive any calls until noon. I'll be glad to take your name and number and he will call you then, or if you'd rather not wait, I'll do my best to help you."

"May I Tell Him Who's Calling?"

When the pastor is wanted, a courteous request on the part of the secretary is, "May I tell him who's calling, please?" When the secretary announces the call to the minister, telling the name gives him a moment to collect his thoughts with reference to the person calling and enables him as he picks up the phone to address the caller by name.

Incidentally, this polite inquiry by the secretary may make it possible for her to save the minister's time in cases where she may know the answers. For example, when the caller gives his name, the secretary may say, "Oh, yes, Mr. Griffith, Dr. Marsh received your message. He told me to tell you if you called that he is planning to attend your dinner next Tuesday night and will be glad to say a few words." This will probably satisfy Mr. Griffith, but if he still wants to speak to the minister, no unnecessary barriers should be put in his way.

It is always irritating to one phoning to be transferred from one party to another. Avoiding this if the person receiving the call can take care of the request is good policy. If doing so involves a brief absence from the phone to consult a reference book or to query another staff member, it is well to say, "This will take three or four minutes. Will you wait, or would you prefer to have me call you back?"

People hate to be left dangling at the end of a dead phone. It always seems longer to the one idly waiting, particularly when smothering in a phone booth, than it seems to the person scrambling through the pages of a directory in search of an elusive address.

A HANDBOOK OF CHURCH PUBLIC RELATIONS

There is one discourtesy that a pastor with sensibilities would never commit, although he is often the victim of it. This is for a secretary to put through a call for someone, perhaps on long distance, then not to be ready instantly to take it when the connection is complete. The man at the other end does not enjoy waiting. In fact, if he is busy, he will probably hang up.

In public relations circles there is a true story of a big corporation president who engaged a public relations firm. A few days later the PR man had a call placed to his new client but was not ready to talk when the president answered. He kept him waiting a few minutes.

The PR counselor was immediately fired. "Obviously he is a poor public relations man to treat anyone like that," the president said in justifying his action.

In general it is regarded as courteous to let the caller hang up first. Occasional telephone users, of course, have not mastered the art of concluding. They need a bit of co-operation in terminating.

This co-operation must be given tactfully and the "good-by" spoken in a pleasant voice. Even though the lengthy call is a thoughtless, unreasonable invasion of one's time, it is unfortunate to be patient all the way through only to spoil it by an ungracious ending.

Reaching Your Families by Tele-Corps

Don't overlook the telephone's primary purpose of conveying a message instantaneously in emphasizing their important incidental use in building good will. Get your money's worth out of this priceless blessing.

Two hundred million phone calls are made each day in this country. The church will of course use the phone for its usual business purposes, but its potentials as an instrument of human contact must not go unused. The phone is a communications medium.

Telephones are effective as last-minute reminders. They are a good means to persuade officials to attend important meetings. Letters can be overlooked or tucked in pigeon holes and remain unanswered. It is harder to duck a phone call.

It may be easier to write a letter asking someone to take on a church job, but the chances of getting a favorable decision are greater in the give and take that the telephone makes possible.

Good executives have heavy phone bills and a correspondingly high batting average. People who get things done are on the phone several hours each day.

Many churches divide and subdivide their membership lists to form tele-corps. By such a marshaling of forces the entire constituency is reached with special messages inside of a few hours.

Such a telephone brigade is open to many forms of organization. Ordinarily a military plan is followed. The church families might be divided into five battalions with a major at the head of each. The battalion may be divided into five companies with a captain over each. The companies may be further divided into five platoons, each headed by a lieutenant. The names of persons not named as officers constitute the platoon membership. They may be divided among the lieutenants.

Mimeographed lists of names, addresses, and telephone numbers of those in each battalion should be put in the hands of all the officers of that battalion. These should be arranged according to the organizational pattern of the tele-corps.

Put the plan into operation by a call from the pastor or the church secretary to the five majors, giving the message that is to be conveyed to all the church families. Each major passes the message on to the five captains in the battalion. The major takes responsibility for a captain's calls if that captain is unreachable or temporarily prevented from serving.

The captains in turn call their lieutenants. By the time the lieutenants have called their lists of families, 780 homes have been notified. No one has made more than five calls, except those who might have handled some other person's assignment.

Adapt the amount of subdivision to the size of your church. Using majors and captains reaches 155 families, while dividing each unit four times reaches 340 families, with each person making only four calls.

Art of Letter Writing

One of the fundamental forms of communications is the letter. Letter writing is an ancient art. Egyptians in the fourteenth century B.C. mailed clay tablets to each other conveying messages in hieroglyphics. If the modern minister received his daily quota of letters in that form, he could presently provide enough bricks to pave the church parking lot.

Correspondence when faced in one mood is a bugbear. By the time you have answered the letters that need attention, a new batch has come in.

Thought of another way, letter writing is one of the most effective methods of expressing friendship and building loyalty to the church. While face-to-face contacts have advantages, the interview—no matter how satisfactory—slips into memory and grows dim.

The letter, however, remains. There must be millions of missives written by pastors that are now preserved in drawers, treasure boxes, and Bibles. Brought out from time to time, they reassure the recipient of the interest and concern in them that prompted the letter.

A good letter is written with the reader in mind. To be most effective, it must center about his ideas, his viewpoint, and his convictions. Regardless of how highly the recipient values you, his immediate concern is himself.

Correspondence specialists warn against two letter writers' diseases: "I-trouble" and "We-itis." Try to think when you write that "I" and "me" and "we" and "mine" are offensive words to the recipient. (This of course may not literally be true, but it will help to keep oriented.)

The so-called "You-ability" of letters is not attained simply by the frequent use of the word "you." It is accomplished rather by a genuine interest in and concern for the reader on the part of the writer.

Keep asking yourself not how does this letter look to me but how will it sound to the person who reads it. Try to talk with or to a correspondent, not at him.

Conversational Letters

Letters should be conversations. This means the end of the old formulas. You would laugh in the face of anyone who came into your office and said, "Yours of the 15th inst. received and contents noted." There is no reason to be unnatural when communicating by letter.

What has been said about personal letters is even more pertinent when it comes to preparing the many form letters that churches mail to their entire lists. Somehow a friendly "tone of voice" must be packed into such letters to keep them from sounding impersonal.

More important than vocabulary, grammar, or logic are the emotional overtones, the feeling that the writer likes us. In conversation gestures, pauses, facial expressions, and stress all help the spoken sentences to communicate ideas. In letter writing these aids are not available.

There are others, however, that compensate for this lack. You can give variety to the monotonous lines of a form letter by underscoring words, by indenting for quotations, or by setting apart a sentence or two you wish to make stand out. You can make some paragraphs just a sentence or two long. You can use exclamation points and capitals (sparingly—they are harder to read).

Letters should have eye appeal. Make them look clean. Use a second sheet to avoid crowding too much on one page.

The appearance of a letter should reflect the character of the institution that is sending it out. Adequate white space makes the letter more attractive and also encourages the reader to finish it.

In planning the letter, first ask yourself exactly what it is you are trying to do. Clarify your objective. Then tell the reader as simply as you can just what it is you want him to do or to know, keeping in mind his own interests and point of view.

Length of the Letter

It should be long enough to make its point and short enough not to discourage reading. It is a fallacy to say that it must be brief. If it can accomplish its purpose in few words, it should be no longer than this minimum.

The letter must not be dull; it must not be wordy. It ought not to generalize or to exhort. If you can keep your letter interesting and there is a reason for doing so, it may be longer perhaps than you expected. You have doubtless received two- or three-page sales letters from some of our sharpest magazines.

These sales managers know what they are doing. This is mentioned not to justify verbosity, which is never warranted. But if you need to explain situations, if you can keep your letters readable and "You-able" throughout, let them tell their tales to the end. Long letters obviously require more effort, both in the writing and in the editing. Each sentence must say something. All padding—each word that can be spared—must be blue-penciled.

Postscripts are particularly useful. Readers are likely to glance at the signature before they start the letter. They see the postscript and read it first. But it is not wise to put the "pitch" of the letter into the postscript because the reader may think he has already found the purpose of the letter and fail to read the main body. Put something in the postscript that will whet his curiosity about what the letter says.

Series of letters build up interest in the projects they promote. The Westwood Community Church in Los Angeles carried on a direct-mail campaign involving seven weekly mailings. No direct response was asked for until the last letter. The promotion centered about the headline, "Church for Sale." The cost, including postage, was less than $2,000. The amount raised was $180,000.

A Wisconsin church asked several of its laymen each to write the copy for one of a series of post cards to be mailed weekly over the signatures of their writers to the constituency. The cause promoted was church attendance.

Don't hesitate to make a fresh approach. An original method of conveying an idea may make a letter unforgettable.

An illustration of this is one mailed by *Time* during World War II to a million prospects. The edges of the letters were burned after having been brushed with kerosene. The charred page, when removed from the envelope, read: "The Nazi flame is licking the coasts of England."

Direct-mail specialists go so far as to believe that the kind and color of stamps used in mailings make a difference in the response. Tests show that commemorative stamps, if used immediately following issue, will increase results. Other factors being equal, purple stamps or purple meter markings get most attention.

One would naturally expect first-class mail to produce the best results. This is the normal finding of tests. However, some studies of third-class mailings metered in purple ink proved that this combination pulled better than first-class mail.

While these tests are related to sales letters, the findings measure attention-getting powers of the letters. It would seem that these principles might apply equally well to mailings from churches.

With higher rates of postage it may pay to do some testing yourself. Send one mailing one way and others in other class mail with differing stamps. Decide which combinations are most effective for you.

TELEPHONE AND POST OFFICE WORK FOR THE CHURCH

To the Editor

Letters to editors, when the minister or some other spokesman of the church has something significant to say about a public issue, are often well worth writing. This method of communication reaches large areas of the public who are otherwise out of range of the voice of the church.

It is hardly gratifying to editorial writers, but surveys have shown that the letters published from persons who wish to have their points of view considered enjoy a better readership than the formal editorials.

Occasionally pastors write indignant protests against editorials or speeches or actions reported in the paper. Sometimes these letters are phrased during the heat of righteous wrath and mailed before the writer has returned to his normal, pacific state of mind. Letters written in such a mood, when they appear in the paper, usually make their writers wish they had used more moderate language.

Magazine editors agree that the most bitter, ill-spirited invective comes from ministers. There is, of course, a reason for this: the clerical complainants feel under a mandate to denounce sin, and they write in this mood. Gentlemen—and particularly Christians—are never justified in taking a name-calling, motive-questioning approach.

The average reader of such ill-natured outbursts is tempted to laugh at them and to regard the writers as intolerant cranks. His mind does not operate from the same premises as does the mind of the protestor.

"Nasty" letters hurt the reputation of the writer and of his profession. Courteous, well-reasoned protests are far more persuasive than illiberal tirades. Even if the argument does not convince, it is still regarded with respect.

The "letters" columns are used with considerable effect in correcting errors and misrepresentations of the church. Several religious bodies, notably Christian Scientists and Seventh-Day Adventists, are particularly well organized in this respect. Each local church has its committee to watch for misleading references about it in any of the media. Immediate letters, written in most courteous terms, are dispatched whenever an inaccuracy is spotted. The publication of the letter or of a correction almost always follows.

It took just one well-written letter, friendly in tone and devoid of threats or pressure, to secure from a British playwright the elimination of an offensive line in a play about to open in New York. In the play a religious fanatic seized with a vision rushed into the jungle without clothes and prayed for the deliverance of an artist's soul from hell.

This crazed eccentric was identified as a Seventh-Day Adventist. The letter to the author simply pointed out the discrepancies between the beliefs and practices of this church and those of the erratic zealot, suggesting that the author would surely want to take this inconsistency out of his play. The author apologized for his error and thanked the letter writer for the opportunity of setting the matter right.

Some of the most influential public relations accomplishments, for better or for worse, result from either good use or misuse of these everyday assistants, the telephone and the U. S. mail.

The odd side of it is that the deepest impressions will be made not by our more studied and planned campaigns but at times when we are least public relations conscious.

It was not so much the big scheduled events of Jesus' life that revealed the character that has drawn millions to him. It was instead the kindly, thoughtful things he did on the way to do something else. Many of these incidents are introduced in the gospels by the words "As he journeyed . . . ."

Church workers, as they journey through their daily routines, picking up a phone, dashing off a letter, will find that it is then and not in the big moments that they unconsciously reveal themselves and the true measure of their concern for their fellows.

CHAPTER XVIII

Sermon Titles Have Public Relations

"A ROSE BY ANY OTHER NAME WOULD SMELL AS SWEET," Juliet declared. What about sermons?—not that sermons smell, at least not many, though some seem a little musty. What about the names of sermons? Do titles make a difference?

Suppose pastors were to cease placing such a strain on their imagination each week and instead of inventing titles for their sermons started numbering them as certain composers do their productions—"Opus 3518." Would the congregation count suddenly drop? Would listeners go woolgathering more or less frequently? In other words, do sermon titles have public relations?

The children of this world can teach preachers much about the importance of giving alluring names to the products of their homiletic efforts.

Those family counsels at which expectant parents name the coming baby are as nothing compared with the proposals and counter-proposals of the advertising, sales, and publicity staffs of a firm about to launch the latest model or a new product. Indeed, back in the days when prospective parents searched the Bible rather than *Photoplay* magazine for suggestions for names for their offspring, a product which was to become an occupant of every kitchen shelf was itself named from the Bible and in a sense was christened during Sunday morning worship.

Mr. Gamble, a good Methodist, seated in his comfortable pew in a Cincinnati church, his mind no one knows where, heard the minister announce his text. It was the Forty-fifth psalm, verse eight: "Out of the ivory palaces, whereby they have made thee glad."

"That's it!" shouted the excited Mr. Gamble to himself. "Ivory—Ivory Soap! That's the name we've been looking for."

As the world knows, that's exactly what they called their new white floating soap. Mr. Gamble probably never sat through what seemed like a longer sermon, so great was his haste to get away and share with Mr. Procter this inspiration.

Titles

Publishers, with an eye to the best-seller list, almost invariably suggest improvements in the original names on accepted manuscripts, usually to the author's dismay as well as to his profit. Some changed titles on the famous Haldeman-Julius little five-cent blue books actually doubled sales.

Motion picture, radio, and drama producers hold lengthy and repeated conferences to find the best possible box-office name while their preparations proceed under a working title marked "tentative" on the script. Often they engage public opinion research firms to find which of several suggested titles has the greatest pull. The wrong title has caused many a production to close.

Commodities such as toiletries—perfumes in particular—seem to count largely on name and packaging for their sales. Some years ago a great hotel in New York changed its name because the management discovered that prospective visitors were not sure how to pronounce the name. They would hesitate, then give the taxi driver the name of another hotel rather than risk the embarrassment of mispronounciation.

Now and then a good product overcomes the handicap of a repulsive or inappropriate name by sheer superiority. The prize for this might well go to "Birdseye" frozen foods. A serving of birds' eyes, even on a lettuce leaf with French dressing, does not tempt the appetite. The textile connotation of "Birdseye" is no more appealing.

Aside from being distasteful, the name is somewhat misleading. My own impression on first seeing a display of the product was of a new diet for canaries—one that put a gay song in their throats, a new light in the bird's eye.

This example suggests that if your sermon is of outstanding quality, an inappropriate, misleading, or even repelling title will not overcome its virtues. Even then the chances are that its excellence will become known and appreciated by a larger number of people if it has a good title.

Isn't titling a literary production equivalent to baiting a hook? The title may, to be sure, serve the further purpose of identification; but even if that were your only purpose in giving your sermon a name, the name would still have the effect either of attracting or of repelling possible hearers.

A sermon title may attract a casual worshiper. It may appeal to his basic interests, promise to supply information on a subject about which he is curious, or offer a solution to a problem which has been troubling him.

Anticipation

The title also has a value to the person who can be depended upon to be at church regardless of the preacher or his subject. A well-phrased title can create in this man a sense of anticipation. It can help to make a more receptive hearer by stimulating thought on the theme in advance of the sermon.

In these days of church announcements and advertisements in newspapers, parish papers, direct mail appeals, and bulletin boards inside and outside, the minister who does not give his best thought to phrasing his sermon title loses potential hearers and fails to a degree to prepare those who do attend.

Select the right words. Public relations counselors give exacting attention to this. "Seat belts" on planes, for example, were at first called "safety belts," until someone pointed out that the newer name described the appliance equally well but avoided the suggestion of danger.

Compare the pulling power of two possible titles for a juvenile book, "Story Parade" or "Excerpts for the Young from the World's Great Literature." The first is a pair of words, both of which produce pleasant sensations in youth. The other is selected by someone obviously far removed from his own childhood.

The language of sermon titles varies from technical theological sesquipedalians to the latest jitterbug jargon. Perhaps one extreme is as bad as the other.

Scriptural language used in titles lends the spiritual authority of the Bible. Expository sermons can be named from the central thought of the passage. It is taking too much for granted, however, for the preacher to approach the exposition of a scripture passage on the assumption that the members of his congregation are at that very moment yearning to know the exegesis of the words and phrases of this particular chapter and verse.

Universal Problems

The minister is most likely to challenge the congregation's interest by announcing that he is dealing with a universal human problem.

Religious educators met the same situation by making lessons pupil-centered. The scripture not only held its place; it became even more cherished. It seemed to students less of a fetish and more of a living, applicable document. You can undoubtedly accomplish more in your exposition by answering a pertinent question which your sermon title has already raised.

Many good titles are quotations or parts of quotations. These may be taken from books, plays, poems, or familiar phrases from the vernacular. Samples of these are: "I Gave Them Christ," "Have a Heart," "Castles in Spain," "Consider the Lilies," "Jobs for Giants," and "Handle with Care."

Often a modified quotation is even better than the original. Consider the surprise element of: "The High Cost of Hating," "When the Roll Is Called Down Here," or "Making Molehills out of Mountains."

The late Dr. Conrad of Brimstone Corner, Boston, loved alliteration in his titles. "The Recoil of Repudiated Responsibilities" was one of his. Other alliterative titles are: "Bossism, Bolshevism, and Brotherhood," "Facing Failure with Faith," and "Residue Religion."

Rhyme and rhythm can be used to good effect, as in: "The Bible—Its Use and Abuse," "Loyal to the Royal in Ourselves," "A New Order or a New Ardor," "Learning Versus Earning."

Some balanced titles play on the sound or meaning of words: "Making the Indifferent Different," "The Importance of the Unimportant," "Roughing it Smoothly," "The Church's Business and the Business of the Church," "The Beast or the Best in Us," "The City of God and the God of the City," "World Christianity or World Catastrophe."

You can introduce contrast: "An Ancient Book in a Modern World" or "Truths That Are Lies."

How-to-do-it titles may be clumsy literary constructions, but they appeal. Books of this nature are perennial sellers, and sermons that promise to help the hearer accomplish something he has always wanted to do always draw listeners. "How to Conquer Your Fears," and "How to Live on Twenty-four Hours a Day" are typical.

Titles that make strong claims, that set forth in honest superlatives something that is biggest or oldest, have great pull. The most famous one is Drummond's sermon on love, which he called "The Greatest Thing in the World." Others of this kind are "God's Greatest Miracle" and "The Church of a Thousand Pastors."

You can arouse interest with a provocative question. "Has Civilization Outgrown the Bible?" "Shall We Change the Name of Grace Church?" "Christians and Others: Is there a Difference?"

A single word, if it is rich and suggestive, can make a good sermon title. "Dreamers," "Deserters," "Dawn," "Camouflage," and "Antiques" have all been used. Hundreds of others are at least as good.

A preacher in his laudable desire to avoid the trite and commonplace sometimes risks giving his sermon a title that lacks dignity completely or smacks of the super salesmanship that makes so many television commercials disgusting.

Despite the bad odor surrounding the words "sensational preaching," the danger is not of touching off sensations and arousing emotions. Sin's power grows out of the emotions it arouses. To combat sin, you must attack it on the battleground where human sensations are found.

A sermon title may, to be sure, be "sensational" in the sense that it is undignified, grotesque, or bizarre. Good taste and a sense of the "fitness of things" are always necessary. A suitable title for a musical comedy may be grossly out of place as a pulpit topic.

Isn't it possible, on the other hand, that in our effort to avoid the sensational we have too often been dull and lifeless?

Truth in Advertising

Another danger, to which I for one must plead frequently guilty, is that of concocting a title that is much better than the sermon itself turns out to be. Doubtless there are other penitents whose titles sometimes create an expectancy that the sermon does not fulfill.

A tricky title may lure people to church once. It will not do it again unless the churchgoers have heard a sincere, earnest effort to solve the problem the title has raised or to furnish the information that implicitly has been promised.

The only guarantee to the listener is the integrity of the preacher. The half hour spent listening to the sermon can never be returned if the homiletic goods are not as represented.

It is called the "sacred desk," but this does not mean that practices which would be of doubtful ethics outside the pulpit take on sanctity because they are practiced in the pulpit. This includes mislabeling homiletic merchandise.

The title has its important mission. It is well worth all the time it takes to think it through.

The thought you expend is repaid, if no other way, by its clarifying and impressing on your own mind what it is you really wish to communicate. When you are completely sure yourself, you will have little difficulty in getting through to the congregation.

But let no one be deceived. It is not the title but the sermon itself —backed by a consistent life and divine help—that instructs, inspires, convicts, invites, and converts.

CHAPTER XIX

Public Relations Pointers for Pastors

"Pray without ceasing, shave every day, and be prompt in your correspondence."

This formula for success in the ministry was the advice that the late Dr. George Butters of Boston gave in lectures to divinity students. A moment's reflection on these simple phrases reveals the discernment the modest symbols imply.

"Pray without ceasing" includes all that is involved in a minister's own personal, spiritual life. It is the minister's number-one requirement.

"Shave every day" carries with it implications of much more than the regular application of razor and lather to the cheeks and chin. It suggests that being a minister means being a gentleman, a person of sensibilities, of good taste and refinement. The same consideration of others that he shows in not offending them with grisly facial stubble will lead him to set a pattern in dress, in congeniality, and in good manners generally.

"Be prompt in your correspondence" symbolizes the whole area of a minister's business procedures—his self-management, the conduct of his office, the keeping of church records, the preparation of reports, and the meeting of personal obligations.

The striking fact about this simplification of the characteristics that constitute a good Christian minister is that two of the three are clearly in the area of public relations.

Dependence on Good Public Relations

Ministers carry an appalling responsibility. To many people they are the church.

The minister may disclaim this idea himself, but the fact that he carries a religious title and is in most cases the only full-time church employee makes him seem to be the personification of the institution he represents. What this involves in his personal character and in his qualities of spiritual leadership, although of supreme importance, is not for this book.

The fact that a minister cannot separate himself from his vocation has significant public relations aspects. Arthur Krock in his column in *The New York Times* once wrote that "among the anomalies of the American scene is that public relations is an art which often is comprehended least by those who most depend upon its sound practice."

This is not quoted because of any suspicion that ministers do not understand good public relations. Probably no other profession is as genuinely concerned in the well-being and happiness of followers than the ministry.

Krock's sentence does, however, mention certain persons "who most depend" on good public relations. Clearly ministers, if anyone, belong in that category.

A Pastor's Inward Look

Every minister has noted in churches of which he was once pastor, when returning for a visit or when reading their parish publications, that there are now among the active workers persons who did not respond to his own ministry. Likewise he realizes that in his present church there are those who seem to have been dormant during his predecessor's pastorate but who have come to life during his.

Probably much of the cause of situations like this is in the realm of the intangible. However, a minister might do well to do some soul searching and, perhaps, a little questioning of trusted friends to learn whether he has attitudes or mannerisms that without his knowledge tend to keep him from getting close to certain people or even to estrange them.

Jesus himself, it might be remembered, in order that he might know the best approach to make to people conducted a kind of inquiry. "Whom do men say that I am?" he asked his intimates.

For a pastor such a process of inquiry and self-examination could be carried to the point of morbidity. If he is the teachable kind, though, he may discover some aspect of his own public relations which, if changed, may increase his influence.

Members lose interest in the church and drop activity in spite of the pastor's most faithful service. The aggregate number of losses in all churches for all reasons is appallingly large.

No pastor ought to feel comfortable in any case of developing disinterest unless his conscience is absolutely clear of sinful feelings of omission. Remember the series of letters you received from the last magazine whose subscription you dropped? What concern the publisher showed over losing just one subscriber!

Can a pastor content himself with less of an effort to dissuade a member from slipping into indifference?

The most significant loss is in the spiritual cooling-off experienced by inactive members who withdraw from the warmth of Christian fellowship. There are also consequences of negative public relations when members drop out. These if not the primary reasons are incentives for pastors to seek not merely to expand membership but also to hold the loyalty of those they have.

A growing church will increase much more rapidly if the loss out the back door is kept at a minimum.

Occasionally ministers sense that they have failed to achieve the same degree of esteem and loyalty with which some of their predecessors are remembered or that their neighboring pastors seem to enjoy.

Recall once more the southern bishop's observation that "given character and a modicum of ability, nine-tenths of a minister's success or failure can be charted in the field of his public relations."

Such a pastor, sincerely searching for what is wrong with himself, might be wise to start his introspection in this area. Here are some of the questions he might ask himself.

Do my laymen have the impression that I do not work as hard for my living as they do for theirs?

No doubt laymen expect a minister to devote his hours industriously to study, to pastoral work, and to church administration. They will concede some time for recreation, but there are definite limits to the amount they will approve. They dislike to see the pastor dawdling or loitering, particularly during the hours they themselves are at work.

Many pastors are overworked, it is true. Their hours extend late into the night. Week ends which relaxed lay people enjoy so much are periods of even tighter than usual tension for the minister and his family.

On the other hand, it is unquestionably true that some of the criticism of clergymen is deserved. Usually the pastor is not consciously skimping on his job. Many ministers need to study some books on personal efficiency. Were they to keep a record of the hours of each day for a week, the total time spent in productive service to the church and parish in many cases would seem shamefully small. Often this is the result of a distorted sense of values, with so much time given to unimportant things that could be delegated or even omitted that more important duties are left undone.

While I am not a blowhard, do my church members misconstrue things I say so that they think so?

This is worth exploring. Probably many ministers might have done as well in some other profession, or even better. It is not good public relations, however, nor should it really be necessary when it is true for a preacher to keep describing to his congregation the fabulous position he might now be holding if only he had chosen another vocation.

This possibility might do something for the parishioners' appreciation of their preacher if they discovered it for themselves. It can be stated categorically that the minister's saying this about himself will have a different effect. The inevitable reaction to the minister who makes such a statement is, "Maybe he could; maybe he couldn't," or "What's stopping him if that's what he wants to do?" or "Why blame us? We didn't decide his profession."

Another angle: travel, whenever it can be financed, should be part of a minister's experience and education. Some preachers, however, unwittingly allow these experiences to come between themselves and their members.

Whether the psychological reason is simple jealousy or something more complex, people who have never needed a passport suddenly register resistance when an ex-tourist pompously starts a sentence, "When I was abroad...." One board of deacons offered the minister a trip to Europe on the condition that he would not tell them about it when he returned.

The situation since World War II has vastly improved. Much wind has been taken out of the traveled minister's sails because the ex-GI's, a considerable proportion of his congregation, have traveled farther and stayed longer in foreign lands than he has. "Fly now, pay later" travel and reduced costs of transatlantic transportation have made it possible for many members of the church to benefit from a summer in Europe.

Certainly the preacher should not deny himself the opportunity to illustrate his sermons with experiences and observations growing out of his contacts with faraway parts of the world. There is an inoffensive way of doing this that should be thought out and mastered.

Could it be that my desire for an adequate salary is interpreted by my church board as avarice?

The minister is placed in a serious dilemma in the matter of his personal finances. He knows that he must maintain his financial integrity in the community or the church suffers. On the other hand, to do this may put him in the position of seeming to violate Paul's injunction not to be a money lover.

He has seen his colleagues, because of the easy credit extended ministers, become obligated beyond their income and in their frantic efforts not to hurt the church become victims of loan sharks. He knows that if he falls embarrassingly into debt, he not only scars his own reputation but hurts that of the ministry as a whole.

Tortured by these fears, ministers quite understandably have sometimes evidenced what looks to finance committees like an unreasonable concern for the adequacy of their salaries.

Many passages in scripture recognize a congregation's financial obligation to the preacher. Paul wrote the Galatians that "those who are taught must share all the blessings of life with those who teach them the Word." It is better that those charged with responsibility for the church budget relieve the pastor of any embarrassment by making as generous provision for his needs as they can.

Some committees may take the position that as long as the minister does not ask for more, the amount he is receiving is satisfactory. Under these circumstances it may be necessary for the pastor to present his financial needs frankly and fully.

All of the minister's public relations abilities will need to be mustered if this becomes necessary. He must not be demanding. Neither can he with self-respect be indifferent to the needs of his family.

Most ministers testify that salary increases that come in consequence of an unprompted vote of the finance committee are much more enjoyed than those that are sought by the minister. There is also a strongly held conviction that when a minister is giving himself devotedly to his work, the congregation is likely to do their best.

Thousands of successful ministers to whom salary increases have come as their needs have mounted never throughout their careers mention the subject of their compensation to church officers. It is also obvious that a balance in the treasury at the end of the year considerably facilitates the granting of an increased salary.

Barring hard times, no one is more responsible for that happy condition than the pastor.

Personalized Pastoral Remembrances

Most of us are sufficiently egocentric to appreciate the kind of thoughtfulness which is expressly for us. This is the reason many ministers regard their anniversary lists as one of their most important pastoral assets in the building up of a spirit of good will, Christian fellowship, and loyalty.

Were it necessary to give up one or the other, a wise pastor would sooner cease the use of Christmas greetings than of birthday remembrances.

Birthdays

One does not have to share his birthday with friends as he does the Fourth of July and New Year's. When we receive a Christmas card, we know that our name has been on someone's lengthy list. When our birthday is remembered, we know that we were thought of individually and singly.

No one can feel that the birthday cards were heaped upon a table, addressed and stamped by extra helpers, and mailed by the basketful, as everyone knows must be the case at Christmas.

The pastor can give to birthday greetings, distributed over 365 days, a personal touch which is impossible with the wholesale distribution of Christmas or Easter greetings. Incidentally the cost, when spread over a year, is trifling; but in a large parish the bill for cards and postage is overwhelming when faced at the expensive holiday season.

On your desk keep a file box containing a large card for every day of the year. Divide these by tab cards into monthly groups, with each filed in its proper order. Such outfits can be purchased at any stationer's or easily made at home. On the card for each day are listed those whose birthdays come that day, with street addresses and in the cases of children and older people the year of birth. Keep the box open on the desk as a reminder. When the necessary cards and notes have been written each morning for the following day, that card is slipped to the back of the box, and the one next to be used comes into place.

Wedding Anniversaries

Not only birthdays, but other anniversaries as well, are recorded on these file cards. From the church record and in pastoral visiting one can learn wedding anniversaries. These, when remembered by the pastor, are particularly appreciated, for comparatively few people know this date; and too often the parties themselves have overlooked its arrival until they receive a brief note of congratulation from the pastor. Usually there is something personal which may be said. Have these persons had a hard year? Have there been sorrows? An allusion to their Christian fortitude in meeting these trials is in place. Have their children accomplished something—were they graduated or promoted or did they appear publicly? If you are a parent, you know how you appreciate a reference to the success of your marital partnership at the point of maximum importance—the upbringing of your children.

At this point a word of caution might be offered, as the result of an unfortunate error on my part. In recording on my file marriage anniversary dates from the church record, I allowed for the possibility of second marriages. I did not want to congratulate Mr. Jones and his second wife on the anniversary of his first marriage, but on one occasion that is exactly what I did. Knowing the maiden name of the present wife, and finding on the church record that this was the name of the bride, I felt entirely comfortable. However, it turned out that the man after his first wife's death married her cousin of the same family name. Since they were good friends, I was forgiven.

Anniversaries of Sorrow

Ordinarily in these cases one would not go further back than the beginning of his pastorate. Anniversaries of bereavement are particularly hard for many people. They feel alone at these times and build up a consciousness of their loss. A note of sympathy from the pastor indicating that his thought is with them on this day, together with a suggestion of a scriptural passage of comfort, cannot fail to endear the church to those whose grief has been freshened by the return of the day.

One easily accumulates these dates by noting them on the proper card when he sits down at his desk to prepare for the funeral. Then automatically the card appears a year later, and the event is recalled.

In a new parish it is natural in going over a visiting list to note how long each member has been connected with the church. Reviewing these facts in pastoral conversation helps to get acquainted, is an improvement on small talk, and is likely to lead to deeper subjects.

If it is discovered that certain individuals are soon to arrive at the twenty-fifth or fiftieth year of church membership, one may look up the date on the church record, note it on the date card, and at the proper time send a note of congratulation and appreciation.

Obtaining Birth Dates

Getting the children's birth dates is easy, since if they are not already on the pupils' enrollment cards, you can ask the teacher to see that they are added either on the card or in the class book, suggesting for the sake of completeness that the children include their own birth dates, omitting the year if they wish.

It is not so easy to learn the older members' birthdays, although it is surprising how they pop out inadvertently in conversation. If the pastor in his interest in people makes note of them as they come up, he will soon develop a sizeable list. Then the members who revealed their own birthdays will have forgotten it and will wonder, when they receive the minister's greeting, how he knew. How many times have you heard elderly people say, "If I live till next March, I'll be eighty." All you need to say is, "Your birthday isn't on St. Patrick's day, is it?" Nine times out of ten you'll get what you want. "No, but I didn't miss it by much. It's the fifteenth."

One minister obtained the birth dates of his official members and later of members of his men's club by a little pardonable trickery. At an entertainment each was asked to fill in small blanks with his weight, the day and month of his birth, and his guess as to the total weight of the crowd. Someone totaled the weights, and a little prize was given for the nearest guess. This served as an icebreaker, provided the pastor with a list of birthdays to transcribe to his daily file cards, and everyone was so diverted by the weight guessing that no further thought was given to the birth dates.

At big church dinners or social gatherings cards can be similarly signed, then those born in the same month can be asked to sit at the same table or to prepare an impromptu stunt or program feature. Although the registration cards would not be necessary to carry out such a program, the fact that the months were used later in the program made their use seem logical.

There are several ways to remember birthdays in addition to the ordinary birthday card. Probably a handwritten note, containing a warm, personal greeting is best of all. Use a special notepaper for that purpose, on which a few sincere words fill the small page and convey the greeting effectively. It costs less to send a letter than a card, and it is much more appreciated. Allusions to recent joys or sorrows, triumphs or defeats, can be made to personalize the message.

A calendar which contains the birthdays of the great is suggestive in writing to children. If a lad is born on Franklin's birthday, perhaps he does not know it; and some allusion to the fact may be made which will be both pleasing to the child and inspirational.

When you use cards, try to make them as personal as you can by writing on them. They can be purchased in quantity from some of the church and school supply houses at extremely low prices. "Happy Birthday" buttons, which cost less than cards, are also available. For little folks one can write a brief message on a correspondence card, pin the button to the card, and enclose both in an envelope. These are much appreciated.

There are particular birthdays which are worth a special comment in your birthday notes, if you have the year of birth. On a twelfth birthday you can make reference to the boy Christ and quote the passage concerning his growth in wisdom and in stature and in favor with God and man. Rightly done, this can bring a sense of identity with Christ to a boy just turned twelve. At thirteen comment upon the satisfaction and the responsibility of being in the teens. At eighteen and twenty-one, those great days of "coming of age" for girls and boys, give a word of pastoral counsel on being a Christian citizen. At twenty-five a "quarter of a century is past." A young man of the right kind might be reminded on his thirtieth birthday that it was then in Christ's life that he began his ministry of service to the world. At thirty-five the "threescore years and ten" are half gone. "To the work!"

Older folks often think they are forgotten and that their years are a handicap to them. A greeting which implies that another birthday is a new honor will please and encourage the aged.

Finding Time

Naturally one asks the question: "Where can I find time for all these personalized remembrances?" Another question answers the first—"Is there any better use of pastoral time outside the direct personal evangelism and ministry to the sick and the sorrowing?"

In the time it takes to make a single pastoral call, one can after a little experience write a dozen or more notes and cards which will be cherished long after a call is forgotten and will arrive at a time when the recipient is particularly responsive to personalized attention.

There is no substitute for pastoral calling. It is one of the primary public relations activities of the minister, but personalized pastoral remembrances, the recognition that a pastor makes of individuals as such, makes the calling when it is done more effective. It helps the person to realize that the pastor's interest in coming is personal as well as professional. It helps him to know that the minister is there as a helpful, interested friend and not simply because while calling on that street he has arrived at that house.

If God is personal, should not his ministers endeavor to render in his name a personal ministry of helpful, friendly interest and concern for every soul committed to their charge?

CHAPTER XX

A Live Public Relations Committee

It is clear that the more complex our designs for living become, the more necessary it is that the public relations of all organizations be under the studied, centralized control and direction of competent persons. Churches are no exception to this rule.

Public Relations Committee: How Many and Who?

Local churches differ in organizational patterns so much that any suggestions made here as to the desirable number on a public relations committee might be wrong for a particular church.

Such a committee can be broken down into at least six subdivisions.

Were a member assigned responsibility for each one, the minimum number would of course be six.

However, many churches like to have this committee as representative of the whole church as possible. In this case certain persons are selected on the basis of their competence in the general field of public relations, others because of experience and knowledge of one or more of the media to be employed, still others because they are the publicity chairmen of constituent groups and organizations.

Certainly if possible someone with actual experience with the working press should be on the committee. Lacking this, someone should be chosen whose college years included a course in news writing. A teacher of high-school journalism would be well qualified.

Preferably the person to represent radio and TV interests should have worked in this field or studied the uses of these media. If someone who has not been well schooled in these areas is given responsibility for them, select a person of the type who will inform himself through books and direct contacts with newspaper offices and broadcasting studios.

Here is a recipe for a church public relations committee that has some merit: an older person with a good memory of the church; a high-schooler with crazy ideas but with ambition and drive; the church secretary, who knows what is going on; a trustee who knows about the property and the resources of the church; an amateur poster artist; a shutterbug; a mimeographer of skill; a newspaper person; a radio-TV person; and the publicity chairmen of all organized groups in the church.

Meaning of Public Relations

The best assurance that your church public relations committee will do a successful job is for the committee members themselves first to come to some agreement as to what they mean by "public relations." Next, they should formulate their objectives. Later they can list and allocate responsibilities.

There are endless definitions of public relations—some simple, some involved. One corporation explained it to its employees thus: "What everybody in our company does to earn—or lose—the public's good will." This conception easily transfers to a church setting.

Another brief definition says that public relations is "everything involved in achieving a favorable opinion." Frequently quoted by

PR men is this simplification: "Doing a good job and getting credit for it."

More scholarly efforts to explain what is involved in public relations are these. "The art of analyzing, influencing and interpreting a person, idea, group or business so that its behavior will conform to the greatest possible degree with public interest." "Public relations is a management function which evaluates public attitudes, identifies the policies of the individual or organization with the public interest and executes a program of action to earn public understanding and acceptance." *

I regret that I am not able to credit all of these definitions to their originators. The phrases and ideas, however, are all more or less the common property of the profession, and each publicist makes his own arrangement of them as he defines public relations.

One excellent definition which can be credited is that of Professor Stewart Harral of the University of Oklahoma, a writer on college pubic relations who has made an equally great contribution to church public relations. "Public relations," he says, "is a social science which seeks to bring about a harmony of understanding between any group and the public it serves and upon whose good will it depends."

For the purposes of this book I have stated earlier my belief that all the definitions can be boiled down to "making friends for Christ and his church."

Exactly what words the church committee on public relations chooses to define its field of responsibility is not as important as that the matter be given thorough consideration and that the members come to one mind about what it is they are to do. Particularly it should become clear in the discussion that public relations means vastly more than "press agentry" and "publicity."

Their common conviction should be that basic to all public relations procedures is the Christian character and practice of those who compose their church. The reputation of the church must, in the end, be measured by the service it renders to individuals, to the community, and to the world.

General Objectives

The second logical step for the church public relations committee is the formulation of objectives. At this stage this should be done in general terms. Later on you can list specific duties and suggest a division of responsibilities.

* *Public Relations News.*

It is better to work out your own objectives as a committee. You might begin this with the "brain-storming" technique. Each committee member will make suggestions as they pop into his head. Neither participants nor chairman will make any evaluation of comments at this time. Every contribution is written down or tape recorded as it is made. The same method is good for listing "things to be done."

This procedure is designed simply to stimulate the flow of ideas. Not until after the brain-storming session is over will ideas—no matter how wild—be weighed. Spontaneity and lack of inhibition must be fostered. Later meetings can pass judgment on the merit of the ideas put forth at this session.

In determining general objectives, you may wish to assign certain ones priority, depending upon the areas of greatest need. One or two public relations activities may already be very well handled. Direct your committee's attention first to points where little or nothing is being done, or where a negative situation needs attention.

Here are a few suggested objectives you may wish to consider when your committee formulates its general goals. They are the author's "brain-storming" and are not evaluated or organized. Some suggestions overlap and duplicate others. Toss around any of them you like with the results of your own brain-storming. Then work out a statement of objectives that meets your own church situation.

To help the public know our church is alive and doing vital things.
To add to the church's reputation.
To merit public understanding and acceptance.
To find ways of discovering and welcoming newcomers.
To encourage contributions.
To help people who don't go to church understand what churches are really like.
To promote acquaintance and fellowship among members.
To prevent misunderstandings and misinterpretations.
To change people's queer ideas about churches and churchgoers.
To win deeper loyalty of constituency.
To bring more people under the influence of the church.
To plan projects providing every member with something to do.
To win public friendship for our church.
To make the whole congregation public relations conscious.
To make our church attractive to people.

To learn public attitude to our church through surveys and research.

To analyze the several publics of our church and to adapt our interpretation of the church to each public.

To create a favorable climate for evangelism.

To learn why people come to church and to do more of it.

To learn why people neglect church and to try changing what it is that keeps them away.

The following six areas of public relations, with numerous subtopics not included here, were phrased as a proposal for a state-wide denominational public relations program. They may furnish suggestions for a statement of objectives.

I. Commend the church to the public by the loyalty of its members.

II. Make the church plant attractive outside and inside and worthy to be called the "House of God."

III. Make adequate use of tasteful printed and mimeographed matter.

IV. Educate the constituency in a knowledge of the denomination and of the ecumenical movement.

V. Make maximum use of the daily and weekly press.

VI. Develop understanding and co-operation with local radio and TV stations and with denominational and interdenominational sources of audio-visual recordings for both broadcast and local church use.

General-Policy Principles of Committee

Before laying out the detailed projects to be undertaken, set up some guiding principles of the public relations committee. Determine and announce to the governing body of your church the broad policies under which you plan to operate.

Here are suggestions that with others of your own might make up your list:

To set and maintain a regular schedule of meetings of the Public Relations committee in order that changing situations may be met as they develop and be provided for without delay.

To maintain impartiality in dealing with all news outlets.

To endeavor to provide fair and proportionate public relations assistance to each group within the church.

To work through, and not bypass, properly constituted officers and committees of the church when public relations objectives lie within areas for which others are responsible.

To participate so far as possible in all local co-operative efforts to advertise and promote church life, doing this not only for its results in our own church but also as a testimony to the basic oneness of the Christian community.

To work in co-operation with similar public relations agencies of our denomination.

To aid our church community and city to obtain full advantage of the Religion in American Life (RIAL) November, and continuing, national advertising campaign in the interest of churchgoing.

To see that the appreciation of our church is made known to those whose media have been used in disseminating our news.

Public Relations Subcommittees and Their Duties

Some public relations committees will prefer to operate as a whole and to rotate duties among members, giving attention to their tastes and qualifications. Other committees will wish to organize into somewhat independent subcommittees, each with rather well-defined responsibilities.

Certainly in a larger church the second plan is to be recommended. At first glance it may seem from the number of interests listed that the public relations committee is out to reorganize the church and to usurp the authority of others. Many of the "duties" listed below are regularly constituted functions of special officials, boards, commissions, and committees. There is no intention to disturb any of this.

The mention of several of these responsibilities in connection with this committee is made because each is one of the elements composing the total public relations impact that the church is making on its several publics. This puts them into the purview of the PR committee.

Should there be a breakdown noticeable at any of these points so that the church loses influence or reputation, the public relations committee has the duty of consulting those who are responsible in the area of failure and of encouraging them to bring about the desired change.

If this approach does not succeed, the next step is to bring the matter tactfully before the governing body of the church for action. In cases of this kind the committee, putting into practice its best public relations manners, becomes a gentle agitator.

For example, painting a church is ordinarily a function of the trustees. Listing "paint-up and clean-up campaigns" among the concerns of the PR committee does not mean any shifting of responsibility. If the lack of paint is making a church shabby and run-down, it is the function of the committee to create a desire on the part of fellow members that it be painted and to build up a willingness among them to help finance the enterprise.

The committee's responsibility is that of a gadfly. The duty of the trustees to contract the painters and to raise the money remains unchanged. In areas where the responsibility belongs to others, the public relations committee serves only to point out needs and to offer co-operation in securing changes and improvements.

The following six subcommittees are suggested, along with a list of duties that might properly be assigned to each. Of course nothing is inflexible about this proposal. Every committee should feel free to adapt its internal organization to the needs of the particular church it is serving.

Perhaps your committee will choose to combine some of these subcommittees or to reallocate certain duties here assigned to one subcommittee to another to which it seems more appropriate. Several of these borderline duties might be handled as well by one as by another.

SUBCOMMITTEE ON PRESS RELATIONS

Appoint one person through whom all press contacts are to be made and an assistant to serve in his absence.

Instruct news source within each organization to release only through this press chief.

Maintain file of brief biographical materials on pastor, organization presidents, and other leaders.

Maintain file of photos of pastor, leading local leaders, and top denominational leaders of your conference. Include church activity and human interest pictures.

Watch for feature-story subjects. Write and release, or tip off reporters.

A HANDBOOK OF CHURCH PUBLIC RELATIONS

Watch participation of your church members in wider denominational and interchurch events. Publicize locally.

Appoint a church historian to keep scrapbook of newspaper clippings about church and church members.

Stimulate courteous letters to editors in cases of the church being misrepresented or misinterpreted.

Stimulate expressions of appreciation for services rendered the church by the news media.

SUBCOMMITTEE ON TELEVISION, RADIO, AND FILMS

Become familiar with sources of audio-visual materials and of subjects available. Encourage church organizations to use what would be helpful.

Take charge of all visual-aid projection in church. Promote purchase of adequate and efficient equipment.

Take responsibility for providing and utilizing tape recorder.

Promote installation of public address system if needed.

Promote use of interdenominational church attendance trailers in local theaters.

Promote use on local stations of religious TV films and radio recordings prepared by denominations and/or interchurch bodies.

Promote the scheduling by affiliated local broadcast stations of nation-wide religious programs available from their networks.

Co-operate with local council of churches and ministerial association on radio-TV committee.

Encourage local stations to use Religion in American Life church promotion film clips and radio tapes and scripted announcements.

Promote and help finance documentary film of your church for annual meeting made by amateur photographer.

Encourage still photographers to take human interest and news pictures for use on local TV stations.

Arrange for TV or radio interviews with visiting speakers whose experience, special knowledge, or important position give them news interest.

Arrange for the showing of the Martin Luther film and similar films dramatizing the lives of your own denominational founders such as John Wesley and Roger Williams.

Stimulate letters of appreciation to station managers for time donated to religious programs.

SUBCOMMITTEE ON PRINTING AND LITERATURE

Supervise and promote parish paper.

Take responsibility for Sunday bulletin.

See that correct and complete mailing lists are maintained.

A LIVE PUBLIC RELATIONS COMMITTE

Prepare and circulate yearbook, including annual reports.

Prepare and distribute promotional view book for newcomers illustrating church activities.

Publish church directory, listing members, officials, and organizations.

Purchase or publish pew cards for visitor registration.

Help design special printed promotional pieces such as blotters, bookmarks, invitations, knob hangers, bumper cards, car cards, and others.

Consider desirability of printing pastor's sermons in handy pamphlet form and if approved, take responsibility for carrying out.

Maintain book table and literature racks.

Supervise securing and distributing promotional literature from denominational boards, such as missions, stewardship, education, evangelism, temperance, Christian social relations, and so on.

Co-operate with finance committee in preparing every-member canvass literature.

Promote circulation of denomination's magazines.

SUBCOMMITTEE ON ADVERTISING

Decide your church policy on paid newspaper advertising. In co-operation with pastor prepare copy and contract for space.

Join with other churches of your denomination in co-operative newspaper advertising.

Utilize Religion in American Life material (300 Fourth Avenue, New York 10, N. Y.) for promoting church attendance.

Organize a telephone corps to reach quickly the entire church with special announcements.

Prepare exhibits and displays.

See that colored souvenir post-card pictures of your church are on sale in local stores.

Provide at cost Christmas cards with photo or drawing of your church—also correspondence folders.

Consider billboard advertising, either independently or in co-operation with other churches and church bodies.

Co-operate with other churches in publishing a joint leaflet of information for strangers and newcomers about the churches of your community.

Consider use of flyers advertising church services for large scale distribution. Make sure they are dignified and in good taste.

SUBCOMMITTEE ON CHURCH PLANT AND EQUIPMENT

Maintain standards of immaculate housekeeping.

Guarantee well-kept lawns and landscaping.

See that buildings are painted and kept in good repair.

Encourage satisfactory lighting, within and without.
Develop floodlighting possibilities.
Promote memorial tower chimes or carillon, if there is none.
Take responsibility for sign boards: identifying, informational, directional.
Provide and service indoor bulletin boards.
Foster church lending library.
Inspect rest rooms frequently.
Provide wheel chair for comfort of aged and invalids.
See that broken and torn hymnals are repaired.
Promote provision of adequate storage space and trucks for handling tables and chairs. Don't let your parlor be a warehouse.

SUBCOMMITTEE ON HOSPITALITY

Organize regular visitation of members beyond the every-member canvass. Don't let members say "they're interested only when they want money."

Contact absentees during the week to learn of illnesses and other emergencies.

Organize "greeters" to supplement ushers.

Conduct "get-acquainted coffee hours" following services.

Provide guest book with attendant.

Plan occasional congregation registrations at which all present sign a card and drop it in offering plate. This provides names for follow-up and is a check on members' addresses.

Maintain liaison with Welcome Wagon hostess to learn of newcomers. See that hostess uses leaflet of information about community churches developed by advertising committee.

Place framed invitations to services in hotels, depots, YMCA, and YWCA. One pastor wrote personal letters on Saturdays addressed to names on local hotel registry books, inviting strangers in town to come to his church or another church of their choice.

See that the sick and hospitalized are visited if they can receive visitors. Encourage "get-well" cards.

Organize car pools to bring elderly members to services.

Explore the possibility of reduced-rate or free taxi service for churchgoers.

Maintain close relations with college and theological students and young people in the armed forces.

Plan social occasions at holiday season when students are home.

Survey social needs of church. Is there need for new interest groups, such as musical, camera, dramatic, athletic, recreational?

Contact members who have moved away for special occasions.

Arrange reunions, "old home" Sundays, and Founders' Days.
Provide drinking fountains as needed.
Provide and supervise nursery.
Supply church with first-aid kit and equipped medicine cabinet.

Persons responsible for the organization of church public relations committees and for sparking them to action will find all time given to clarifying and formulating objectives an excellent investment.

A wide division of duties involving as many persons as possible, both within and outside the committee, is in itself good public relations. This is particularly true if the persons assigned responsibility are not the "old faithfuls" but members and attendants who have hitherto had no specific duties.

One further continuing service that this committee can render may, perhaps, be its most useful one. Without using the words "public relations" or slinging any slogans or exhibiting any charts or attempting to be professional about it, the committee can quietly pervade the whole church with a genuine, friendly family feeling.

Courtesies extended as a part of a self-conscious public relations program often lack the most important ingredient. There must be in both the motivation and the execution a genuine love for people and a deep-seated, Christlike concern for their well-being.

CHAPTER XXI

Getting Personal About Public Relations

WHAT IS THE BEST FORM OF PUBLICITY FOR OUR CHURCH?
No public relations counselor, however enthusiastic he might be for a particular medium, would hesitate a moment in answering this question. The whole profession is unanimous—*word-of-mouth publicity*. This is the most effective.

More powerful than gimmicks and gadgets is personal testimony. Incidentally, it is also the least expensive medium. Many an advertising and public relations campaign has as its direct object not immediate sales but the stimulation of favorable conversation about a product. This in turn does the selling and does it more effectively.

GETTING PERSONAL ABOUT PUBLIC RELATIONS

Is it not anomalous that about the time that modern advertising agencies began in a big way to publish personal endorsements to promote the sale of merchandise and services, the evangelical churches which had long made conspicuous and successful use of personal testimony began to abandon it? Whether dropping out "testimonies" and "experience meetings" from the church schedule was good or bad may be debatable, but whatever the reasons, none of them applies to a Christian talking favorably about his church to his friends and neighbors.

Texans, Californians, and Floridians are not noticeably shy in saying a good word for their states when occasion arises. Indeed they have even been known to create opportunities to give their personal testimonies. They all seem to be born WOMPs, believers in Word-of-Mouth Publicity. Why should Presbyterians or Baptists or Methodists hang back in telling people about the attractions of their church homelands, of the enjoyment, the enrichment, and the strength for living that they find there?

Important as are all the media and techniques that have been described in earlier chapters, churches could, and indeed do live, and sometimes thrive without them. But denied word-of-mouth publicity the church would languish and die.

Protestantism in Spain is an example. In this country the law denies to Protestant churches all use of the usual methods of communication. Regulations require the churches to be inconspicuous and architecturally unidentifiable. No sign or symbol is permitted either directional or to mark the building as a church.

Public notices either as posters or in newspapers are forbidden. Completely dependent on word-of-mouth publicity, the devoted church members take it upon themselves to notify one another of services and activities and to invite the attendance of those they would like to interest.

That these churches are maintaining their vitality by word-of-mouth publicity alone suggests two conclusions. First, that this simplest of all forms of communication is basic and indispensable. It is so important and productive that its use should undergird the employment of every other medium.

Second, were we to utilize the word-of-mouth method as faithfully as do these Spanish Protestants, then employ all the other communication methods available to us, we would be compelled to double the number of our churches. We would clarify the vague and distorted conceptions of our purposes and programs which others sometimes have. The resultant enlarged respect and status of the church would make its contribution to social, economic, and political life highly influential.

Good Rumor Man

It would be difficult to overestimate the power of word-of-mouth publicity. A well-researched study was made by David J. Jacobson, published under the intriguing title "The Affairs of Dame Rumor." In it he revealed the ways in which persons have organized the launching and transmission of rumors destructive of the reputations of products and of persons.

In war rumor is a weapon. In finance it is a tool often used to facilitate unscrupulous manipulation. At election times it feeds prejudices to influence voting. In salesmanship it is often fraudulently used to undermine the competition.

Here is a ridiculous example of the way in which rumor seems deliberately to have been circulated to serve a cause. In the fall of 1948 it was almost impossible to dislodge from the minds of Brooklyn school children the belief that if Thomas Dewey were elected president, they would have to go to school on Saturdays.

Happily the tremendous power of rumor can be directed to the advancement of good causes quite as easily as for dubious ones, and perhaps better. When so used, it gains the propulsive power of truth.

The mathematics of rumormongering, whether for a good or for a questionable cause, is incredible until you take out your pencil and verify the statistics.

The possibilities of person-to-person communications are breathtaking. Suppose ten members begin on noon Sunday to talk about the warm, friendly atmosphere at Old First Church. If each tells just one other person every half hour throughout the day and those who learn the good news repeat the story to someone new every thirty minutes, by midnight 167,772,160 persons—almost every American citizen—will have heard about the hospitality of Old First Church.

Never forget that people are media.

Believers and Communicators

"In one respect, Protestant churches are crowded to the doors with Roman Catholics," asserted a startling editorial in *The Christian Century* some years ago.

Begging the question as to whether with some exceptions the churches are "crowded to the doors," the writer pointed out that the Protestant churches rest on three principles, two of them privileges and the third a duty. Protestantism holds that no one can stand between a man and God. No intermediary is required. Access is direct.

The second principle is that no one can stand between a man and the truth. A preacher may give his congregation the benefit of his wisdom, but in the end the believer himself must decide what is true for him.

Wouldn't it be just as you expected that in general we Protestants accept and exult in the two principles that present us with privileges but ignore the one that requires effort on our part? That is exactly what we have done.

The third axiom of Protestantism is that no one can stand between ourselves and our fellow men. In violation of this principle we have allowed the pastor to come between us and those to whom we ourselves should be ministering.

Instead of being the leader who organizes and inspires Christian workers to services of friendliness, of comfort, of evangelism, we have laid these duties, impossibly heavy, upon one man. Little wonder that the church grows so slowly.

To be sure, the minister is supported by his church members. He appeciates the privilege thus provided to follow his vocation and to devote full time to the service of Christ.

But no contribution toward the budget—even though it helps pay for the minister's time—can ever relieve a Protestant of his own personal responsibility. No one must stand between each of us and our fellow men.

In addition, the layman should want the portion of the pastor's day for which he has paid to be used as effectively as possible. This should mean the minister's acting as general rather than carrying out detail which should be done by sergeants, corporals, and buck privates.

The original Society of Friends and certain other churches feel so strongly on this point that they do not maintain a professional ministry. They believe that one's individual responsibility is something that cannot be transferred. The presence of a minister might be a temptation to do so.

Belief in "the priesthood of all believers" underlies the Protestant conception of both Christianity and the church. In this relationship priesthood includes "pastorhood" as well.

Society of Aaron and Hur

A pastor at River Rouge, Michigan, was discouraged over the dearth of lay leaders. "What can we do?" he asked the local school superintendent. The next day the layman turned up with a plan.

"I'm going to organize a society of Aaron and Hur," he announced.

"We have too many organizations already," the minister countered.

"This one is different. It will have no constitution or by-laws, no officers, no dues, and no meetings." The official recalled to the minister how Moses from a hilltop encouraged the warring children of Israel in their battle with the Amalekites.

"Whenever Moses held up his hand, Israel prevailed; and whenever he lowered his hand, Amalek prevailed." Aaron and Hur, seeing that "Moses' hands grew weary" and that the Amalekites were advancing, rushed to the side of the venerable leader. As flying buttresses support a cathedral wall, they lifted high the patriarch's arms. Courage returned to the fighters below, and at the setting of the sun, according to scripture, the Amalekites were routed.

What the new pastor needed, said the superintendent, were Aarons and Hurs to uphold his arms.

This wise layman told fellow members of the congregation that whenever any of them had said or done something to uphold the arms of the minister, he should regard himself as a member of the Society of Aaron and Hur. As such he would be privileged to recruit new helpers.

Church of a Thousand Pastors

How many pastors does your church have? One? Then at best it is only hobbling along. If a church depends upon its pastor to do all the pastoral work, it will be disappointed. With all the other responsibilities loaded on him, the minister will not find hours enough.

Does your church have a thousand members? Then it should be a church of a thousand pastors.

No Christian church can remain Christian that regards itself as a passive group to be ministered unto. A church is a working force under the guidance of a leader. In no other way can the Christian religion overcome the world.

Even were the clergy twice as efficient and twice as diligent, they couldn't do the job alone. There simply are not enough of them. Figure it out. Ministers constitute only .02 per cent of the population.

Every member must in one way or another be a communicator. How did Christianity rise and spread? "It flew like hallowed fire from heart to heart."

On one and only one occasion was it reported that Jesus "rejoiced in spirit." Do you remember when it was? Many suitable occasions in his life suggest themselves. Was it his baptism? Or when he came down from the mount a victor over temptation? Or on another mount when he preached a sermon that would live for centuries? Was it at the Transfiguration or the Resurrection?

No, nor was it at any other of the many occasions which involved him personally. The answer reveals how in this day we can renew exultation in the divine heart. Jesus rejoiced in spirit at the hour when seventy unordained lay members, who had gone out two by two in his name, returned with enthusiastic accounts of their success.

More Than Techniques

"We commend you for the excellent job you are doing interrupting the church to the public."

This was the rather disconcerting way a letter, addressed to a colleague, concluded. Since the general tone was friendly, we preferred to believe that the writer's secretary had erred in at least one word. Sufficiently familiar with shorthand to know that the word sign for "interrupting" is almost identical with the one for "interpreting," we considerately allowed ourselves to believe that he had actually dictated "interpreting."

The incident, however, gave us serious pause. It is all too easy to "interrupt" the church in its onward march. It can be done by unintentional misrepresentation or by inconsistencies in our lives that distort its true nature to those who without our knowledge may be trying to understand the church through us.

This, however, is not the most likely way for persons committed to the church to "interrupt" it. Our danger, if we are not on guard, is through omission. Through the sin of doing nothing we default in our duty to make our church and our faith more widely and more favorably known.

Whether layman or minister, if we fail in our pastoral responsibilities to our fellow men, if we miss or do not make opportunities to talk up the church, to give it the signature of our personal testimonies, we have thereby, perhaps unwittingly, "interrupted" the church in its progress toward the allegiance of the world.

If in the numerous ways in which the church makes contact with its several publics—through its plant, its business methods, its printed matter, its human representatives, its services of worship, its program of service—if through any or all of these, people are repelled rather than attracted, then the church has most certainly been "interrupted."

If there are media for communicating the message and mission and spirit of the church that have been open to us but to which we have been indifferent, we have "interrupted" the church.

Or if in our use of these media—newspapers, radio, television—we have done less than our best to obtain maximum value to the church, once more we have "interrupted" it.

When it comes to "interpreting" it, much space has been given to the mechanisms through which the church may be made known and to the most effective ways of using them. This chapter has centered on the primacy of word-of-mouth publicity. These are the good ways and the better way, respectively. Publicity-wise it is doubtful if there is anything more effective or persuasive than the spoken word.

But there remains a factor without which no publicity can be helpful. Backing up the broadcast and the news story, the form letters and the parish paper, the signboard and the poster, the glowing spire and the landscaped edifice, there must be a reality. There must be a church that is a church. There must be a fellowship of Christians worshiping together, studying together, working together, building better lives, a better community, and a better world.

GLOSSARY

OF TERMS COMMONLY USED IN PUBLIC RELATIONS

Compiled by Arthur West

Here are only a few of the terms most frequently encountered in dealing with newspapers, radio, and television. Obviously there are many technical terms that cannot be included in this list, which is planned especially for the churchman rather than the professional publicist.

A.B.C.—Abbreviation for American Broadcasting System; also Audit Bureau of Circulation, an organization which compiles statistics on the circulation of publications.

Across the Board—A radio program presented the same time each day for five days a week.

Ad—Abbreviation for advertisement.

Ad Lib.—Speaking without a prepared script.

Advance—Story about something which is to take place in the future.

Agate—The smallest type used by modern newspapers, 5½ points in depth. Column lengths and advertising space are generally measured in agate lines.

Alive—Type or copy still alive for use.

A.M.—A morning newspaper.

Angle—A particular slant or emphasis given a story by a newsman.

AP—Associated Press, one of the major wire services providing news to member papers.

Art—All newspaper illustrations are called art.

Back-timing—Timing the last two or three stories of a newscast so the newscaster will get off the air on time.

Banner—A headline stretching across the top of a page; also called "line" or the "streamer."

Ben Day—A photoengraving process which permits the use of several shadings for zinc line engravings.

B.F.—Abbreviation for bold face or black face type.

Bleed—An illustration trimmed so that it runs off the edge of a sheet is said to "bleed." "Bleeds" are common in magazines and brochures; seldom used in newspapers.

Blow up—To enlarge a photograph.

Body Type—The type in which the greater part of a newspaper text is set, usualy 8 point type.

Booklet—Six or more pages of printed material arranged with a cover and usually stapled together.

Box—Type enclosed by printed borders or rules.

Break—The point at which a story must be continued to another page; also refers to the availability of news.

Brochure—A booklet of several pages, usually containing a number of pictures and more elaborate layout than just a "booklet."

Bulletin—Last-minute news printed before the lead of a story to which it is related; also the brief announcement on the air of an important news event.

Bulletin Interruption—The act of breaking into a regular program to give an important news bulletin.

By-line—The author's name at the top of a story.

Call Letters—Letters identifying radio or television station as assigned by FCC.

C. and l.c.—Abbreviation for capital and lower case letters.

Caps.—Abbreviation for capital letters.

Caption—Usually refers to picture headings and accompanying text to describe the picture.

C.B.S.—Columbia Broadcasting System.

Center Spread—Two center facing pages of a publication, printed on a single continuous sheet. Often used in booklets for a picture spread or a map.

Circular—Usually a one-sheet printed piece used for promotional purposes.

City Editor—A key spot on a newspaper's staff, specifically, the editor in charge of the city room. One who handles or supervises coverage of local news.

Clips—Abbreviation for clippings from current newspapers or magazines or clippings found in files of library.

Coated Paper—Enameled stock paper with a hard, smooth finish, especially suited for halftone reproduction of pictures.

Col.—Abbreviation for column.

Continuity Writer—Radio or TV writer who writes copy other than news.

Copy—All written material. Also used to describe any illustrations to be reproduced by photoengraving.

Copy Desk—Where copy is edited and given headlines before publication in a newspaper.

Cover—To be responsible for getting and writing a story of a particular event.

Cover Stock—A sturdy paper stock used for covers for booklets and pamphlets.

GLOSSARY

Credit Line—A line giving the source of an illustration or other copy.

Cropping—Reducing or changing the size or proportion of a picture so that it will fit into a particular layout. Frequently used to eliminate dead areas or unnecessary details of the original photograph and to accentuate important features.

Cue—A signal, either in word or by sign, given by a program director on radio or TV.

Cut—Any metal plate bearing an illustration. When used as a verb, "cut" means to eliminate some of the copy or type to shorten the story.

Cut line—The caption for a cut, consisting of overlines and/or underlines.

Date Line—The city from which a news story comes and the date of the dispatch.

Deadline—The last moment to get copy in for an edition.

Delete—To omit or take out of prepared copy.

Dingbat—A decorative bit of type, printer's ornament.

Dummy—Sheets of paper cut to resemble the finished leaflet or booklet. Sometimes proof may be pasted up to look like the completed job.

Dupes—Contraction for "duplicates." Carbon copies of news stories or manuscripts.

Edition—Copies printed during one press run.

Editorialize—To inject opinion in a news story.

Electrotype—A duplicate of a photoengraving, cast from a mat made from the original cut.

English Finish—A paper stock smoother and less bulky than antique paper; especially suitable for folders, booklets, and others.

Exclusive—A news story is "exclusive" when it is the property of only one newspaper or station. A "scoop."

Filler—Short items that may be placed anywhere on page, sometimes used simply to rectify the column. Hence, quite literally, "filler."

Flush—Even with margin.

Flyer—A giveaway or mailing piece of printed material, usually one page long and rather inexpensive.

Folder—A four-page printed piece.

Folio—A page; the page number.

Follow—A story with new details: that is, often related to one in an earlier edition.

Font—A complete assortment of type of a particular style or design.

Format—The size, shape, and general make-up of a publication.

Four-Color Process—Using yellow, blue, red, and black inks to reproduce full-colored illustrations.

FYI—Abbreviation of "For Your Information."

Galley—A metal tray on which printer keeps type ready for use.

Galley Proof—A proof of the galley of type.

Ghost Writer—One who is employed to write under another's name.

Glossy, Glossy Print—A shiny-surface photograph, preferred by photoengravers for reproduction purposes.

Green Proof—First proof taken, one not yet corrected.

Halftone—Ordinary cut printed from plate consisting of small dots. (See Photoengraving.)

Handout—Publicity material, copy supplied by a press agent.

Head—Headline above a story.

Human Interest—News with an emotional appeal. Material which contains stories and illustrations about interesting people.

Insert—A paragraph or more to be inserted in copy already written. Also an extra page or pages which may be inserted between pages of another publication.

Jump—Break a story from one page to another.

Jumping Cue—Act of starting a program before it is scheduled to start.

Kill—To remove material from copy or to destroy type already set.

Layout—Arrangement of pictures or other art work and textual material on a page.

Lead (pronounced lēēd)—Opening paragraph or two of a news story which gives the essential facts.

Lead (pronounced led)—Thin metal pieces for spacing lines of type so they are more readable.

Leaflet—A printed piece, usually about four pages, often containing promotional material.

Letterpress—A printing process by which ink is applied to raised type and then by direct pressure to the paper.

Lithographic Printing—The transference of an inked image from smooth surface to paper by chemical process, as in offset printing and photo-offset.

Make-up—Placing articles in position for printing on a page.

Manual—A book or booklet giving detailed material and instruction in a given area.

Masthead—The matter printed in every issue of a publication, usually on the editorial page, to show the name of the paper, the publisher, place and date of publication, and so on. Also called "the flag."

Mat—Papier-mâché impression of a photograph from which a lead casting can be made easily and quickly. Mats are particularly useful to weekly newspapers and small dailies.

M.B.S.—Mutual Broadcasting System.

Media—Various channels through which materials reach the public—newspapers, magazines, movies, television, radio, books, filmstrips, and so on.

Mimeographing—Process of reproducing material typed or written on a stencil by means of a rotary-operated machine. Inexpensive method.

Monitoring—Listening to or checking on radio and television shows.

More—When "more" is written at the bottom of a page of copy, it indicates that the story is still running and that there is more to come.

Morgue—A somewhat outmoded newspaper term to designate its reference library.

GLOSSARY

Mortise—A cutaway section of a photoengraving into which type can be set.

Multilithing—A special process of duplicating large quantities of typewritten material.

N.B.C.—National Broadcasting Company.

News Analyst or Commentator—One who reports, analyzes, and comments on the news; an editorial writer or columnist of the air.

Newscast—Radio or TV program of straight news.

News Editor—In radio or television a newsman who rewrites, edits, and supervises news programs.

Newsprint—Paper used for newspapers and other inexpensive printed materials.

Offset—Printing process of lithography.

Overset—Additional type for which there is no room.

Photoengraving—A picture photographed on metal, which is then given relief for printing reproduction by being etched either chemically or electrolytically. A halftone is a photoengraving photographed through a screen, with the dots in the light sections etched away to offer little printing surface. A line engraving or a zinc etching is a photoengraving made without photographing it through a screen.

Photo-Offset—Printing process by which copy is first transferred to a rubber blanket and then from the blanket to the paper.

Pica—Twelve-point type.

Pix.—Abbreviation for pictures; any newspaper illustrations.

Play Up—To feature or emphasize some factor.

P.M.—Afternoon paper.

Point—One twelfth of a pica (about 1/72 of an inch), a unit of type measure.

Proof—First impression of set type on which corrections are to be made.

Publics—The vague term "the general public" is replaced in modern public relations by consideration of the several "publics"—groups with common interests whom a public relations program is calculated to reach.

Public Relations—The art of interpreting an institution or a product to its various publics and influencing them favorably toward it. The public relations director seeks to execute a program of action which will gain understanding and acceptance of the cause he represents.

Spot News—Fresh, live news.

Spread—An ad, related group of photographs and copy, occupying two facing pages.

Stet—From the Latin, meaning "let it stand." Used to indicate that matter marked for correction or omission is to remain as it was originally.

Stuffer—Small printed piece for insertion into envelope or packages along with some regular mailing.

Subhead—Small headline insert in the body of a story.

Tabloid—Newspaper slightly more than half the size of regular newspaper usually with five columns to the page and featuring pictures.

Thirty—Written in figures on reporter's copy or news release indicates its end.

Tight—A paper is said to be "tight" when there is not much room for news material because of heavy advertising and the like.

Trim—To shorten an article so it will fit allotted space.

UPI—United Press-International, a major wire service representing the merger of United Press and International News Service.

Wash Drawing—Water-color or India-ink brush drawing which requires halftone reproduction.

Watermark—Trade-mark identification left in texture of paper; can be read when held to light.

Wide Open—Considerable room for news material. The opposite of a "tight" paper.

Widow—A very short word or part of a word standing alone on the last line of a paragraph of body type.

Zinc—Common term for a zinc etching, a cut without a halftone screen.

The above glossary has drawn extensively upon lists of newspaper terms found in the following books:

Bastian, George C., and Case, Leland D. *Editing the Day's News.* New York: The Macmillan Co., 1956. Pp. 385-98.

Campbell, L. R., and Wolseley, R. E. *Newsmen at Work.* Boston: Houghton Mifflin Co., 1949. Pp. 525-28.

MacDougall, Curtis D. *Interpretative Reporting.* New York: The Macmillan Co., 1948. Pp. 692-95.

Stuber, Stanley I. *Public Relations Manual for Churches.* New York: Doubleday & Co., 1951. Pp. 265-70.

INDEX

Aaron and Hur, Society of, 242
Accrediting reporters, 114-15
Accuracy, 51
Advance stories on conventions, 106-8
Advertising in parish papers, 182
Advertising, subcommittees on, 235
"Affairs of Dame Rumor," 240
Air conditioning, 171
Air-line courtesy, 202
All Church Press, 189
Alliteration in titles, 215
Amateur groups, booking problem, 147-48
Anniversaries, 90-91, 95
Answering telephone, 203
Appreciation to press, radio-TV, 75-76, 122-23, 135, 147, 154
Architecture, church, 18, 159-60
Areas of local church PR, 231
Art in church public relations, 18
Asbury, Bishop Francis (quoted), 23
Auchincloss, Douglas (quoted), 27
Audience promotion, 134

Backdoor losses, preventing, 219
Backgrounds, distracting, 85-86
Bad news, handling of, 72
Benson, Charles Francis (quoted), 57-58
Biogs of speakers, officials, 111
Birthdays, remembering, 222, 224-25
Boners, how to handle, 65-66
Borman, James, 70

Brainstorming, 230
Broadcast, first church to, 19
Brodhead, Charles D., 99
Buckley, James M., 182
Bulletin boards, 163-66, 169-70
Butters, George S. (quoted), 217

Captions, photo, 87, 88
Carnegie, Dale (quoted), 18
Catastrophe makes news, 33
Chapels in churches, 168
Childhood, church interest in, 172-73
Chimes, tower, 236
Christian Advocate, 182
Christian Century, 57, 241
Christian Science Monitor, 155
Church editor's confusion, 63
Church, first PR practices, 17-23
Church plant and equipment, 235
Church-school news possibilities, 175
Church schools practice PR, 173
Church services, broadcasting, 138-40
Cleanliness in churches, 167
Clergy on newsmen, 56-58
Clinton, John, 97
Clippings, exhibiting, 120
Comfortable worshipers, 170-71
Conferences, covering, 103-26
Conflict makes news, 33
Conrad, Dr., 214
Contacting absentees, 236
Conventions and conferences, 103-23
Conventions, covering, 103-26
Conventions, news values of, 104-5

251

Conversational style on air, 139
Co-operation with press, 70-72
Coors, Bishop D. Stanley, 101
Courtesy toward guests, 196
Creating news, 89-102
Cushman, Bishop Ralph S., 100
Cut lines, photo, 87-88

Daily Courier, Waterloo, Iowa, 30
Daniels, Jonathan (quoted), 26
Date lines, 49-50
Deadlines, 54-55
Definition of public relations, 228-29
Dial-a-prayer, 168
Dionne, Papa, 89
Documenting Radio Programs, 145-46
Double spacing copy, 46
Drama on radio-TV, 146-48
Dramatizing news, 100-101

Ear appeal in script writing, 155
Editor and Publisher magazine, 49
Editorial writing, 186
Editorializing, avoidance of, 39-40, 155
Editors, dealing with, 56-76
Editors vs. clergy, 56-58
Efficiency, personal, 220
Eliot, President Charles, 30
Errors, how to handle, 65-66
Exclusives, 68

Fact sheet, use of, 40-42, 113
Feature stories, 42-43
Feature writers, helping, 118-19
Felmly, Lloyd M. (quoted), 58
Fighting the evil, not the editor, 73-74
Fillers for parish papers, 185-86
Filming church school, 177
Finances, minister's personal, 218, 221-22
Financial appeals on radio-TV, 135

Fine arts as public relations, 18-19
Flesch, Rudolph, 51
Floodlighting, 236
Freedom of pulpit and press, 73-74

Gamble of Procter and Gamble, 212
Glosary of PR terms, 245
Good Rumor Man, 240
Ground breaking, 96-97
Guest appearances on air, 141

Handwritten copy, 47
Harral, Stewart (quoted), 229
Hartman, Bishop Lewis O., 29
Headlines on releases, 49
Homiletics vs. news style, 36, 155
Honoring churchmen, 92-94
Hospitality, 194
Hospitality, subcommittee on, 236
Housekeeping, church, 166-67
Hutchins, Sydney, 195
Hymns that invite and instruct, 20

Identifying source of news, 47-48
Illumination, 160-62, 171, 236
Importance as news element, 28-31
Installations of officers and teachers, 175-76
"Interrupting the church," 243
Interview programs, 140-43
Inverted pyramid news style, 38-39

Jacobson, David J., 240
James, Edwin L. (quoted), 24
Janitor, briefed on courtesy, 202

Kansas City Star, 52
Kniskern, Maynard (quoted), 57
Krock, Arthur (quoted), 218

Landscaping, 160
Lead, writing the, 37
Letters to editors, 209
Letters, length of, 207

INDEX

Letters, series of, 208
Letter writing, advantages of, 206
Libraries, local church, 236
Lighting, 160-61, 171, 236
Linen, James A. (quoted), 23
Local church PR objectives, 230-31
Luncheons and dinners for press, 115, 117
Luther, Martin, 22, 234
Lutherans, Augustana, 101

Magee, Bishop J. Ralph, 99
Making friends with editors, 58-59
Manuscripts, advance, 112
Marble Collegiate Church, 166
Margins, wide, 46
Marvin, Dwight (quoted), 70
Minister-reporters, 109, 114-15
Ministers, not enough, 242-43
Miss America, 80
Modesty, ministerial, 220-21
Moralizing in news writing, 39-40
Mortgage burning, 97-98
Motion pictures, 177
Music as public relations, 19-20

Names, handling of, 52
Names make news, 31
Nasty letters, 209
National Religious Press, 189
Network programs, promoting, 128-29
New York Times, The, 24, 29, 155, 218
Newark (N. J.) *News*, 58
News, acceptance for religious, 23-25
News, broadcasting religious, 149-55
News, defined, 27
News, how to write, 35-43, 151
News, ingredients of, 31-33
News possibilities, 34
News sources for broadcasts, 153-54
News, what makes, 26-34
Newscasts, religious values of, 153

Newspapers, number of, 23
Newspapers vs. broadcasting, 150
Newsweek magazine, 27
Nicknames, 53
Nomenclature, ecclesiastical, 62, 63
Numbers, notable, 92

Objectives for PR committee, 230-31
Obligation to broadcasters, 128
One side of paper, why, 45
Overstreet, H. A. (quoted), 33

Palmquist, Theodore H., 100
Panel programs, 143-45
Parish paper, weekday or Sunday, 179
Parish papers, editing, 184-86
Parish papers, financing, 181
Parish papers, head writing for, 188
Parish papers, make-up and layout of, 187
Parish papers, values of, 180-81
Parking provision, 162
Pastoral appointments, handling, 119
Patience in press relations, 62-64
Paul (quoted), 222
Periodicals, denominational, 23
Personal testimony, 238-39
Personalized pastoral remembrances, 222-26
Photo backgrounds, 85-87
Photographer, official church, 82
Photographers, working with, 79-80
Photos (news), qualities of, 80-82
Photos, warnings and hints, 83-88
Pictures, importance of, 77-78
Pius XII (quoted), 127
Postscripts, value of, 207-8
Press conferences, 117-18
Pressroom, equipment, etc., 109-11
Press tables, 111, 116

253

Printing and literature, 234-35
Programs, plan with press in mind, 105-6
Promoting church periodicals, 235
Protecting the pastor, 203
Protestant restrictions in Spain, 239
Proximity as a news element, 31
Public relations committees, 227-37
Public relations defined, 228-29
Public Relations News (quoted), 229

Quotation in broadcasts, 139-40
Quotations as titles, 214

Radio-TV, disadvantages of, 132
Radio-TV news writing, 151
Radio-TV preaching, 138-40
Radio-TV program ideas, placing, 133-35
Radio-TV station relations, 135
Reader's Digest, survey of, 24-25
Recordings, use of, 168
Refreshments for reporters, 117
Registering congregation, 236
Release dates, 48-49
Release heads, 45-46
Releases, preparation of, 44
Religion in American Life, 232, 234, 235
Reporters, dealing with, 56-76
"Rev.," misuse of, 54
Rhyme and rhythm in titles, 215
Rose, Billy (quoted), 74
Rumormongering, 240

Salaries, ministerial, 221-22
Scan-a-graver, 83
Second-class mailing, 183-84
Self-seeking, ministerial, 221
Seney, George I., 182
Sensational sermon topics, 215-16
Sermon and news writing compared, 35-36
Sermon titles, 211-21

Seventh-Day Adventists, 210
Signs, 163-66
Sinatra, Frank, 74
Singing commercials, 20
Sorrows, anniversaries of, 224
Special days, 22, 91, 95, 141, 176
Spence, Hartzell, 71
Storage space in churches, 167
Street numbers, use of, 53
Subcommittees in local church, 232-37
Supple, James, 52

Tampa (Fla.) *Tribune*, 57
Taylor, Senator Glen H. (quoted), 29
Teachers, PR importance of, 178
Tele-corps, 204-5
Telephone Corps, 235
Telephone manners, 201-4
Telephones for pressrooms, 109
"Thank you," saying, 75-76, 122-23
Thousand pastors, church of, 242
Time magazine, 23, 27, 51, 208
Timeliness as news element, 30
Troy (N.Y.) *Record*, 70
Truman, President Harry S., 99
Trusting reporters, 67
Truth in advertising, 216
Typing releases, rules for, 50

Ushering, 190-99
Ushers, bibliography for, 199
Ushers, "don'ts" for, 197
Ushers, "do's" for, 196-97
Ushers, few or many, 192-93
Ushers, organization of, 192
Ushers, personal appearance of, 193
Ushers, training of, 199

Valentino, Rudolph, 30, 31
Van Kirk, Walter W., 152
Vanderbilt, Commodore, 68
View book for local churches, 235

INDEX

Visitors, obtaining names and addresses of, 197-98
Voigt, Bishop Edwin E., 101

Walker, Stanley (quoted), 57
Wayside pulpit, 164
Webb, Captain Thomas, 93-94
Wedding anniversary greetings, 223-24
Welcome Wagon hostesses, 236
Wesley, John, film, 235
West, Arthur, 5, 245

White space, importance of, 187 207
Williams, Professor Talcott (quoted), 23
Women's names, 53
WOMPS, 231
Word of mouth publicity, 238-40
Words, choosing the right, 139, 214

"You-ability" in letter writing, 206